WHERE CLARE LEADS, IRELAND FOLLOWS

For My Mom and Dad

WHERE CLARE LEADS, IRELAND FOLLOWS

Richard Fitzpatrick

with illustrations by

Greg Murray

MERCIER PRESS
WHAT YOU NEED TO READ

MERCIER PRESS
Cork
www. mercierpress. ie

Trade enquiries to CMD Distribution
55A Spruce Avenue, Stillorgan Industrial Park,
Blackrock, County Dublin

ISBN: 978 1 85635 606 0

10 9 8 7 6 5 4 3 2 1

A CIP record for this title is available from the British Library

 Mercier Press receives financial assistance from the Arts
Council/An Chomhairle Ealaíon

Printed and bound in the EU.

CONTENTS

FOREWORD

Micheál Ó Muircheartaigh

It is not today nor yesterday that Clare has led the way and others followed; wasn't Brian Boru a solid Clareman who, on becoming high king of Ireland, set about wresting control of the country from the Danes? Clontarf – not too far from where the hallowed Croke Park now stands – turned out to be the site for the decisive battle. The greatest exodus of people from Clare to that date in 1014 converged on Dublin in support of the great Brian, and the magnetism of the leader brought an equal response from other quarters. Even his political enemy, the deposed Maolseachlann, decided that the cause was a worthy one, and placed his army at the disposal of the high king. Was it any wonder that the Danes were routed?

Ní neart go cur le chéile.

As forewords to books are best when brief, I will now take a leap of almost seven hundred years forward in history to give another example of vibrant leadership coming from the Bannerland. Once the Jacobite/Williamite war ended with the Treaty of Limerick in

1691, the remnants of Patrick Sarsfield's army headed for the bigger European stage, where they gained great renown. History records that the Clare Brigade – 'those homeless troops, the banished men, the exiled sons of Clare' – were to the forefront in battles like Fontenoy, driven by a noble ideal 'for faith and fame, and honour, and the ruined hearths of Clare'.

A century later, the homeland of Clare was once again propelled into the limelight when Daniel O'Connell's campaign for Catholic Emancipation needed a major boost. The Liberator, as he was later labelled, decided to stand for election to the mother of parliaments for the constituency of Clare. The right of secret ballots was not yet in vogue, but, nevertheless, the people of Clare openly voted for the Kerryman and returned him as MP to Westminster. It was a significant moment in Ireland's history, and the example of the brave voters of Corca Baiscinn was soon taken up nationwide. I often wonder why Eamon de Valera opted to stand in Clare for the historic election of 1918!

And so to the present, and Richard Fitzpatrick's treatise on a selection of Clare people of modern times, all of whom rightly merit the accolade of leader; they are a varied lot – men and women, lay and clerical – but still similar on account of the common bond of excellence in their chosen pursuits. Richard guides us into the many fields of sport, the arts, music, politics, religion, minority causes, the media, social issues and outlooks, and much more. His personal observations and research on each of those featured makes for memorable reading, but quotes and asides from others add considerably to the enjoyment of the content.

The names of the anointed are known nationally, and some have shone on the mirrors of a wider world; their names, as chronicled on passports, are rarely needed for instant recognition, and I say with confidence that you, the readers, will have no problems in identifying the following: Anthony, Keith, Sharon, Ger, Smyth, Michael D., Harry, Marcus, Brian, Jamesie, etc., etc., from start to finish.

Of course, you will have your own favourite among them, and why not; as for myself, I have many, but somehow a certain Anthony is unique – he is and will for evermore be the first Clareman to hoist the Liam McCarthy Cup aloft in triumph.

Anois má sea, fágaimis siúd mar atá sé, tá raidhse ceannairí iomráiteacha curtha in bhur láthair ag Risteárd; bainigí sásamh as a shaothar.

Micheál Ó Muircheartaigh

INTRODUCTION

There's a category in Wikipedia, the online encyclopaedia, which lists famous people – dead and alive – from each of Ireland's thirty-two counties. Of its living worthies, there is one midlands county – which shall remain nameless – that has a celebrity chef and a few local politicians and Gaelic footballers of note to mention. It might also have a Sky News weather forecaster.

For its size, County Clare, with little over 100,000 in population, has produced an inordinate amount of prominent people, across a range of disciplines. It is the home of traditional music. In sport alone, it has given us the inaugural World Rugby Player of the Year; the most distinctive face in British sports' broadcasting; arguably, the finest horseracing jockey of his generation, and, thanks to its county team in the 1990s, the most compelling chapter in the history of hurling. Rarely, it seems, has its personalities done things meekly, touched as they are by a particular type of devilment and fecklessness.

'Clare people tend to carry their views very strongly,' argues Liam Griffin, who led Wexford to an All-Ireland hurling title in 1996 and played hurling for Clare in the late-1960s while studying in Shannon. 'They tend to be very determined in their point of view, which is a sign of great strength but it also probably gets them into confrontational situations from time to time. That West of Ireland trait – I mean it's in my own family; it's in my own father, a Clare man – that breeding, from a place that's not exactly the Golden Vale, it's a tough, hard landscape and it's going to be reflected in its people. It moulds the man and that's what makes a lot of Clare fellas tough and hard and now that they're at the top, they're very definite in their views.'

I find this penchant to entertain and infuriate in equal measure intoxicating. It has informed the selection of the people who are profiled in this collection. In assessing sporting prowess, for example, longevity is the great benchmark; in this, the talented, unruly Tom Morrissey, a (shooting) star from Clare's 1992 Munster Championship Gaelic football-winning team, falls short, but none of his teammates are his match for colour and warmth of personality. He lights up a dull sky. To be boring, isn't that one of the only great sins in life?

For inclusion, a lot of the names picked themselves, reflecting fields of endeavour in which the county's sons and daughters have excelled. Inevitably, the range betrays a certain bias; for that, I make no apology. Sadly, some of the key personalities of our time – namely former president, Dr Paddy Hillery and the industrialist, Dr Brendan O'Regan – passed away during the writing of the book.

I took certain liberties, spreading the net wide to include the Clare Diaspora for some of the candidates, chiefly the story of Kevin Sheedy. Star of Ireland's Italia '90 adventure, his father, a Clareman, left for the UK aged 20. Michael D. Higgins, the great icon of left-wing politics in Ireland, was born in Limerick and moved to Clare aged five, but he passed the acid test: when asked who he would support in a match between the two counties, he chose Clare. Likewise, the hurler James O'Connor, who moved to the county from Galway at ten years of age, and who would question his Clare credentials?

My motivation has been to find out what makes interesting, successful people tick and to harvest some of their impressions and recollections, many of which are from, at the risk of sounding mawkish, a disappearing County Clare. To hear, for instance, accounts of what Eamon de Valera's visits to the county were like, when he used to be ushered along in a procession like the return of a triumphant Caesar. Also to quiz them about some of their contemporaries, characters such as Christy Ring, Muhammad Ali and, literally, the mythical figure of Dolly Parton.

The portraits are, by their nature, incomplete biographically. They are a mix of reporting, anecdote, observation and analysis. I've eschewed linear, factual accounts of the chosen lives; for those, you will have to go elsewhere. The profiles attempt to bring the reader as close to the subject and their area of expertise, to their story, as possible. They try to capture the public lives and glimpses of the private selves. They present certain angles of a life, a career and, essentially, a conversation, touching on the gamut of human emotions, from triumph to injustice and bereavement.

The profiles are heavily coloured by third-party contributions, drawing as the book does on over ninety interviews. This was important. I was particularly keen to gather the reflections of the protagonists' peers and, in some cases, their critics about major achievements and tribulations; to hear the opinions of folk like Eamon Dunphy, Kevin Myers, Nell McCafferty, D. J. Carey and Dr Garret FitzGerald. Alas, some contributions, such as racing pundit, John McCririck's were so contentious they had to be culled.

The characters – obsessive, outspoken, original in differing degrees – encompass a few of the great sagas of recent Irish history. There's the Munster rugby team's Homeric assault on the Heineken Cup; the daily drama of jockey Kieren Fallon's life; an examination of how the FBI and the Archdiocese of New York tried to get a gay rights activist priest wrongfully imprisoned for child abuse; and a report on an unseemly distancing between key personalities in Clare's hurling community.

In my job as a journalist, I've been lucky enough to meet some extraordinary people – from Nobel Prize winners to Death Row inmates – and to hear some spellbinding stories, but few memories remain as vivid for me as the recollection of James O'Connor's description of the moment he ran onto Páirc Uí Chaoimh, a natural amphitheatre, for the 1997 Munster hurling final.

It was a beautiful July day; Clare was playing Tipp, the high-water mark of a tumultuous, decade-long rivalry. The ground shuddered as the teams ran out onto the pitch. Such was the rush of adrenaline, O'Connor, who was a natural livewire as a player, started jumping around like he was on a pogo stick. I nearly began bouncing around his sitting-room myself so infectious, so dramatic was the picture he sketched. For a second, I'd transported myself back there with him. What, dear God, must it feel like to tap into that energy ... to play the Main Stage at Glastonbury ... to win the Aintree Grand National?

I don't expect you to leap from your armchair while reading this book of profiles – or even to let out the occasional Banner Roar – but hopefully, in patches, you'll experience some of the excitement, some of the wonder I felt from hearing the stories of these 20 remarkable Clare people.

Richard Fitzpatrick

GER LOUGHNANE

In the days before corporal punishment became unfashionable, Ger Loughnane used to keep order amongst the students in his National school – St Aidan's, in Shannon, County Clare – with a big, brown stick. If pupils were unruly, they'd be sent to wait outside the principal's office. There, they would be given time to stew over their misdemeanour before being invited into his office for some 'hot chocolate'.

Few in the country brew and dole out the 'hot chocolate' like Loughnane. Whether it's opposing teams (Limerick, 'the third world'), Munster Council administrators ('Donie Nealon, and the mad eyes on him staring at us!'), Clare County Board delegates ('mushrooms, the more shite you feed them, the faster they'll grow') or his own players ('You're too fucking slow! That's why you were destroyed! That's why they were laughing at you last year!'), nobody administers the lash with quite the whip of Loughnane.

On the other hand, no one speaks more eloquently about the soul of hurling. Fiercely intelligent, he has a remarkable facility with language. Former Clare hurler James O'Connor once remarked that, of all the functions he went to after the Clare hurlers won the All-Ireland in 1995 and 1997, he cannot recall Loughnane ever making the same speech twice, and yet he always had 'the audience in the palm of his hand'. In the league of the opinionated, along with Eamon Dunphy and Roy Keane, he is one of the country's most compelling characters. There are few as fearsome and as feckless.

In a lazy-afternoon interview with him in his school office – which, given the meticulousness of his management style, is surprisingly cluttered and dishevelled-looking, with papers strewn here and there on his desk – he's relaxed, directing the intrusions into his lair calmly, as students pop in and out casually to empty his bin or deliver a message. There's no sign of the hot chocolate. Not yet, anyway.

When Loughnane shakes hands, he swings out his shoulder like a golfer's three-quarter air backswing. He has those cobalt eyes, a pair that would serve him well at a Texas hold 'em table, and, of course, the magnificent jawbone – the kind, says portrait painter Mick O'Dea, that 'Samson could have used to beat the Philistines with'.

He's full of charm and has a noticeable habit if you interject with an agreeable comment of repeating the three or four key words of the interjection, which is a very empathetic quality – what psychologists would call 'mirroring'. And sure, the man is mighty entertainment. Obviously candid, but it's the giddy, colourful turn of phrase in his stories and the mountainy-man aspect to him that makes him such good company.

Born in 1953, Loughnane grew up in Feakle, County Clare, a hinterland renowned for its traditional music. Loughane's father, John James, who was an able long-distance runner, also played the fiddle. The *cuairt* was an almost nightly occurrence in the house, where neighbours, mostly single ones, would drop by for chat, cards, music and dancing. Loughnane, who has been known to serenade Clare hurling teams with a song, never warmed to the impromptu *céilís*, though. 'I never took to it, at all, at all. I'd a very bad experience the first time. We were all taught to dance the set. You know the thing where you spin around in the set? I used to always get sick – because if I go up on one round of those chairoplanes [at the funfair], I am sick – so it was that which turned me off Irish music. Whenever I hear one of those Irish music things, that feeling comes back in my throat again.'

If not the music, what did his father instil?

'Definitely one thing – hard work, hard bloody work,' he says, hammering out each word for emphasis, and points out that when he was young, he had a reputation for working hard. He talks, for example, with pride of the job satisfaction he accrued from twelve-hour shifts spreading turf in the bog – 'back-breaking work' – but rails against the romanticisation of de Valera's rural Ireland. 'No, no, [Ireland today is] a far better place. Way better. Way better. Look at all that hard work – what was it for?' he says rhetorically.

He has, however, less clear memories of Dev's vision for Irish social life and the contest of athletic youth. 'There was the greatest social scene in the countryside in summer that time,' he says with trademark enthusiasm. 'Every parish, for one week, sometimes for two, had a marquee. The marquee then moved from Feakle to Scariff to Whitegate to Tulla, and everybody would go to the marquees.

'When that marquee, we'll say, came to Feakle, there were a whole range of events organised around the marquee. I remember they had a race with milk churns. Then they had backing a trailer with a tractor in between bales, which is a very skilful thing,' he says with a poker face, 'apart from the normal sports like bicycle races and all that sort of thing. It was just brilliant. It was simple, but it was brilliant *craic*,' he stresses.

'You often say to young lads now, what *craic* have ye? If a young lad is bored, they want you to invent something for them. We could entertain ourselves. I remember when we went to school in Feakle – [our teacher] Seán Harrington, he must have been a bloody saint, because what we used to do when we were in the old school, like hunting was a big thing with us, one fella would set off with a 'hare' out across the fields, and we'd come up along the street, and all the rest of the school would be coming up along the street as if they were the beagles chasing the hare and the hare's job was to get back to the school before he was caught, and if he was caught, he was murdered halfway up the street,' he says, struggling to keep in the laughter.

'Totally innocent fun, and the funny thing was the people made no word of it. If you saw a gang of people doing it now, you'd say, "Lock 'em up".'

Incarceration came soon enough. Loughnane highlights the length of time that one boarded, as he did, in a school like St Flannan's College. Having gone in – along with his fellow boarders – at the start of September, he wouldn't return home until Christmas, a pattern that was repeated for the other two terms.

'It was a matter of adapting,' he says. 'It taught you how to adapt to your surroundings and how to survive. You know, you have five or six hundred lads together – even the competition for food at the table was very competitive. It was a bit like the gunslingers in the Wild West. You'd to go in. You'd a big, long table, and you'd to sit at your seat, and all the potatoes would be in the middle of the table, and then the priest would sit above and he'd say the grace before meals, and the minute it was over there'd be a massive grab. It was, like, who had the fastest gun would get the best spuds or would get the best brown bread. You had to have your wits about you, and you had to be competitive. It was literally survival of the fittest.'

He made all his school hurling teams, winning an under-15 White Cup – his only Munster-level win, he points out – and losing a Dr Harty Cup final. Both teams, incidentally, were trained by Bishop Willie Walsh and Fr Seamus Gardiner, and included future teammates on the Clare hurling team, Colm Honan and Johnny Callinan.

'Ger was no more opinionated than a lot of the rest of us,' says Callinan about those days. 'We all thought we knew it all. He was a very driven fella, there's no doubt about that, and he was a fecker to mark, and he had a ferocity about his play. I'd never regard him as being dirty, but you earned everything off him.'

17

Sport was a passport to an improved existence for him, but after so bleak a schooling experience, he has not been to a Flannan's Dr Harty Cup hurling match since.

Teacher training at St Patrick's of Drumcondra in Dublin was a different story: a world of unimagined freedom, of time frittered away in the college's common room, and the hurly-burly of life-or-death inter-house matches on the campus across a range of sports, including rugby. 'I was only allowed play one game,' he admits. 'I wasn't so sure of the rules. It was one of the few times in my life that I was banned. We were playing against another house. It was our first game in, and I was playing at centre. I thought rugby was anything goes, so a fella passed me out and I just reached out and he had a big head of fuzzy hair and I grabbed him by the hair and 'twas then I learned that it wasn't allowed in rugby. I was sent off and advised not to come back again,' he says, as devoid of remorse now as then.

His first year in St Pat's was also the first year in which there were female students in the training college, which 'added to the excitement of the whole thing'. During Rag Week, someone hatched a plan to get a mixed hockey brigade from Trinity College to play in a compromise-rules game – a cultural exchange between the culchie hurlers of St Pat's and the West Brits from College Green. 'They were running rings around us. Now, we had the hurleys but we were playing under the hockey rules, so anyway, at half-time we got together and we said, "Right, we'll change over to the hurling rules." We flaked the living shite out of them. All our prejudices were brought out … these nice, little polite boys from Trinity … and I don't remember any social gathering afterwards,' he says, emitting a slow Count Dracula cackle.

His St Pat's hurling team, which included Brian Cody in the half-back line with him, swept to a Dublin under-21 title. He was also trucking back down to Clare at weekends to play under-21 and senior hurling, making his senior debut against Tipperary in 1972, the same year he played in a Munster under-21 final in Cusack Park in Ennis with a team that included several of the best other Clare hurlers of that era: Callinan, Honan, Jim Power, Enda O'Connor and Séamus Durack. 'The reason we were beaten was as simple as this,' he says, flicking through the famously fat Rolodex of Munster finals he lost – thirteen in total – as a player or mentor before 1995. 'It was the old bloody thing. Séamus Durack, the best goalie around, was playing wing-forward because one of the selectors was from Clarecastle and he wanted a Clarecastle goalie. Séamus Durack was above wing-forward, and the goals we let in were as simple as could be, and we were very narrowly beaten.'

Inter-county glory of a kind came in 1977 and 1978 when he was part of a Clare senior hurling team that won back-to-back National League titles at a time when the competition wasn't the pre-championship training exercise it is becoming these days. But those two heady afternoons are overshadowed, in particular, by the Munster senior hurling finals he played in and which were lost to Cork's three-in-a-row All-Ireland team. 'I suppose he wouldn't be too unlike John Gardiner in lots of ways,' says John Allen about Ger's stick work, having played against him in the 1978 Munster final. 'Now, John Gardiner's bigger, obviously, but Loughnane did his business. He was a good striker. He was a good reader of the game, which is important at wing-back.'

To look at footage of him as a player – with that 'walk like a crouch', as Babs Keating remarks – is to see a tidy, hard, no-nonsense operator. Clare's first-ever recipient of an All-Star, in 1974, he was a hurler who was rarely caught out, maintain those who analysed him during his career.

'It was in the *Examiner* one time, a big heading: "One Glorious Day at the Park" – some Cork guy that went mad – "One day", it was always referred to afterwards – "One Glorious Day at the Park". Now, Loughnane wasn't that sort; he was the guy that you could depend on every day,' says RTÉ radio commentator, Micheál Ó Muircheartaigh.

'He was the one fella that I always remember would question things,' says Colum Flynn, who was the physical trainer of the Clare team at that time. 'You knew with Loughnane: what you saw was what you got. There was no talking behind your back. I always remember one night, one of the lads was giving out – Jimmy Mac [McNamara]. Jimmy was after taking a bit of a pasting. He was a fine hurler, but he didn't take to the physical training very well. Jimmy said inside in the dressing-room, "Ah, for feck's sake, my lower back and legs are goosed. That was too much now tonight."

'I was just outside the dressing-room. I heard Loughnane: "Ah, for goodness sake, Jimmy, why don't you speak out for yourself if you feel you're being hard done by?" That obviously shut him up, pronto.'

'He was a very dedicated player,' says Justin McCarthy, who trained Loughnane on those league-winning teams in the late 1970s. 'He was very single-minded, but so was Seán Hehir, so was Johnny Callinan – a very single-minded guy – so was Durack. I couldn't at that stage pick out and see that this guy was going to be something different.'

What he did do differently – certainly to Hehir and Durack, who both went on to unsuccessfully manage the Clare senior hurling team – is that he had the gumption to absorb some of McCarthy's hurling philosophy when his time came to manage the team in the mid-1990s – chiefly an obsession with speed.

'Always his training sessions revolved around speed, even when we were under-14,' says Brian Lohan, who played on under-age teams with Loughnane at Wolfe Tones and later with the Clare under-21s and seniors.

Exactly how much Ger Loughnane owes to McCarthy has been a contentious point. 'The legacy of Justin's time with Clare is Ger Loughnane's team,' argued Callinan in an interview in 2002. 'It's irrefutable. Justin kept on talking to us about speed, speed, speed. That was Loughnane's mantra as well. I have seen Loughnane coach at close quarters, and it was obvious to me – who had played under Justin – that it was a development of the McCarthy School.'

Yet Loughnane has shown some reticence in acknowledging the influence McCarthy has had on his coaching style, revising an assessment he made in an interview before the 1995 All-Ireland hurling final of McCarthy as 'the best I ever saw' to the watery compliment that appeared in his book, *Raising the Banner*: 'For his time, McCarthy was a good coach.'

Success has many fathers, as they say. Beyond the coaching antecedents, trying to determine where Loughnane's part in ending Clare's eighty-one-year All-Ireland famine starts and finishes is like trying to unravel the drivers behind the Northern Ireland Peace Process. Would those fifteen young bachelors – Lohan, McMahon, Doyle *et al.* – have swept to victory at some stage anyway?

Clare, remember, won six Munster club titles in a row from 1995 to 2000. How important was the role played by physical trainer, Mike McNamara – General MacArthur to Loughnane's Eisenhower? What about the charismatic captain, Anthony Daly? And where did Biddy Early fit into it? Wasn't she just a nineteenth-century healer?

'Whether he would have found that extra grain within that Clare team is debatable,' says hurling analyst Liam Griffin, getting ethnic on the Great Question. 'Maybe he would, but on the law of averages, he mightn't. I think it would have needed a Clareman to get that final bit of inspiration out of them. And in fairness to Loughnane, the management he assembled … Mike McNamara is an unusual character and so is Tony Considine; they were all very different, but as a combination they were a fairly potent force. You'd have to give credit to his team, but at the same time Loughnane was the fountainhead of that team. He was the right man in the right place at the right time. He was also – like everything in life, you make your own luck – a bit lucky with the late goal against Cork [in the 1995 Munster semi-final], and I suppose you could say they were lucky again in that Limerick were in the final and Clare, traditionally, were never afraid of Limerick.'

'If you were Loughnane coming in – and Mike Mac – in 1994 and drawing up your plan, you'd have had a list of criteria,' says James O'Connor, with a logician's hat on. 'Okay, is it physical fitness? Right, well, we're going to take that away. We're going to be the fittest team in the country. Is it speed of our hurling? Well, we'll make sure to do whatever we can to maximise that. Is it organisation? Is it the back room? Whatever it is, one by one, you take all the excuses away. Players just have to go out and play because everything else is right.'

Tony Adams, the former Arsenal footballer, once cited a US study into champions and their coaches over a twenty-year period in which it was concluded that the maximum impact of managers is ten per cent. Even if Loughnane's contribution was to only add one per cent, it was probably the difference that was required. And if that little bit had a name, it was his preternatural we're-going-to-do-it self-confidence. After whippings in the 1993 and 1994 Munster finals, Clare stormed to a league final in the spring of 1995, but got a lesson from Kilkenny. 'The common word after that final,' says Ó Muircheartaigh, 'was "the same old story" because they came to it with a good chance ... the same old story, the same old story, but Loughnane said that evening, "We'll win the Munster championship." Nobody believed him. I didn't believe him, but I was convinced later that he believed it himself.'

During Ger Loughnane's tenure, Clare won two All-Irelands and three Munster championships. It was an unprecedented haul. The goading, the bullying, the bloody skulduggery he employed to achieve it is the stuff of legend. He would stop at nothing to win, an embodiment of a rugby forward's if-you're-not-cheating-you're-not-competing attitude, as a snapshot from the 1998 Clare–Cork championship match – recorded in Brian Corcoran's book, *Every Single Ball* – illustrates. In the closing few minutes, Cork were two points down. They won a sideline ball inside Clare's 40-metre line. Just as they were lining up the ball, Loughnane kicked it away. It gave Clare time to regroup. Clare won back the ball and swept down field in an attack that resulted in a Stephen McNamara goal. While Clare's 'Sparrow' O'Loughlin was being treated for an injury, Loughnane rushed in to complain to the referee, again sucking the wind from Cork's sails. 'I roared at Ger to get off the fucking field,' writes Corcoran. 'I was fuming.'

Loughnane quarried for similarly competitive individuals to make up his team. 'If you look at Davy Fitz [Fitzgerald] – so determined – if you look at Brian Lohan, look at Daly, look at Ollie Baker … he moulded half a dozen guys around him that were very similar to himself, and those half a dozen were going to get the best out of everybody else,' D. J. Carey points out. 'He hadn't his own personality and everyone else was different. He had six or seven like-minded guys – guys who wanted to win, and wanted to win badly.'

In addition, Loughnane had an eye for plucking players from obscurity. 'His biggest strength was the way he was able to pick out players who certainly I wouldn't have noticed before,' argued Brian Lohan in Joe Ó Muircheartaigh's book, *The Time of Our Lives*. 'McMahon was the prime example. After the Munster final of 1993, Loughnane told me that I would be full-back and that McMahon would be outside me at centre-back. He did the same thing in relation to Michael O'Halloran. He was never on a county team. He did the same with Alan Markham, who was on the senior team before he was on an under-21 team. Niall Gilligan made the county team before he played a full match for Sixmilebridge.'

In the same interview, Lohan states that players from other inter-county teams spoke about Loughnane's presence on the field; in effect, that he was like a 'sixteenth player'. He certainly made his presence known at training, where the stick was favoured over the carrot. 'Invariably, in an awful lot of the challenge matches we'd play in training, I'd be marking Rusty [Chaplain] or Rusty would be on me,' says James O'Connor. 'A wet, dirty evening, Rusty might have cleared the first two balls in the match and Loughnane would be, "G'man Rusty, you've him fuckin' cleaned." But that was it. What were you to do? You were gritting your teeth and making sure you were going to win the next ball and shove it down that bollix's throat. And he was doing that to everybody.'

Daly wondered if he was on something for his throat, as the berating would last nonstop for the duration of the training session.

Pictures of him, particularly in 1997, show the toll it took on him, his face drawn and gaunt-looking. And, of course, it wasn't only the players who suffered the sergeant-major treatment in the Clare camp. One evening a County Board official was given a simple task for training. 'The old way for training matches was to puck around with three or four hurling balls,' recounts a witness. 'Every time one went out over the back, play had to be halted. This fellow was told to bring two dozen balls to this training session or more even – it could have been three dozen – and he arrived with a half dozen. Loughnane came out roaring his name, "You bollix, you! Where are the hurling balls?"

'"Oh, I've some more out in the car."

'"Well, get out and get them." So he hunted him out like a dog. The car was parked out by the gate. And when he came back in with them, Loughnane said, "Now fuck off out that gate again!"'

Outside the camp, the country was treated to dramas of high farce, as controversy piled onto controversy. There was the listing of dummy teams, to the annoyance of the GAA authorities and the press.

After Clare's All-Ireland victory over Tipp in 1997, Loughnane availed of a post-match celebratory slot on television to lambast RTÉ analyst Eamon Cregan for his overly critical assessment of the most dramatic All-Ireland final in memory, insinuating that Cregan was 'looking after his job' in Tipperary as a building-society branch manager.

And during one glorious summer, while the country's politicians rested poolside during their silly season, Loughnane took to tilting at windmills, thundering on air during a 70-minute interview on Clare FM radio about the murky murmurings of three priests high up in the stands of Croke Park, and the illegality of the Munster Council's handling of Colin Lynch's three-month suspension.

'The greatest thing is when you look back on it that you did it,' he says about the summer of 1998. 'I mean, the easiest thing would be to walk away from it and not do it. It gives me massive satisfaction now to look back on it and say, "Jesus, wasn't it great to take them all on, fuckin' have a go at them," you know? You got an insight into the workings of the GAA,' he says, buoyed by the memory, 'that you'd never have got. The instinct to protect the institution became a fanatical desire for the hierarchy in the GAA. That goes from president down. Protecting the institution, that was their instinct. That's what they were going to do. No matter what, and no matter what rules they had to invent or to circumvent, they were going to do that, and that is the way it works.'

Loughnane stepped down as manager of the Clare team in 2000 after they were knocked out in the first round of the Munster championship by Tipperary. 'Always the hardest decision is to tell players their career is over, players that have served you very well,' he says about the toughest challenge he experiences as a manager. 'Telling the likes of the Sparrow that his career was over,' he adds with a heavy heart. 'Clare wouldn't have won any All-Irelands without the Sparrow. You take in the Sparrow's contribution towards the Munster championship win the day [in July 1997] below in Cork against Tipperary and the punishment he took that day was just incredible in order to give the ball to David Forde. I mean, fellas who had laid down everything they had for the team, and then the time comes when you have to tell them that the show is over, but that is what you have to do for the good of the team.'

The forcefulness with which Loughnane – in his role as a hurling critic in a weekly column in the *Star* newspaper and on television's *The Sunday Game* – sought to curtain-call the careers of so many of his former Clare players has caused trouble lately. In his capacity as a hurling pundit, he persistently belittled some of his ex-players' performances. Some of them, he moaned, had become 'big-game chokers'.

Regeneration is a key dictum with Loughnane. The problem, observers note, was that when he was calling on Daly – as Clare hurling manager from 2003 to 2006 – to retire older players such as McMahon and Lohan, there was no one near their stature to replace them. Should Daly have discarded McMahon in order to groom

Conor Plunkett at centre back? Would, as a parallel, the Republic of Ireland have beaten Italy and qualified for the knock-out stages of the 1994 World Cup finals if Jack Charlton had jettisoned Paul McGrath in favour of sprightly Alan Kernaghan? Could Kernaghan have then gone on to be the backbone of the Irish team for the next five years as a result of the exposure? Unlikely.

Furthermore, the language Loughnane employed – acceptable when used to goad his players in training sessions behind closed doors – caused grave offence when presented in cold print for the public's titillation. Baker was a 'spent force' in 2001 he proclaimed; Niall Gilligan, Barry Murphy and Forde, 'nearly men'. Clare supporters 'visibly cringed', he stated, when James O'Connor reappeared for the second half of a qualifying game in 2004.

'It never affected me too much. I always thought that Loughnane did an awful lot for us when we were there and if there was anyone entitled to criticise us, surely 'tis him. I wouldn't have felt the criticism; then I probably didn't hear it, either, but I would never have had any problem with criticism from Loughnane,' says Brian Lohan in Loughnane's defence. He is a lone voice in a straw poll of several former Clare players, the rest being at best bemused, at worst peeved with Loughnane's over-the-top criticisms.

Aside from the criticism being expressed in scathing terms, it often seemed contradictory, as has been highlighted in forensic examination by Denis Walsh. Writing in June 2005, he noticed how Loughnane announced 'a new era was starting for Clare hurling' when they had defeated Tipperary in the first round of the Munster championship in 2003. Four weeks later – after Clare were knocked out of the championship by Galway – he declared that 'Clare are at their weakest in terms of personnel, morale and ability than at any time in the past 10 years.' What happened to the new era, wondered Walsh.

A year later, after an honourable defeat to Kilkenny in a two-match quarter-final encounter, Loughnane declared that 'Anthony Daly really showed his mettle as a manager on Saturday and he is the man to take

Clare forward.' The following summer, he had revised his opinion, declaring Daly to be 'indecisive, and timid, lacking the confidence and cockiness that marked him as an exceptional captain. Worst of all, his team reflects this.' Before that year's league final, in May, Loughnane announced that, apart from the Cork hurlers, Clare had the 'best goalkeeper, defence and midfield'; several weeks later, he was calling for retirements in all of those areas.

Amidst these inconsistencies, what remained consistent was his demand that Daly clear out members of his support team, though he declined to name them. 'He would have done Daly no favours now would he ... when he [Daly] was managing the team? When Clare was going badly, no one was telling Len Gaynor to get rid of his back-room staff,' points out Fergie Tuohy, alluding to the days in the early 1990s when Loughnane served as a selector under Gaynor.

'I still have desperate respect for the guy [Loughnane] for what he did for us, but relations at the moment are nothing short – and I've no problem in saying this – of sad,' says Daly. 'Things are sad, and if I've contributed to that ... I'm not so sure I have. I did nothing as far as I'm concerned, and even last year – my first year – on the auld panel [*The Sunday Game*], there was a lot of controversy, and I tried to stay clear of it as much as I could, and yet every time Tony [Considine, 2007 Clare hurling manager] had a bit of bother, Ger put it down to the fact that he was only trying to clear up that three-year mess [Daly's management reign]. You know, what did I do to deserve this? If he has problems with Harry [Bohan, former Clare selector under Daly] ... Harry doesn't know where that's coming from either. The players are still great friends. I don't meet fellas now [regularly] ... we try and go away twice a year for a game of golf – in the summer in Glasson, and then go away for a golf weekend before Christmas. So they [Loughnane and Considine] won't go anymore because they know there's tension. That's the way it is now. Look, if I'm the cause of the tension, I'd be the first to hold my hands up. I don't think I am. I can look in the mirror and say, "I didn't cause this." It's sad. It's sad,' he says, shaking his head. 'That's the only word to describe it. You know, I meet fellas from other counties and they say, "Jeez, it's feckin' awful." From talking to lads, you know the Cork–Tipp rivalry – Babs [Keating, former Tipperary manager] would be in the thick of it: "You remember that day, Nicky? You kicked it past Cunningham. Hah?" They'd still have brilliant days out. They'd meet up with the Cork lads and they have an auld golf tournament with each other.'

'He is stone mad,' reckons Keating, reclining in the psychiatrist's chair. 'I got the job of analysing the book [*Raising the Banner*] for the *Sunday Times*. When I went through the things he wrote, the things he said about his own county men, it sickened me. Then I cut him to pieces in the paper. The following September, we were both asked to do something for charity, sponsored by Toyota. I said it to the wife going off, "I dread this meeting, now." I got there and I was having a meal. Now, if he wrote about me, I'd have hit him a box. He came in, and he was all over me, shaking hands and "Great to see ya." He couldn't be nicer to me. I was saying to myself, "What kind of fella are you at all?" Hah? I was sitting down thinking, "I'm not too sure he's right". That's the way he is.'

'Ah, there's a streak of madness in Ger all right,' adds former Clare hurler, Michael O'Halloran. 'There is. I talked to other people from other counties and they'll all say the same – you know he could say something about you on *The Sunday Game*, and if he went into Dublin to a hotel and met you that night, he'd have the big shake-hands. There is that streak of madness to him, and maybe that's what drives him as well. Maybe that's what made him good in the first place – I don't know – but he's definitely not your normal, sober kind of a Brian Cody or Nicky English or any of these fellas.

'And the thing is that once he started, he wasn't rowing back. That's the thing about him. A bit like 1998 – once he got on his high horse, there was no bringing him back down from it. I think once people started carping and he saw there was a bit of a reaction, for some reason he decided I'm not gonna flinch here, I'm not gonna back down.

I'm gonna keep calling it as I see it. The only other thing about Ger is – and I've heard it in Cork [where O'Halloran lives] particularly – is that it would have killed him to see someone else winning with basically his team. He should have acknowledged in 2000 when he stepped down that he had done what he could, he'd taken them as far as he could, and move on, much like the Kerry manager steps down – Jack O'Connor steps down and Pat O'Shea comes in and wins an All-Ireland, and it's great. Jack O'Connor doesn't start slagging off the Kerry team.'

Daly is troubled, too, by American writer Gore Vidal's old adage that 'it's not enough to succeed, others must fail, especially your friends'. 'I think there's something inside of him,' he says. 'I have to admit now: that *he* was the man that had won for Clare and I think inside in us all, deep down, we must overcome that at times. If I had won club championships for Clarecastle … somewhere deep down, there's a morsel … anyone's a liar that tells you that you're not thinking, "Jeez, someone else now is stealing my bit of glory on me." You must overcome that as a human being. You have to say, "Damn it. It's my club. I'm bigger than this. By Jaysus, I'll back him to the last." I think it overcame Ger a bit. That he was a little bit scared that we would get there … and we almost got there. That's my honest opinion. I could be well wrong … I could be well wide of the mark.'

'I'm fond of him, but I could see where you'd fall in love or you could get sucked in with that whole guru, celebrity [status],' suggests a successful inter-county manager of his generation. 'I really think you have to step back and not believe your own publicity, maybe. There could be an element that he has believed his own publicity a little bit, and that has distanced him from the team, and I'll be straight about it, there's no way I would distance myself from the players I was involved with because I'm a different personality. I wouldn't be able to live with myself if I did, but Ger is quite comfortable in his own skin doing that, and maybe he's a stronger character because of that. It wouldn't be my way, but in fairness to him, that's his way and he's entitled [to it].'

Although this is a sentiment you will hear repeated – that Loughnane suffers from hubris – the logic doesn't wholly apply. He's not an ostentatious man. He's still rooted in the simple, rural locale in which he grew up. His behaviour hasn't altered in the last fifteen years, or, indeed going further back; it's just that his platform has broadened. He's always been wildly opinionated and zealous. 'I first got a taste of managing from a school's team in Shannon,' he writes in his book, *Raising the Banner*. 'I remember once we were playing in Newmarket. The referee, a teacher from the other school, got so annoyed with me that he threw the whistle over the line and walked off the field! He said, "I've enough of this lunatic," and disappeared!'

You get the sense that if Baker's fortuitous goal against Cork in June 1995 hadn't gone in and changed the course of hurling history, Loughnane would probably be busy today making a nuisance of himself with Department of Education heads rather than GAA authorities.

'With Clare, there was no time you ever thought of pulling back [in your criticisms]?' I ask.

'No. No.'

'There was no way of sugaring the pill?'

'No. No. No.'

'You weren't worried about upsetting relationships?'

'Listen,' he says, laughing, 'when players played under me, I told them exactly how they played when they were inside in the field. I told them who went to town on them. They all knew exactly where I stood. Now, funnily enough, when they heard me say it on television, there was a lot more resentment on their part because they imagined that I was still manager of the Clare team, that I was a manager. It's very hard for a player to separate in their mind … if they're with you for five or six or seven years, there is a huge bond there between you, but when you are doing analysis on a team, it's a completely different thing. You have to look at it from a totally different point of view.

'It's funny, one Saturday night I was looking at Alan Hansen and [Alan] Shearer on *Match of the Day*; pure fluke that I should turn over, and they were drawing Shearer about becoming involved with Newcastle, and Hansen was encouraging him to become involved, and he saw him as the number one, and the presenter says, "Yeah, you'll be his number one and in three months' time, you won't be talking to him."

'It's gas, isn't it? That's what it is. Because if you do it properly – and I wouldn't do it unless I was going to do it properly – but if you do it properly, you have to cut yourself away … you're no longer in the dressing-room, you're no longer in the Clare dressing-room, you're in nobody's dressing-room – you're looking at it from a totally different point of view.

'I wasn't the manager of the Clare team when I was on television, I was gone from it. I was totally divorced from it, but it's very hard for a player in his mind to divorce or separate me as manager of Clare, and me, not being manager anymore, now analysing the thing on television and having to come at the thing from a totally different perspective. Some would see that as being disloyal to them, but if I was loyal to them and tell lies to them on television … in other words, to say you're playing great when you're not playing great …'

'But what about Daly? Is that a travesty or does that upset you, if relations aren't the best anymore?'

'The way I look at it is there's always going to be a certain amount of resentment when you say it first, but as you let time go by – if you let five or six years go by – that'll all fade away. That'll all be totally different. Whatever about Daly, when Daly was captain of the Clare team, nobody had greater admiration, and I've always professed it – the admiration I had for him – and I have never, ever seen a better captain than him. Anyone you want to captain a team, you want them to model themselves on the way he was as captain, but he has to remember there's a difference between Daly as captain and Daly as Citizen Joe, as well – there's a big difference – or Daly as manager.

'When I'm commenting about Daly's decisions as manager, it's as a manager, it's not as Anthony Daly, the captain of the Clare team,

Anthony Daly as a person, Anthony Daly as a hurler; it's Anthony Daly as manager of the Clare team. Now, again, he probably finds it very hard to separate that, but for me it's totally different.'

'But ye would have had a bond or [shared] mutual respect, and that's impaired now, isn't it?'

'In Anthony Daly's mind, I'd say it is, but I still have the same regard for him now as I had when he was captain of the Clare team, even though I had to tell him at the end of his career that he was no longer captain of the Clare team, as well. That cycle always comes,' he says, chuckling.

'He knows that I was dead honest when I told him that I think his time for the captaincy was over, and that he must be struggling hard enough for his place on the team the last year he played, and that we're better off to move on to a new captain, and he respected that.

'Now, the same way when I moved out of the Clare dressing-room, I was commenting on his performance as a manager, not his performance as captain and he was never used to any criticism because I had no reason to ever criticise him as captain of the Clare team because he was exemplary. Players find it hard to differentiate between that. I suppose it's because of their youth as well.'

'Does that upset you?'

'Not in the slightest. Not in the slightest,' he says with a smile. 'It doesn't upset me in the slightest. In time, they'll realise that that is what it is. Once you take on a job, whether 'tis as a manager, or as an analyst or whatever you're doing, if you're not really true to yourself, first of all people are going to see through it very fast – even though you might think they won't – and secondly, you'll get no satisfaction out of it. Whatever job you're given, unless you do it to the best of your ability and in the most honest way possible, you're going to get no satisfaction out of it.'

It is this loose observation that maybe relations are impaired 'in Anthony Daly's mind' but not in his own that hint at a defining trait of Loughnane. The guy has rhinoceros skin. If somebody says something critical about him, often he doesn't seem to harbour any ill-feeling (a good quality), but, equally, if he says nasty, overly personal things about others, he seems oblivious to their feelings (a not-so-good quality).

A couple of the players he managed to All-Ireland success in the 1990s no longer speak to him. Men he had soldiered with. What is it all for, you wonder? Loughnane believes maybe this animosity has been caused because of 'their youth', and that they will come around. But who has acted immaturely in creating the rift, they argue? 'It's a pity,' says Tuohy. 'If you look at all the good managers, if you look at Liam Griffin, he has a great rapport with his old troops. Jimmy Barry Murphy would have the same, Donal O'Grady, John Allen, Cyril Farrell above in Galway, [whereas Loughnane] doesn't give a shite who he pisses off.'

Maybe it was written in the stars that Loughnane would grow apart from his former team, just as Alex Ferguson's schism with Roy Keane led to the player's departure from Manchester United. Loughnane always maintained a distance of sorts, but for it to happen so dramatically seems a tragedy. Sure, he has been true to himself – a most civilising quality – in his role as a pundit, but maybe to uncivilised lengths.

'People can turn around and say, "He says what he thinks and that's good." Yeah, yeah,' says D. J. Carey, each affirmative word drawn out slowly like a question mark. 'It's all right, if the tune is not changing every day. At the end of the day, no matter what anyone says in any sport, we're all human. None of us go out to play bad. None of us at inter-county level are bad players. It just may not work out on a particular day.'

After a six-year hiatus, Loughnane stepped back into inter-county management with a different tribe, being unveiled as the Galway hurlers' manager in September 2006, brashly proclaiming that if he didn't deliver an All-Ireland title in two years he'd be 'a failure'. Boy, did he fail. As misadventures go, it ranks with Cloughie's forty-four-day reign at Leeds United. Both seasons Galway didn't even manage to get past the quarter-final stages, losing – in a particularly listless performance – to fourteen-man Cork in the qualifiers in July 2008.

'It's hard to know what exactly went wrong,' pondered Daly in his Digest for RTÉ, 'but at the end of the day I guess if you haven't paint you can't paint and how he must have longed halfway through the second half to have some of his old foot soldiers like Baker, Lohan, Lynch and McMahon to stem the rising Rebel tide. Making rash statements like winning the All-Ireland within two years is loose talk that to me only serves to heap pressure on shoulders that are hardly able to carry it, but then Ger always struggled a bit in that department.'

Removed from the post in October – his three-year contract cut short by a year – who knows what lies in store for Loughnane? It's hard to imagine the hurling landscape without his irreverent presence, even the muzzled version on display last season. In Clare, because of the controversies he has created, the enmities he has aroused in the hurling community, there is an eaten-bread-is-soon-forgotten feeling about his legacy. As his good friend, Colum Flynn remarks wistfully: 'The evil that men do lives after them; the good is oft interred with their bones.'

Though no Caesar and certainly not godly, to paraphrase American writer, Padgett Powell, Loughnane is still a kind of god in the county. Like all gods, he's loved by some (mostly from a distance) and not by others.

KIEREN FALLON

During the court case at the Old Bailey in late 2007 in which Kieren Fallon was charged, farcically, with conspiring to defraud the betting exchange company, Betfair, he was asked if he knew of the practice of 'stopping a horse'. He said he had read about it in Dick Francis stories and seen it in Mickey Rooney films. In a quieter, private moment, Fallon may well have wondered was it all a bad dream. But even Dick Francis would have been pressed to come up with a novel as preposterous as Fallon's life story.

Although Fallon is probably the greatest flat-racing jockey of his generation, and some would argue of any generation, he was eighteen years of age before he mounted a horse with a saddle. It's a mind-boggling thought. It's as if someone told you that Tiger had taken up golf at the voting age rather than as a toddler. Yet this incredible detail flounders among the footnotes of his story when set against the drama of his life on and off the track.

So when Fallon was a teenager – instead of riding out like Frankie Dettori or Christophe Soumillon did as youngsters because it was in their blood – boxing was the sport that used to keep him out of harm's way. And in the Mickey Rooney film of his life story, the Spencer Tracey character would undoubtedly be Jimmy Regan, his wily old boxing coach.

Regan is in his late sixties now, but you wouldn't know it to look at him. He'd still take you in a ring. He's five-foot-eleven, but stands four-square, and the flesh on his nose is pressed back towards his cheeks, courtesy of the three hundred-plus fights he boxed in his prime. He lived in the UK for the first half of his adult life, once receiving a winner's medal for the British tug-of-war championship from Queen Elizabeth II. Having worked in Broadmoor Hospital for seventeen years – tending to inmates such as Ronnie Kray and Moors Murderer, Ian Brady – Regan came back to Ireland to continue working in psychiatric care. When the thirteen-year-old Fallon turned up at his gym in Gort – on the Galway–Clare border – Regan took to him. He liked his attitude. Fallon would find his little space, and work away, always having to be told when to stop his drills on the bag or the time ball. Fallon was clever. He'd listen to advice. If Regan told him he was dropping his left hand when he was sparring, he wouldn't drop it twice. And when Regan walked on the stomachs of his charges like a man using magic stepping stones to get across a lake, Fallon wouldn't wince. Although invariably there was nothing in Fallon's stomach. Regan challenged him one evening, wondering if he was getting his food. When Fallon muttered unconvincingly about having a sandwich in his bag, Regan told him to drop by his house the following evening at half-six so he could have some food with himself and his wife Jane before going on to the gym. It became a routine.

Fallon's boxing was coming on nicely, so, having won his counties and receiving a bye in the 'Connaughts', he arrived at his first inter-provincial series kitted out in a vest 'that you'd nearly have to tie between his legs,' says Regan, referring to his forty-two-kilo frame of 'pure bone'.

'As it happened,' he continues, 'when we went into the dressing-room, I looked across and I said to myself, "I know this guy. I've seen him before." He was from Cork city. Joyce was his name. So I went over to him and said, "Is your name Joyce? Are you boxing a guy from Gort?"

'"That's right. I'm boxing Kieren Fallon."

'I said, "I've seen you before. Have you been up to Dublin?"

'"Oh yeah, I've been up there." He had an Irish title at twelve.

'I called his trainer over. I said, "Hold it a minute now. I don't know who made this match, but I think your boy is far superior to my boy.'

'And he said, "Well, there's no secret about it."

'I said, "How many fights has he had?"

'"Oh," he said, "Thirty, forty fights."

'"Well," I said, "our fella's just had three or four fights."

'"Ah, I wouldn't agree with it," he says.

'I said, "Thanks very much. At least you're honest."

'So I went away across to Kieren. I said, "Kieren, that's your boy over there."

'"Yeah," he said. He never opened his mouth to speak. The energy output was very little.

'I said to him, "Kieren, he has a lot of fights." And he listened, and I said, "I don't think the match is correct. What do you think?"

'He said, "I think he's only got two hands."'

So in Fallon went. Round one, round two – pop, pop, pop. He was getting pasted, but for the third one, he stormed out to the middle of the ring and clocked Joyce with the first punch of the round. Knockout. 'He went home,' says Regan, 'with a trophy as big as himself.'

Fallon was always a jockey in stature. It was said that when he arrived in Our Lady's College (Gort Community School), he was the smallest boy in school, and when he left shortly before his Leaving Certificate five years later, he was still the smallest pupil in the secondary school.

Born on 22 February 1965, he didn't get it easy growing up, being one of six children in his family. 'He had a very, very tough upbringing,' says Regan, remembering that Fallon would think nothing of walking the seven miles from Gort on dark, wild, winter evenings to his parents' forty-acre farm seven miles away in Ballinruan – the last mile of the journey being up an old, unlit bog road – and would thumb everywhere: into Ennis for the shopping with his mother, and to school, since, inconveniently, the bus would have dropped him at the school gates an hour before class started. And he was never in a rush to get into class.

'I was the thickest in most schools I was in. I had to be the thickest,' says Fallon with that endearing honesty of his. 'Nothing would register at school at all with me, but sometimes I'd put up my hand because if I didn't put up my hand they'd ask me. They'd always ask the one that don't put up their hand. They'd say: "Hands up all who know the answer." Who's he going to ask? The thick eejit who doesn't have his hand up. What's the point in asking him? If he knew the answer, he'd put his hand up. That's one I couldn't understand, one of the mysteries of my school anyway.'

Academically, he struggled, failing most of his Inter Cert subjects, although he bagged an A in woodwork. Literacy is still a bane. 'I can't spell my own name,' he says, and he's only half joking. Writing text messages is a painstaking operation, taking two or three times to get it right, and he says he might have read three books in his life.

When he wasn't at school or working on the farm – 'bog land that's really no good for nothing,' he admits – he laboured, mixing plaster for his father, who worked as a plasterer. Without the luxury of a cement mixer, he'd horse the plaster together with a stick, and, going to a new job, he'd dread arriving at a driveway with a two-storey house as that meant scurrying up and down a makeshift ladder with buckets of wet plaster.

Years later, in one of the perverse pay backs that life occasionally affords, he realised that the crushing pattern of early mornings and physical work he endured as a child stood to him when it came to mucking out stables and the like as an apprentice jockey, where he got to work with 'lovely three-pronged forks,' he says affectionately – the way a fisherman might talk about a favoured brand of rods. 'I loved work,' he says simply and convincingly. 'Racing isn't difficult. Compared to farm work, stable work is a piece of piss, really.'

He got the racing bug by osmosis. 'Whatever I was on, I always thought it was a horse, from watching telly. Getting on a wall, with a rope across a wall pretending you were on a horse or with a stick, or even riding your bike, you'd think it was a horse. Whatever I was on, I always thought it was a horse,' he says, while you're picturing him on Sunday afternoons, glued to old Westerns on a black-and-white television, sitting astride a blanket on the end of a couch riding along with the posse.

'You can't explain it, but you're living out the country there, and all you're doing is going to school and back; there was no life other than boxing, hurling and sports on a Sunday,' he says, referring to the communal sports days in which his mother used to always win the married women's race, while his father used to row in with one of the tug-of-war teams.

They had an old Connemara pony called Isabel – a wild one that was never broken in – on which he got his first real taste of riding. 'There was a big old slab of black rock out the back. I used to stand up on that and have a carrot or grass, and encourage her to come around so she's parallel; and then when she did, I'd be feeding her, rubbing her back. Next thing, I'd slide on across her without her even knowing. She'd feel me on her back and she'd take off across the field,' he says, slapping his thigh.

'Because she didn't have anything around her – if you put a saddle on a horse, because you put the girdle around them, that's what makes them buck – she used to never buck. She used to take off, flat out, racing down through the fields for miles. I would tuck in behind her, hold onto the mane – no tack, no bridle, no nothing – like a jockey, not knowing what to do but ... it was instinct,' he says proudly. The only way to dismount was to be thrown off. 'It's amazing when you're a kid like that – you bounce like a rubber ball,' he says. Indeed.

The horseplay came to an end one day when his father spotted him from across the fields. Isabel was gone the next day.

'You must have been heartbroken,' I venture.

'What?' he says, looking at me disbelievingly. 'Look it, back then, there was no such thing as fucking "heartbroken",' his voice lowering. 'Years ago, you got on with whatever you had to do. You just got on. You had to do your chores …'

In his last year at school, he came across a 'how to become a jockey' book, which included a list of Irish trainers. He got his mother to do up a letter, and with a reference letter from Regan, he fired a set off to Andrew McNamara, Edward O'Grady, Dermot Weld, Jim Bolger and Kevin Prendergast. Prendergast replied and gave him a job. The Leaving Cert exams could wait for another time, he reckoned, and he took off, arriving at Prendergast's stables in February 1983, on the cusp of his eighteenth birthday. It didn't take him long before he could ride everything in the yard, piloting his first winner, *Piccadilly Lord*, the following year in Navan – although his late arrival to the game contributed to his unusual technique.

'He wouldn't have the most orthodox of styles,' says racing trainer and pundit, Ted Walsh. 'Technically, some fellas have a certain style. He hasn't got the crouch of Johnny Murtagh or Dettori; he stands a little bit upright, and he always rides a little bit different. He's a very good rider, now. Horses run for him. Everyone who rides has their own identity. You'd look at some fellas and say, "He's a beautiful style." You'd pick Fallon out, but you wouldn't say he's a lovely stylist. He's good hands, now, and he's very strong, but not a stylist. It doesn't matter – every cripple has his way of walkin'.'

'He's very kind to horses,' adds Eamon Dunphy, one of racing's more colourful pundits, drawing attention to the empathy Fallon has with horses. Along with his scratch-your-eye-out determination, Fallon's great gift is his innate understanding of horses, experts argue.

'With two-year-olds, they can get beaten up,' continues Dunphy. 'They need tender introductions into racing, which he gives them. He doesn't beat them up to win first time out, necessarily. He'd give them a nice introduction to racing, and they'd improve because of him being on board, whereas other jockeys might beat them to death to win by a short head. He's very professional, very patient, and then when he needed to be strong with experienced horses on the big day, he always was.'

Fallon stayed with Prendergast for five happy, carefree years – sharing a flat with Charlie Swan – before moving across the water to take up a job with Jimmy FitzGerald, whom he credits with teaching him the most in his career, though the biggest-single lesson he learned in racing came from 'the long fellow': 'I was riding a horse for Eric Alston, one of the first good fillies I ever rode. She used to like to make the running. I was in the stall and [Lester] Piggott is sitting next to me, and looking at me, not that he'd want to be talking to me or anything: "What are you doing?"

'I couldn't wait to tell him what I was doing. "Sir, sir, I'm going to make the running."

'"Yeah, you'll definitely make the running!" I was riding one of the dangers. He was riding the other one. There was a big field. When you're riding in those sprints, it's great to be able to know what to follow because he had choices of different ones to follow, but you usually like to follow the one that's definitely going to make the running. In those sprints, you can't give an inch away. So anyway, I bounced out,' he says, whistling for effect. 'And I'm looking at the video afterwards and who's sitting up my fuckin' tale, using none of his energy, getting no wind resistance? With a half a furlong, he just buzzed out and got me on the line. Got me on the line. If he beat me by three or four lengths, I'd say he was on the better horse, but got me on the line.'

So what was he like, the 'Housewives' Favourite'?

Fallon makes a slow, buzzing sound to go with a scrunched-rat's face. 'He'd do that at you, fucking eejit. I'll tell you one thing, apart from that, if I was on something I fancied and anyone asked me what I was going to do, I wouldn't be telling them, anyway,' he says, tossing his head wearily.

Racing is a taxing sport. When he's racing, Fallon enters a thousand races a year, legging around the country from racecourse to racecourse, and from continent to continent. While riding in Australia, he used to have to set his alarm clock to wake him every couple of hours so he could get fluids into himself to keep his weight up because he was perspiring so much. It's probably a luxury he has that most other jockeys don't – he doesn't struggle to keep his weight in check. 'You keep yourself fit by riding,' he says. During his younger days, he would have taken various tablets such as Thermolift or Duramine – which have since been banned – to help keep his weight down. His stomach – or his appetite – has shrunk as a result.

Racing is also a ruthless game. You get the impression from Fallon that there aren't many high-fives exchanged between jockeys in the weigh room.

'Is there any *craic*, any banter?'

'Where? In racing?' he asks, looking for my second head.

'You know – before or after races?'

'Ah yeah, when you're out on a night or whatever. But fuck it, hey, somebody wants your fuckin' job. You know everyone wants the good jobs, and not just the good jobs, the good rides as well. You get on a good ride, you want to keep it 'cause you know there's five or six others trying to get on there as well, and if they don't, their agents will.'

More than once, Fallon's temper has spilled over on the course. In 1994 he picked up a seven-day ban for cracking fellow jockey Chris Rutter with his whip. The same year, he got a six-month ban for violent or improper conduct after a clash with the jockey, Stuart Webster. 'It's a bit like watching the hurling,' he says, using an analogy from his favourite spectator sport. 'If you had somebody that you're having a niggle with or somebody wants to cut your fuckin' throat

– and he was trying to cut mine for a long time, and [we] ended up in a race that he put me on the floor. I went down on my head. I nearly got killed. So by the time I came up, I chased him but I didn't realise he'd won the race and the camera was on him. When I went up to pull him up over it, he told me to fuck off. I was just in a rage. I just grabbed him.'

'He nearly took your life?'

'But they weren't worried about that,' he spits. 'They're worried about what is bad for racing; what's seen on camera. Not that you could have got killed in the race. There's something like twenty run a race and I've got eighteen cunts behind me, and he's right underneath my neck, clipped his heels … [I] nearly went down. But anyway …' The altercation concluded in the weigh room where, apparently, Webster came off worse. God bless those boxing tips, Mr Regan.

Fallon picked up the first of his six British Champion Jockey titles in 1997. (Piggott has won the award eleven times; Dettori, three times.) Over one recent five-year stretch, he amassed prize money of £22 million, from which he would have earned a ten per cent cut. He's ridden a lot of winners – over 200 each year for three years in a row when he first teamed up with trainer Michael Stoute in 1997, and 221 in 2003, his best year.

'What days stand out?'

'He's had millions of them,' says *Sunday Times* racing correspondent Donn McClean, before adding, when pressed: 'Just after he started the Coolmore job, he won the 2,000 Guineas on *Footstepsinthesand* and the 1,000 Guineas on *Virginia Waters* in 2005. There would have been a lot of pressure on him to bag a winner and he won both, the first two classics of the year.

'Later that year, he completed a remarkable one-day treble at Longchamp. He won first with *Rumplestiltskin*, then with *Horatio Nelson*, before squeezing home for his first Prix de l'Arc de Triomphe win on board *Hurricane Run*. John Magnier remarked to friends that it was probably his most enjoyable afternoon at a racetrack.

'There is any number of really good rides,' adds McClean. 'I remember him on *Ad Valorem* at Royal Ascot two years ago. He shouldn't have won. He just gave the horse a helluva ride. The horse wasn't the best horse in the race, and Fallon got into the right place, and he's just strong and he made sure to keep the other guys in the pockets on the rails.'

Fallon, not surprisingly, struggles to isolate particular days, but mentions *Dylan Thomas* in the 2007 Prix de l'Arc de Triomphe, and the ride *Islington* gave him to win the Breeders' Cup Filly & Mare Turf in 2003 at Santa Anita Park. He singles out other fillies, such as *Ouija Board*, and a special day at Epsom – a track he rates as being 'very hard to ride' and scene of his three British Derby victories – in 1997.

'There's something about *Reams of Verse* that I loved,' he says. 'I won the Oaks on her when I probably shouldn't have done because I didn't ride a great race and Jimmy Fortune came down the outside, blocked me in, which obviously should have ended our race, but she's big-hearted; she battled back and she got me out of trouble.'

Fallon would certainly identify with her redoubtable spirit. He is one of sport's great comeback kids. His career in racing has been a history of triumph over adversity – some of it, admittedly, of his own design. But not the spill he suffered during the Ascot Stakes in 2000 in which he found himself in a four-horse pile-up. 'Head first, over two horses – it's what we call a "motorbike accident" because of the shape of our helmets ... our heads twist violently. I should have really broken my neck, but thank God I've got great bones,' he says.

He severed a main artery and the main nerves in his left shoulder. He said at the time that he thought his left arm had detached from his body. The doctors said he would never ride again, but by knitting the nerve endings back together in time before they died, the medics managed to preserve the use of Fallon's left arm, and he was back in the saddle in 2001, when he captured the first of another three-in-a-row British Champion Jockey titles.

Exhilarating stuff, but while he should have been basking in these glory days, Fallon was about to feature in a most odious saga. In

September 2004, a couple of months after he had ridden his third Epsom Derby winner, the racing world looked on in shock as he was detained (along with two other jockeys, Fergal Lynch and Darren Williams) as part of a police investigation into the alleged fixing of over eighty races in the previous two years. The jockeys were charged with 'conspiracy to defraud' people placing bets with Betfair by interfering with the horses to ensure they lost.

In 1998 Fallon had successfully sued the now-defunct newspaper *Sporting Life* for £70,000 when it alleged that he had 'cheated' when losing on *Top Cees*. Here, six years later, was more smoke that the public was led to believe must originate with fire, but in what has been dubbed as horse racing's 'trial of the century', it was the prosecution's case that went up in flames as, halfway through the case, the judge threw it out of court, telling the jury to acquit the defendants as there was 'no case to answer'.

The prosecution's case cost Fallon an estimated £750,000 in lost earnings, as he was suspended from racing in the UK for the duration of the investigation – a seventeen-month period – in a guilty-until-proven-innocent stance that reflected poorly on the British Horseracing Authority, the UK's racing regulatory body, which, notably, changed its name three times during the investigation in an effort to improve the sport's ailing image.

Meanwhile, the court case against Fallon cost the British taxpayer £10 million, and involved 500 interviews, 5,000 exhibits, and 40,000 pages of 'evidence' furnished by the City of London police, whose competence was called into serious question, as was much of the case itself. The prosecution's expert witness, Ray Murrihy – the chief steward of racing in New South Wales – was woefully unfamiliar with British racing, and was at a loss regarding details pertaining to several of the horses, jockeys, trainers and racecourses involved. While Murrihy dithered at one stage, Fallon's defence counsel – racehorse owner John Kelsey-Fry QC – drew some laughter when he told the Old Bailey court that it was 'not Mr Murrihy's fault he is Australian'.

For Fallon, unfortunately, it was no laughing matter. Although, remarkably, he kept riding winners through the lead-up to the case, it was an unnerving few years of doubt, surveillance and harassment. In fact, he steered *Dylan Thomas* to victory in the Arc on the eve of the trial's commencement, which is testament to his singular focus, but he admits the spectre of a possible jail sentence rattled him, and affected his riding. 'I would be a lot, lot better rider if it didn't happen to me three years ago,' he says. 'I would have ridden a lot more [winners]. When the gates opened I could usually focus and turn on and get involved in the race, but I wasn't getting the same thrill from winning. I knew that "that" was always at the back of my mind, and it's the lift you get from winning that gives you confidence for the next race, and if you're winning and winning, you're giving yourself confidence rather than thinking about "whist",' he says, making a whistling sound, 'and back into that zone again. All you're thinking [about] is a prison cell if you go down. Even though we knew there was nothing [to the prosecution's case] … you never, ever know.

'I knew I'd done nothing wrong. Looking at the races, the other lads didn't look as if they'd done anything wrong because I'd have picked it up straight away if they did,' he says, snapping his fingers. 'And, if anything, they were trying harder. In these so-called "stopped races", I saw Fergal Lynch in one of them, being blocked – he got two days for barging because he was barging his way out,' he says incredulously. 'That's why it didn't make sense.'

'Ah, it was all bollocks,' says Dunphy, climbing down from the fence. 'He was found not guilty. He wasn't guilty. He did nothing at all except what everybody does – he told people he thought this would win or this wouldn't win, but every jockey does it. It's not illegal. There are people probably that he spoke to who were shady but he was clean, he was straight, he was completely innocent of that. They just abused him really.'

'Fallon was guilty of no more than giving his opinion,' adds Donn McClean. 'People asking him what he thought, what he fancied and he'd say, "I fancy this. I don't fancy that one." It's common practice … even now anywhere you go in the country or on TV, you see all these jockeys doing analysis. Pre-Cheltenham, you'd see a jockey on the panel and he'd be giving his opinions.'

What is troubling about the whole sorry affair is why Fallon was targeted. Disregarding the irrefutable evidence that no money trail was established to show he benefited from the supposed betting scam – not trying to win isn't in his vocabulary. Owner after owner, trainer sitting atop trainer called on by the prosecution – not by his defence team, mind – drew attention to Fallon's horsemanship and his ferocious drive to win. For instance, when Sir Michael Stoute was called to bear witness regarding six of his horses – five of whom were ridden by Fallon – he left the court in no doubt about Fallon's integrity in the races involved, remarking that Fallon gave *Daring Aim*, for example, a 'brilliant' ride in a victory at Newmarket. 'She was not helping him,' recounted Stoute. 'He gave her one smack and, as she really resented that, he put the whip down quickly. That won him the race.'

In fact, ludicrously, Fallon's strike rate on races he was meant to lose was significantly higher (29.4 per cent) than his average in other races (19 per cent). Something is amiss about the whole affair. Dunphy is in no doubt as to what it is. 'Because he was a big star, they could get the story onto the front pages and appear to be "cleaning up racing",' he explains. 'He was a victim of circumstances. He'd nothing to do with it. He was a very convenient scapegoat in a very murky operation, indeed. It was a terrible injustice.'

Coolmore Stud – Fallon's employer – stood nobly behind their number-one jockey throughout the investigation, retaining him as their stable choice for races outside of the UK and inside the jurisdiction while ploughing £3 million into his legal defence.

However, any delight Coolmore might have experienced at the case's verdict was replaced quickly – overnight, in fact – with dismay. On 8 December 2007, the day after the Betfair case concluded, French racing authorities announced that Fallon was to be banned worldwide for eighteen months after testing positive for a banned substance. Fallon had failed a test after he landed a winner on the aptly named *Myboycharlie* at a race at Deauville the previous August. It was the second time the French authorities had doled out a ban to the jockey. In November 2006 he was suspended worldwide for six months by France Galop for testing positive for a banned substance – even if it wasn't a performance-enhancing one – following a race in July of that year. 'The time before that [July 2006], I had done something ...' explains Fallon in his defence; 'something like eight days before [the race]. It was still in my system because it was the time I got charged, right, and I wasn't riding all that week, but because I got charged, I was fuckin' depressed instead of flushing it out of [my] system by drinking water – if you drink loads of water you can flush your system out – but I wasn't even thinking. I was out and had a few glasses of wine or whatever, and that's why it was in my system.'

'Kieren has been under intolerable pressure,' said his trainer at Coolmore, Aidan O'Brien, on hearing news of Fallon's second ban in December 2007 – which ultimately cost him his job with the stables – 'and his temperament is fickle enough at the best of times. It's a big shame and a big mess and he will probably never get over it. Obviously, he will have to get a lot of counselling.'

Thanks to the glare of the media, another chapter in Fallon's struggle with his demons was being played out for the public's titillation. In January 2003 *Daily Mirror* reporters shamelessly knocked on the door of the Aiseiri Centre, a rehab clinic in Tipperary he had fled to in an effort to sort out a drink problem.

'I've messed around my gift over the years,' admits Fallon. 'Look it, I enjoy life,' he says, while you hear echoes in the room of the hotel porter's famous question: 'Mr Best, where did it all go wrong?'

'You've no regrets?'

'No.'

'But you could have achieved more?'

'There've been some little blips. I wish I could do it again, but I've won some great races and I've enjoyed it. There's plenty more to come. I'm really looking forward to getting back now.'

It recharges the batteries, I suggest, perversely, about another stint in the wilderness, this one having cost him his position as number-one jockey with the leading stables in the world.

'It does. I was only telling a friend of mine the other day. I was out golfing and you'd be hitting a Pro V there and you wouldn't even bother looking for it. And that's wrong really, you know? You've lost – what's the word? – your perspective in life. It's not right. I'm a lot more careful now, and I'm gonna *try* to do things right … Thank God, I don't think I've had a bad year [in his career] even with the wild times I've had. The years were unbelievable.'

'You say you'd do it again. What mistakes did you make?'

'Well, just the wild bits really. In saying that I've seen the lads who are dedicated, so dedicated and doing everything right, and they just can't seem to do anything right when they get out there. I could name lots of jockeys there, that are great jockeys, just not … when they get out there … they just can't seem to motivate the horses the same. There's one or two very good jockeys struggling to ride classic winners. Look at Richard Hughes. You know, he's a polished rider. He's dedicated. I don't think he's ever won a Classic. You know, he comes from a good family, a racing family, gets great rides, big jobs, you know? And he's not on his own. It doesn't mean to say that I'm gonna continue being a lunatic.

'You see, the thing is, all the big boys want the classics. You can win as many championships. You can win as many handicaps. You can have a thousand winners in a year; break all the records … Seb Sanders, a Champion Jockey. [Jamie] Spencer? He rode one in Ireland, a Guineas, when he was eighteen, but what has he won since? He'd some great opportunities when he was riding for Aidan, but he just kept fucking up.'

So does Fallon – you're thinking – but in more dramatic style. He is such an enigmatic character. Separated from his wife Julie – also a jockey – they have three children: twins, Cieren and Brittany, and Natalie.

Acquaintances of his in Clare stumble over each other like a horse-and-jockey pile-up to impart stories of Fallon's selflessness, of him popping in to visit elderly neighbours and relatives, of guided tours around Coolmore Stud, of his delight in helping out with local fund-raising efforts, of the money he has lavishly spent on his family's welfare. Meanwhile, his own wealth, it is estimated, is a fraction of what it should be given his success in racing for the past fifteen years.

To meet him is to be bowled over by a man of genuine humility, and his conversation is characterised by a childlike inability to censor his thoughts. It's not for nothing that he still has a boyish grin. All the back-slapping, all the adulation, hasn't altered his sense of self. He's still the same humble lad who used to turn out corner-forward for Crusheen hurlers as a kid.

'He's a great character and he's got an infectious personality, and yet he could be here and you wouldn't notice he was here. He's unassuming and yet he's a champion. He's a champion of champions,' says Jimmy Regan, hinting at the incongruity of elements of Fallon's personality.

His self-destructive tendencies, Fallon pleads, have affected nobody but himself. 'Look it,' he says, 'the thing is I've done nobody any harm except myself. I've helped a lot of people along the way, and I'd do anybody a good turn.'

'He's a little bit unworldly,' argues Dunphy, 'like a lot of great people who are into their own thing, and maybe one or two people have got him into trouble, but he himself is a man of great personal integrity. Fallon's a mighty man. I think everyone who's ever worked with him thinks he is. He may have been foolish with the drink, but none of us are perfect.'

He is flawed, surely. He patently doesn't learn from his mistakes and, fatally, he is impressionable and easily misled. This gullibility in Fallon's personality – the foolishness that Dunphy alludes to – is it innocence, you wonder?

'I wouldn't say it's innocence,' says Regan, before pausing for a moment. 'He's cute. You know he's a cute guy. Without question. The fire in his eyes is always there. Have you seen his eyes? Have you looked at his eyes? There's fire there. And when he's telling you something, when he's talking about horses, by jeepers, the feedback you get from his eyes is incredible,' he says, pausing again for a second. 'He's a smart guy. Oh, he's smart.'

FR BERNARD LYNCH

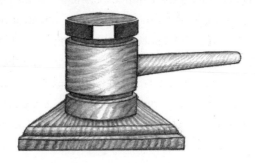

This tale would bend your bones. Dismayed at his championing of gay rights in the 1980s, the archdiocese of New York, in cahoots with the FBI and the Bronx's district-attorney's office, concocted a child-abuse case against Ennisman Fr Bernard Lynch. Every TV network in the city crammed into the courtroom to report on the proceedings. It was the stuff of movies, but, sadly, with horrendous, real-life consequences.

'The trial was an extraordinarily destructive, dehumanising experience. I'm still not over the trial. I don't think I will ever be over it. To think that my own Church could set me up with something that was so untrue. That knocked the heart out of me,' says Fr Lynch sombrely. 'I just couldn't believe it. It was naivety, because the Catholic Church has been, and is, capable of great good, and has been, and is, capable of great evil.

'It was after the trial that I suppose I had a walking, talking nervous breakdown. I wasn't institutionalised, but, for example, every time I would see a police car I would have to turn and face the wall until it passed. I was afraid to go into a store and ask for a paper. I'd be talking to you here about the game on Saturday, and suddenly I'd break down crying, at completely inappropriate moments. While I believe that I have healed greatly, there is still a residual scar there.'

While growing up in St Michael's Villas, Ennis, there was no inkling of the tumultuous life Bernard Lynch would lead. Born in 1947, he was always enchanted with the Church. Like many of his generation, the pageantry and trappings of the Church were intoxicating – not least, its carpets. While a child, nobody where he lived could afford carpet for their floor. Lynch and his mates would sneak into the Old Ground Hotel to prance around on its carpet before being sent scampering by the hotel's porter. And every Sunday, across the road from the hotel at the Pro-Cathedral, where the sanctuary was furnished with a deep-green carpet with decorative patterns, his eyes would melt with envy as the priest went about his duties.

When this lad from St Michael's Villas became the first from the area to be ordained a priest – in December 1971 – it was a triumph for the neighbourhood. Bonfires blazed along the neighbouring streets to mark his homecoming. A next-door neighbour had to be helped back to his feet, a bit tipsy, after falling to his knees for a blessing, as family and friends fawned over him. As he says himself, he couldn't help but feel like the Pope.

Yet, for all the fanfare, he was unsettled. He was deeply troubled about the growing awareness of his gayness. It would be 1982 before he came out to his parents. And after several years in the rarefied atmosphere of a seminary, he was hopelessly ill-equipped for the harshness of life. 'One of my assignments when I was ordained, just for a summer, was to go to Knock, County Mayo and be a confessor. A confessor?' he says, still incredulous. 'At twenty-four years of age? [Without] Confession at that time … you couldn't go to Communion. That was the only time I ever had a crisis of vocation. When woman after woman was coming into the box saying, "You know, my husband comes home drunk and forces himself on me. I've already got six children." And I'm listening to this and I instinctively knew, this is off the cotton-pickin' wall. My three Hail Marys is not going to change his mind or hers, and what could I say? I remember coming out of the box, there was an older priest with me, and I said, "Father, I can't do this."

'And he said, "You're such a good priest."

'I told him: "This is wrong. This is wrong."'

The situation served to lay bare the brutal logic that underpins the Catholic Church. Its power is based on what Fr Lynch refers to as 'McDonald's Theory' – the *raison d'être* is to open more franchises, and anyone who interferes with this drive isn't being a good Catholic. 'I realised, I suppose, at quite a very young age that the dialectics of power in the Church were about "increase and multiply" irrespective of whether you were gay or straight. Children are a great gift. The reason that we as gay people are so marginalised by the Church is because we don't produce, which to me is also a wonderful gift, given the already over-exhausted earth and problems with population explosion.'

Several years later, it was while facing a population implosion – the very annihilation of the gay community in New York as a result of the AIDS pandemic – that Fr Lynch's character was forged. Having arrived in the city in 1975 to study for an interdisciplinary doctorate in theology and psychology – after a stint working in the missions in Africa – he became more and more involved in gay and lesbian circles, and in the summer of 1977 joined Dignity – a gay/lesbian Catholic support group. 'Within three years, AIDS had hit like a bang,' he says. 'The bottom fell out of our world. I initially thought I was infected. Three of my closest priest friends died of AIDS. Then it became more urgent to care for the sick not out of any pious sense but because there was nobody else to care for them.'

It is difficult to appreciate the scale of the devastation. For most people who contracted the disease in the 1980s, it was a death sentence. Of the 600 people who Fr Lynch tended to as part of his AIDS ministry in the early 1980s, only six of them were still alive a decade later. 'People were diagnosed on a Wednesday and dead on Sunday,' he says mournfully.

Gripped by ignorance, vast swathes of society turned a blind eye to their suffering. Often, meals for AIDS patients in hospital would be left to go cold at their doors because orderlies were afraid of catching the disease. Funeral homes refused to take the corpses of those who died with AIDS. Worse, sons dying of the so-called 'gay plague' were often ostracised by family members unable to come to terms with their condition. In Ennis at that time, he points out, three men died from the illness but their deaths were attributed to cancer: 'Denied,' he says, 'in life and death who they were.'

His heroic work with AIDS patients drew plaudits, and he was a member of the mayor's task force on AIDS in New York City. In 1986 he joined Mary Robinson and Dr Noel Browne as a recipient of the Magnus Hirschfeld Award in Dublin, and the following year, Channel 4 filmed a documentary about his ministry; the programme was entitled *AIDS – A Priest's Testament*. But a coalition of disparate forces was forming with the objective of skewering Fr Lynch.

His involvement in the struggle to secure legislation against the discrimination of gays and lesbians in housing and employment drew the ire of the archdiocese of New York. On Gay Pride Day in 1984 – having delivered the prayers on the steps of St Patrick's Cathedral to bless that year's parade – a TV-news reporter asked Fr Lynch to respond to the archbishop's objection to the mayor's pro-gay legislation. Although his statement was innocuous – 'Employment is a basic human right for all people – men, women, black, white, gay and heterosexual' – it was enough to generate 'PRIEST OPPOSES ARCHBISHOP' headlines, and to provoke a nasty riposte from the archbishop in the *New York Post*, who stated that he would 'close all my orphanages rather than employ one gay person' – a devious insinuation that gayness was to be equated with child molestation.

The battle lines were drawn. Having testified at the hearings for the mayor's pro-gay legislation, Fr Lynch had to receive a police escort to the subway, as right-wing Catholic groups, Hasidic Jews and others chanted 'Shame, shame, put him on a plane'. There was hate mail. A woman slapped him across the face while walking in the St Patrick's Day Parade. Yet, despite the antagonism, he felt compelled to take a stand. 'It's like put your Gospel on the line. People said, "You were very courageous." Even [Bishop] Willie Walsh, when I came out publicly as a gay man, would say: "Great courage but great innocence". That was his line to my father. But I believe if you really believe in the Gospel, if you really believe in the core humanity of people, if you really believe in justice, you have to be naive. Naivety is almost a choice because you believe in something that does not exist, and all the odds are against it in a sense.

'It was amazing. I had politicians that I had never met, like Fernando Ferrere where I lived in the Bronx, saying …' – and here he adopts his best New 'Yoik' accent – '"Fr Lynch, we want to vote for the Bill of Rights; do you think I'll be excommunicated?" I said, "No, I'm going to speak for the bill also. You won't be excommunicated." So the bill passed, after ten years of lobbying.

'My face was on every television channel, every newspaper, and you know what New York media is like – it's the media capital of the world. I was an unwilling celebrity. My mother – God bless her – always wanted me to be a priest, but she never thought I would get on Broadway. It was mega stuff, but, of course, it really rankled with the authorities. They were furious. It was, "Catholic priest opposes cardinal", "Who's Church is it?"'

Trouble was brewing. On St Patrick's Day 1986, as he stepped off the Phil Donahue talk show, a man accosted him, saying, quite aggressively, 'We are going to find a boy to accuse you.' Meanwhile, an Irish priest by the name of Fr Bruce – demented by the death from AIDS in 1984 of his brother, Fr Jeremy – launched a one-man tirade against Fr Lynch, who was a close friend of Fr Jeremy. 'Bruce, it seemed, blamed me not only for his brother's death, but for his very homosexuality as well,' he writes in his memoir, *A Priest on Trial*.

In full clerical garb, Fr Bruce took to picketing the school in which Fr Lynch worked as a campus minister, with a placard that read 'FATHER LYNCH – PERVERT. DO YOU WANT HIM NEAR YOUR SONS?' At a school faculty meeting, a motion seeking his resignation was defeated: seventy-three of the seventy-eight teachers voted in Fr Lynch's favour. No student or parent issued a complaint against him or made a demand that he resign. But under pressure from the archdiocese, the principal's support for him evaporated, and with Fr Bruce relentless in his patrol outside the school – always in full clerical regalia and bearing his infamous placard – Fr Lynch handed in his resignation in December 1984.

By this time, he had become consumed with his AIDS ministry – at the very moment the Church's attitude towards gay people was hardening. In the autumn of 1986 the Vatican issued a letter on the pastoral care of homosexual people, labelling gay people as disordered in their nature and evil in their love.* It was a devastating blow to the gay community. Fr Lynch was blackballed by the cardinal archbishop, who refused him canonical faculties in the archdiocese of New York, thus rendering him virtually unemployable. His superiors' response to the impasse was to send him to Rome in June 1987 for a sabbatical – or to 'recuperate', as they so delicately put it.

By Christmas, even without institutional Church support, he was longing to return to New York. He had just booked his ticket back, with the blessing of his superior, when a priest friend in London informed him that the FBI was eager for his return, too. He was to be indicted on a charge of sexual abuse in the first degree as result of accusations made by John Schaefer, a fourteen-year-old former student of Mount St Michael's, the high school where he had been a campus minister. If convicted, he faced fifteen years in prison.

He was on holidays in Ireland in May 1988 when the Bronx District-Attorney's Office announced the charges in a press conference. As Michael Kennedy, his defence attorney, said in a Channel 4 documentary, *A Priest on Trial*, aired in 1990, 'They immediately poisoned the well of justice by making various false statements, such as that he was a fugitive, and that there were several allegations from

---

* Letter to the bishops of the Catholic Church on the pastoral care of homo-sexual persons, October 1986, his holiness, Pope John Paul II.

several young men. Then they pulled back and tried to hide, leaving Fr Lynch and his supporters to be vilified by the media.'

Facts went unchecked. Shamefully, the worst misrepresentations came from Irish reporters. 'Nowhere was I more of a target for hatred than in the Irish press,' he writes dolefully in his memoir. While praying one day in his digs, he noticed an *Examiner* headline, 'AIDS PRIEST FATHER LYNCH ON THREE SEX CHARGES'. He dropped to the floor, grabbed his stomach, and rocked in the foetal position, crying. He was crumbling.

The tabloids, like buzzards, circled for blood. His mother had passed away in 1982, mercifully saved from the onslaught. His father, a private man, was barraged with phone calls. The *Star* newspaper ran a front-page headline with a picture of him: 'MY SON IS NO MONSTER', it read, even though he had never spoken to the paper.

When his order, the Society of African Missions, based in Blackrock, Cork, found out that the FBI were looking for him, it thought that he was gun-running for the IRA. 'I'm an openly gay man, for flip's sake,' he said to his superior. 'Gun-running for the IRA? Do you want them to go out of operation?'

When the trial began, the media in New York cranked into top gear, with TV cameras capturing the high drama inside the court. As a gay advocate priest directly opposed to the Catholic archbishop of New York, and as a darling of the talk-show circuit, Fr Lynch had good billing. The world-weary hacks covering the story, like much of the public, had already made up their mind on the case. 'Every TV station in the town, radio stations, written press and so on – we all had formed opinions,' explains Bob Teague, a reporter with the NBC television network. 'We had all heard stories about those priests, you know, who are celibate – ha, ha, ha! I think there was a general belief, early on, that a dirty old man had been caught, and let's hope they hang him. This is understandable when you consider that in New York City, as a working journalist, you become pretty damn cynical. It costs the city so much damn money to bring someone to trial that they have to be very, very certain as a rule, and they have to spend all that money and the resources of the city to try and put the accused away. We go into the court – the media, that is – assuming that most offenders are guilty. I mean – that is the reality.'

It was a non-jury trial. Judge Roberts, who presided over it, was the star of the show. He looks a bit like the actor Jason Robards in his later years, with a full head of grey hair, a strong angular face, and the kind of gravelly voice that comes from chewing tobacco. Footage of him on the Channel 4 documentary is the stuff you get your popcorn out for. Twice, he jumped from his seat like a football manager springing from his dugout to berate a referee and clobbered a bunch of law books against his desk in exasperation at the prosecution's attempt to hoodwink him. 'I'm going to give you enough rope to hang!' he would bellow.

Off-screen was the other unfortunate attraction. The judge wouldn't permit the cameras to film John Schaefer, but he was interviewed by Channel 4 for its 1990 documentary. Fr Lynch has great sympathy for him. He, too, was a victim – a confused adolescent hijacked by the FBI in order to construct a case against Fr Lynch. Psychologically, he was a complicated young man. He had been sexually abused by a family member; he was a loner at school; and by the time he was interviewed by Channel 4, he was working as an actor. While on the stand – according to the accounts of Fr Lynch's two attorneys – he seemed to think he was on stage. Expansive and full of bravado, he enjoyed the role initially, but later began to flounder spectacularly. 'The truth is that John Schaefer tried, in a sad, inept but wholly understandable way to seduce me,' writes Fr Lynch in his memoir. 'I am aware that it sounds pretty outrageous that a fourteen-year-old boy should try to persuade a priest to have sex with him. But John, although only fourteen, was sexually very mature, and by his own admission gay. As Michael Kennedy pointed out in court, he had never received any love from his natural father, and in seeking that love from other adult males he was used and abused by them. He grew up believing that in order to receive affection he had to offer himself for sex. I had been aware of his need and of his disturbed state of mind. In fact, on the evening he visited me and suggested we have sex, he talked incessantly about wanting to go to Dignity so that he might meet other gay people … his actual words were, "I wouldn't mind having sex with someone as attractive as you."'

Fr Lynch had reported the incident to the head counsellor the following day, and years later – following his arraignment in June 1988 – he underwent a lie-detector test with one of the top experts in the country, and 'passed with flying colours'; yet, it failed to deter the prosecution from proceeding to trial.

Schaefer's testimony was littered with inconsistencies – at one point, he maintained that on the night he claims to have been molested, his encounter with Fr Lynch lasted twenty minutes; later, he reckoned it was an hour. At first, he claimed that Fr Lynch was drunk; later, he said there was nothing 'unusual' about his behaviour. And, despite the patient probing of Judge Roberts, he couldn't establish the exact year that the attack had taken place. He then began to malinger, and wouldn't retake the stand, which sent Judge Roberts into apoplexy. But it was an earlier admission – coaxed out of him by the judge – that drew an audible gasp from the courtroom, and hinted at the real driver behind the prosecution's case. Schaefer admitted that the District Attorney's Office and the FBI cajoled him – though he was reluctant – to testify. Later, it emerged that they had promised him at the outset that there were a dozen other witnesses willing to testify, too, and that all he would have to do is give them 'something dirty' about Fr Lynch; that the case would never go to trial because Fr Lynch, undoubtedly, would either plead guilty or scarper.

This news – that he had been bullied into the witness box – rocked those following the case closely. 'Naturally, there was a kind of sensationalist quality in a Catholic priest on a public morals charge against a minor,' explained Chris O'Donoghue of Channel 9 News in New York. 'But beyond that, it occurred at a time when the Bronx

DA's Office, which was prosecuting the case, was under investigation itself. Some of their practices and some of their decisions had come under scrutiny and were found wanting. So there was that question hanging over them. And then, of course, the controversial background of the priest himself, Fr Lynch. But when I saw the flimsiness of the case and how it was presented, I began to ask, why did they push this case with such a weak witness and such little evidence? Even the kid himself said he was coerced into testifying prior to even going to court. So who was pushing it? And why would they push something that was so shaky to begin with? Was it a case of bringing a charge that they felt would never go to court and would, at the same time, accomplish their goals?'

Their goals failed dramatically – the trial collapsed after three days. As Bob Teague said, 'At the very end, the judge declared a mistrial, and then gave a verdict exonerating the defendant and finding him not guilty. I've never heard anything like that before.'

Kennedy, Fr Lynch's defence attorney, made a point of commending the judge's clarity in the whole sordid affair. 'Burton Roberts had the courage – and he's one of the few who has that courage – to face the facts, and say publicly as the fact-finder in this particular case, "I find no evidence of guilt here. This man is innocent, and I so find him." That was a courageous judge.'

The champagne flowed, but – as Fr Lynch acknowledges – it was 'a pyrrhic victory' that left several questions unanswered about the role his Church – which professed itself to be the embodiment of love and sanctuary – had played in the affair. 'Father Lynch was a very active political man, particularly here in New York City,' said Kennedy. 'Because of his ministry to the AIDS victims and because of his championing of homosexual men and women in New York City, he became something of a pariah in the Church. Indeed, we know that the Church sought through a variety of ways within the Church itself to have Fr Lynch taken out of New York and returned to Ireland or returned to Africa where he would, it was felt, cause less mischief.'

Nothing when compared to the mischief caused by SAFE: Students Against Faggots in Education, a body that had been set up by a small group of students at Mount St Michael's, and encouraged by certain members of the faculty to purge the high school of its gay staff members. 'There is no question,' said Robert Cammer, assistant defence attorney, 'that SAFE was active in this prosecution because I saw, when I was in Assistant District Attorney Walsh's office, on the table behind his desk, a file folder with the word SAFE clearly written on it. He turned it over so I wouldn't see the name, but I'd already seen it. Of course, I didn't get a chance to look inside the file.'

Fr Lynch was being blatantly targeted. 'When the allegations generally of sexual misconduct were first brought, they were not focused on Fr Lynch,' explained Kennedy. 'They talked about St Michael's in particular. It was not until Fr Lynch was focused on by the Church itself and by the archdiocese in particular that his name began to crop up. As a matter of fact, the FBI was the first to bring up Fr Lynch's name. It was never mentioned by any of the people they interviewed. So, they targeted him. Why did they target him? I think because he was a political, highly visible man.'

And when the defence team, in preparation for the case, sought to uncover possible links between SAFE and the hierarchy in the Church, it was stonewalled. 'We knew that the homophobes from Mount St Michael's had gone to the archdiocese,' said Kennedy, 'and I wanted to get that correspondence to find out what, if any, activity the archdiocese had had with reference to bringing these particular charges. I had, of course, subpoenas to get those documents. They immediately got their lawyer – who is a very fine, powerful, prominent lawyer here in town – to move to quash those subpoenas. They said that under no circumstances did they want Kennedy to have access to those files. And, indeed, I never did get them.'

It was a rather curious stance for the archdiocese to take. In the build-up to the trial, overtures by Lynch's colleagues to solicit support from the archdiocese of New York fell on deaf ears. When a television station erroneously described him as a 'fugitive at large', a colleague – Sr Karen Killeen – called the station to tell them that they were wrong: he wasn't a fugitive, he was on holidays in Ireland. When she asked where they had got this misinformation, she was told, 'From a spokesperson of the archdiocese of New York.'

The archbishop of New York, Cardinal John O'Connor, maintained a stony silence throughout the affair. His only contribution came a year after the trial. Caught by a TV reporter, all he could offer was, 'I have no comment on Fr Bernard Lynch.'

'One of the great ironies,' say Fr Lynch was that, 'they covered up sexually abusive priests – one after the other who toed the party line and said the right things – they came after me.'

Despite the witch-hunt, despite the mental torture he and his family were made to endure – from which he still bears the emotional scars – he doesn't harbour any enmity. 'I don't. That's a real grace,' he says simply, going on to acknowledge that his gay politics didn't sit easily with the go-forth-and-multiply ethic of the Catholic Church.

The *Clare Champion*, the county's primary broadsheet at the time, gave the story a wide berth, declining to do any investigative journalism. It was too close to the bone, the elephant in their newsroom.

His old classmates were baffled. 'My age group were saying, "This guy is being hung out to dry."'

'Without knowing anything – you just don't change all of a shot,' says a local publican who used to serve Mass with Fr Lynch as a boy. 'We knew he was gay, but that was it.'

But if there were people in his corner in the town, they weren't making themselves known at the time. 'Even though my mother, God rest her, was a native of Ennis and her parents and her grandparents, and my father was from Clarecastle, they were well known and well respected, but people wouldn't say anything. There was very little visible support; although there was no condemnation. But with Irish people, you don't talk about it.

'I remember when my father came to visit me in London – this was a few years after the trial – we were chatting and I said, "Dad, what was it like?" I was then beginning to find my feet, as it were, and he said that the morning that news of the acquittal reached Ennis, he went to Sunday Mass, taking up his usual place in the cathedral, and he said people were lining up to shake his hand and congratulate him. He said one woman in particular from St Michael's Villas came up to him from the queue and he broke down crying, and I asked, "Why?" And he said she was the only one when the charges came initially that came up to him. She knocked at the door and he invited her in, and she said, "John, I was born and reared in this town like Bernard. I'd have to see him do it to believe it. Let's take it from there." It gave him such heart – a stranger, a neighbour ... but when she came up [in the cathedral], that really broke him.'

Almost twenty years after being exonerated, Fr Lynch is living in London now, where he moved shortly after the trial, and has a summer house in Lahinch, County Clare. He continued with his ministry to AIDS sufferers when he moved to London, although that work is winding down now as he's understandably all but 'burnt out' from it.

Perhaps because he spent the defining period of his life in the States, his brogue has kind of an Irish-American twang. He still gets over to the US to visit friends every Thanksgiving. Physically, he's fit as a fiddle, courtesy of all that jogging he's done over the years – it's his great passion; along with prayer, it has always been of succour to him.

Legally, he is still a priest. It's no surprise that his email address encompasses the numerals '1971' – the year of his ordination. When invited, he continues to celebrate Mass, mainly for gay friends and acquaintances, for people with HIV and AIDS, and for social occasions such as funerals, christenings and weddings. While still raw, still healing, he met his partner Billy – 'also Irish, from Cork' – in London in 1993. After a five-year courtship, they had their union blessed by a Trappist priest friend, but await the day, he laments, in which they can be married in the land of their birth.

While held as a hostage in the Gaza Strip in 2007 – facing possible execution at any moment – the BBC correspondent, Alan Johnston, used to find strength from words a fellow journalist had said to him years earlier in Central Asia: 'All you can expect of yourself in life is one or two substantial moments.' Fr Lynch has faced his moment with fortitude.

'You have a sense of drama and history and personalities that inspire you,' remarked Teague, the grizzled, middle-aged, black journalist with NBC at the end of Channel 4's documentary on Fr Lynch's trial. 'This was one of the most impressive human beings I've ever met.'

MICHAEL D. HIGGINS

Along with Dermot Morgan, Gerry Stembridge was one half of the *Scrap Saturday* team that used to fillet politicians on RTÉ radio every weekend during the early 1990s. As one of the country's great political satirists, there aren't many politicians for which he would come out to bat.

'When he was minister for the arts, the University of Virginia had put on an Irish seminar,' he recalls of an encounter with the Labour Party's Galway West TD, Michael D. Higgins. 'A bunch of us were over in Charlottesville, Virginia, on a lake, giving talks about all aspects of Ireland and the arts and politics and all the rest of it. Michael D. was a keynote speaker at the occasion, full of the great and the good of West Virginia, and a fair few of the literary mafia from Ireland as well, enjoying the occasion.

'He gave a marvellous speech, extremely well written – clearly written by himself, a rarity among government ministers – delivered well. It was witty. It was intelligent. It was full of humanity. It was one of those rare occasions where I actually felt proud of an Irish government representative. I thought to myself, "Isn't that fantastic now that we've somebody like that to represent us in the arts?"

'The difference was profound ... [after Higgins] you were back to the kind of stumbling, halting reading of a civil servant-written speech, full of all the obvious clichés that went with that. Whereas with Michael D. – here was somebody at home, both with the academics and with the artists. He knew how to speak to them. He knew what to say and how to say it. That is what a minister for the arts should be capable of. Without question, he has been the best minister for arts we've had.'

'There are very few people who are capable of delivering a speech with the kind of passion he naturally generates,' adds Niall Stokes, who commissioned Michael D. to write for *Hot Press* magazine in 1982, an arrangement that lasted a decade. 'There are some very good wits in the Dáil. People can write good speeches – Pat Rabbitte is good. His speeches are generally well put together; [former TD] Joe Higgins, not dissimilarly, but it tends to be stuff they've put in the oven beforehand; whereas Michael D. has that ability to contemporise, and has a real emotional engagement with issues. I think it's one of the most impressive things about him as a public figure.

'I remember hearing him give a speech about education on the radio. This was more of a crafted speech, but I remember somebody coming to me afterwards: "Jeez, I heard Michael D. on the radio the other night – it was just fantastic." I'd heard the thing myself and it was just a really good exposition of the value of education for its own sake, and the idea that the purpose of learning shouldn't be hog-tied to the achievement of grades, that we need to get back to the sense of a more liberated kind of teaching environment, true to what teaching is.

'Here was the genuine intellectual, willing to address things intellectually, the unusual ability to set out arguments very effectively, ... achieving a level of passion and emotion even on subjects that weren't intrinsically emotional. It's different if you're talking about an attack on Tehran by the military.'

And boy, can Higgins get wound up about breaches of the Geneva Convention. In November 2001 he was ejected from the Dáil, having made a fervent plea in relation to Afghanistan. When told he was out of order by the *ceann comhairle*, he bellowed, 'What is not in order is the taking of shoes and gold fillings from prisoners who are being slaughtered. It is not in order to have 160 prisoners slaughtered on the side of the road.'

A year and a half later, on the eve of the invasion of Iraq, he lambasted the government for adjourning for a fortnight without a debate on Iraq/Shannon. As he launched into his tirade – with a sheaf of notes quivering in his right hand – the *leas-ceann comhairle* tried to suggest he was speaking out of order, but gave up and listened. 'By the time this house returns on Tuesday 25 March it is possible that up to one million mothers may be affected by war, there may be 100,000 direct casualties and 400,000 secondary ones – ten to fifteen million people on food dependency may also be affected. That that does not merit a debate in this house is a disgrace.' An inquiry from the *leas-ceann comhairle* – 'I take it the deputy is opposing the proposal [to adjourn]?' – sent the house into convulsions of laughter. For a moment, Higgins looked like he might himself snigger, but held his nerve and wrestled control of the house again.

The silence as he held forth was broken only by some tut-tutting from the government benches when, pointing to the government side, he declared: 'The blood of Iraqi children and civilians will be on the hands of all the people who would not permit a discussion on the issue. It will be on the hands of all these people. They are the ones who would not allow it to be discussed. This parliament will have been shamed. It is a disgrace the Taoiseach does not have an opinion and is not having a debate. It is wrong, wrong, wrong.' Upon which he sat down. Deputies from all the opposition parties burst into a round of applause; there wasn't a peep from the government TDs.

Higgins' oratorical flourishes – his ability to grab an audience by the throat and sweep it along with a lively, cogent argument – mark him out as a rarity in the land. Few can match him for his powers of rhetoric. Even Dr Garrett FitzGerald – who has had too many ideological jousts with him to number since they first locked horns on a Galway University campus in the 1960s – concedes as much: 'He's a brilliant speaker. He speaks with passion. He has very strong beliefs which he propounds in a way that is also unusual.'

Perhaps it is no surprise that he is so effective in debate, given rhetoric is an amalgam of his strong suits: language, performance and ideology, and is, according to Fintan O'Toole, 'the place where politics meets art'. For the politician Michael D. – there are few in Ireland of working age who do not know him by this moniker – is happiest when enmeshed in the arts world.

The Irish people whom he admires – all acquaintances – are a) people such as the literary critic, Professor Declan Kiberd; b) folk from the stage, like Gerard Mannix Flynn, Tom Hickey and Mick Lally (indeed, his wife, Sabrina Coyne – they have one daughter and three sons – is an actor and founder member of Dublin's Focus Theatre); and c) some of the country's finest poets: Brendan Kennelly and Paul Durcan. For Higgins, too, is a poet; he has published three collections of poetry: *The Betrayal* (Salmon, 1991), *The Season of Fire* (Brandon, 1993), and *An Arid Season* (New Island, 2004), and in conversation sends one scurrying for biographical clues to be found in his verse in a manner reminiscent of Sherlock Holmes' teasing of the plodding Dr Watson.

There was nothing gilded about his upbringing. It was hard, the family unit having fractured owing to reasons of health and finance. He was born in Limerick in April 1941, but lived in Newmarket-on-Fergus, County Clare until he was nineteen years of age, having moved there in 1946 with his brother John. His mother's brother had just passed away, and it was felt she wouldn't be able to handle them at the time, so they were farmed out to Higgins' unmarried uncle and aunt on their small farm – relatives who effectively reared their two 'instant children', without question, in their one-room-slated, two-room-thatched house that lacked a toilet or running water.

Higgins, himself, and his brother paid 'intermittent visits' to Limerick city, and there was a brief family reunion in County Clare when he was about thirteen years of age, before the family was scattered permanently, with his sisters going to England. His brother still lives in Ballycar, County Clare, having married one of the Hassetts of Quin.

His family history on his father's side – he came from Ballycar, Newmarket-on-Fergus – is the stuff of a Liam O'Flaherty novel, one of Michael D.'s literary heroes. His father and *his* brothers and sister fought in the War of Independence. The uncles were in the East Clare Brigade, and his father – who had been working in Charleville when the war broke out – in the Cork No. 2 Brigade. During the civil war, his father sided with the anti-Treaty forces, while his uncles took up arms on the Free State side, with his aunt – a former member of Cumann na mBan – betwixt. The family spoke little afterwards about this violent period, he confides.

His father, like many an idealistic nationalist revolutionary, was blighted by the experience – most cruelly, years of sleeping under reeks of turf or by cocks of hay had left him with chronic bronchial ailments; the promise of a republic for him had been utterly compromised; and, frustratingly, as a young man with hopes for a family, he was marginalised economically when he came out of his civil-war internment camp near Newbridge, County Kildare. 'When he came out of the Curragh and came back to County Clare, there was no welcome for him at all because Clare is interesting in a way – Clare is now described as a Fianna Fáil place; it wasn't then … In Newmarket-on-Fergus, for example, anybody who had been involved in the civil war couldn't get a job. My father had had a job before the war. I think he had about £150 a year working for Binchy's [shop] at the outbreak of the War of Independence, and when he came out of the camp at the end of the civil war, he was much older, obviously, but he couldn't get a job – he finally got a job as a live-in junior in Newbridge, Kildare, earning £50 a year. The point was that there was no place for anyone who had come out of the Curragh getting a job at that time.'

His uncle also suffered from ill health, being bedridden, while electricity, he laments, came too late for his aunt and many of her peers: 'You didn't have raised fireplaces, for example, so you had an enormous number of women who suffered from curvature of the spine.' The absence of running water – with the added demand of tending to cattle during long, dry summers – meant that the image of his poor, buckled aunt balancing a bucket of water at the end of each arm is an abiding memory.

He shies away from any attempt to romanticise the brutal reality of his childhood, which was lived amidst the splendours of a rustic hinterland. 'I know the experience of grass between your toes, and I know that a fern will cut you, and I know where butterflies gather, and I know about mosses,' he writes lyrically in a collection of his life's writings and speeches, *Causes for Concern: Irish Politics, Culture and Society*. 'I can remember all these sensations very clearly, but I also remember when my aunt and uncle's house was caving in, and youngsters going past the house saying, "We haven't broken windows in our house", and firing stones at the old couple and their nephews, who were living inside. I remember the quiet cruelty of it; it is dishonest of people to take the quietness and richness and complexity of natural settings and use them as a mask for the cruel social divisions that prevailed in rural Ireland. I was very glad to escape from that poverty. It was only after a lot of healing that I was able to reach back through these memories and rediscover again the colour and sensation of a fern, or a moss or a grass. I really do not have much time for people who try to perpetuate a kind of pastoral nonsense about rural Ireland.'

It had a cost, he adds, sitting in his office in Dáil Éireann. 'The price we paid … was that we lost a lot of our youth. There was a great deal of anxiety that I could have done without. There were the incredible illnesses of my father and others, and there was the business always of my mother who wasn't really a rural person and who had come from a city, really, and spent most of her time aspiring to have a decent house, and liked company. She was a lovely woman, but there was a loneliness associated with her. It's all in Kavanagh as well. You'll get it in Patrick Kavanagh's work – he leaves it too late to leave Monaghan.

71

There's nothing ennobling about it. There's nothing ennobling about any form of suffering. People should realise that, and what you need is discretion and choice.'

Perhaps this is his great glory, that despite the harshness of his family circumstances, emotionally and financially, for him as a child, he is an irrepressibly ebullient person. 'He is so cheerful, optimistic and confident, even on the darkest of days, and I love that in a person,' says Nell McCafferty – someone who has soldiered with him on many a human-rights hustings over the past thirty-five years.

Surely the grinding poverty of his formative years has informed that implacable socialist vision of his. 'He generally remembers and knows poor,' suggests the poet Theo Dorgan – a friend since younger bohemian days right through to the present. 'We're so profoundly reluctant to acknowledge the existence of the poor in this mythical Tigerland that we think we inhabit, but Michael knows what it is to be poor and disenfranchised and cut off, and in that sense he's a spur to conscience. That's probably one of his greatest assets – he really is a spur to conscience. In fact, to have lived the life that Michael has lived, he's an expression really in the generous belief in the goodness of people because he has never become cynical. That actually, when you consider how most of us age, is a remarkable fact. He's still prepared to fight the good fight at quite an advanced age, and in the last year or two, he has been battling quite severe health problems but believes in human goodness.'

This is something echoed by Senator David Norris, who has been to Israel and Iraq on human-rights observations with him: 'He's not cynical. So many people who achieve his level of profile in public life become cynical. He still feels the wounds of the ordinary people. That's what I feel about him. People think in terms of the movement of money and personnel and great sweeps of people, and they're just marks on a map or figures on a piece of paper, but Michael D. just knows the human suffering behind it. It's not just an abstract design to him. It's always something human.'

He also has an acute appreciation for the potential in people and a consequent feeling for the people who have been damaged by life, people whose chance might have passed them by – 'All that might have been', as he puts it. In his own personal life, for example, he cites his mother's hankering for respectability – for a house, for simple things – and how that was thwarted; in his public life, he calls to mind the people he's encountered during his travels while campaigning for human rights in war zones, in refugee camps, and in prisons. 'I met an enormous number of people in my life who were *in extremis* in one way or the other,' he explains. 'I can relate to many people who have struggled to retain hope in a very cruel context. I have a great admiration for the kind of spirituality that [philosopher] John O'Donoghue would have. He saw the ethical possibilities of what might be are not abstract, they're always there. They may yet happen. People who know that it's not going to happen for them, but it should happen for others, always have had my admiration. There's no doubt about it that there are these core decencies that I respect in people. People I would relate least to are neurotic, consuming freaks.

'The main thing is that many people have vision. People have vision who want to see Clare win an All-Ireland, people have vision who want to bring something into existence that wasn't in existence before. I admire imagination. I find that there is an enormous effort being made to consume. If a person can only talk to you about how much they have or how much they are consuming, they're not great company. You have enough of it. You describe the thing "as getting stuck with them" rather than anything else. There's a necessary bit of madness needed, which I admire.'

Growing up, he absorbed a love of books – his great love since about the age of twelve – from his mother, reading everything she had on their visits backwards and forwards. He distinctly remembers going through the entire Annie P. Smithson canon. Education was always his escape to a better future. Fortuitously, he came under the influence of an inspiring national school teacher called William Clune – a brother of the Irish Volunteer, Conor Clune, who was brutally murdered by two guards in Dublin Castle on Bloody Sunday, the day Michael Collins orchestrated the killing of the Cairo Gang and British forces infamously killed fourteen people at Croke Park. William Clune – a graduate of St Flannan's College, like his famous rebel brother – lived in Quin and used to cycle down to the two-teacher, one-room national school in Ballycar every day, taking up one end of the long classroom while a Ms Lucy Hastings took the juniors facing the other end. He imbued in his charges a deep sense of history; a love of Irish and Latin; encouraged an intimacy with their environment; and was commendably inclusive. There wasn't a child who came into his classroom who, testifies Higgins, was not respected as 'a carrier of wonderment'.

Higgins excelled, academically, at St Flannan's College, which he says was put on this earth for three purposes: one, to win the Harty Cup in hurling; two, to win the gold medal in Greek; and three, to dispatch priests to the diocese. 'It was a tough regime. The most benign comment you'll get was that it was character forming,' he says caustically. He spent the first two years there as a boarder, while his remaining three years were spent as a day boy – 'a lower form of life'.

The classroom was a breeze – he got over ninety per cent in seven subjects in the Leaving Cert. He was particularly taken with Canon Maxwell, who was acting out all the parts of the Great Bard long before the Reduced Shakespeare Company began condensing his work into ninety minutes. One minute, he was Iago, the next, Bassanio.

Accolades were not as forthcoming in other realms of school life. In hurling – during a time when his parish was churning out illustrious names such as Jimmy Cullinan, Liam Danagher and Pat Cronin – any team runs he got were 'usually where less skill was demanded' – corner-back, for instance. 'I had a liking for handball,' he adds. 'Now handball is something that the Clare GAA and, indeed, the GAA around the country barely recognise at all. They think the thing is played by the criminal and lower classes, and those who are heading for both. I didn't get very far. I played once in what was called the Gael Linn championships, where you played for half an hour, but I'm afraid I was drawn against [Hall of Famer] Pat Kirby in the first round. That was the end of my competitive life. It was a matter of the humiliation having to last half an hour.'

He cast a weary eye on the regal visits of Eamon de Valera to the region at the time. 'The older people had these mythic stories of de Valera arriving. I remember the band playing at Halpin's Corner as he passed by,' he says, throwing his eyes to heaven. 'He would travel through Newmarket-on-Fergus. All the instruments stood in a galvanised shed between Pat McNamara's house and Halpin's Corner. They used this galvanised shed as a practice room. They used to bring out the instruments when de Valera would be on his way going through to Ennis.

'There were old stories that when he used to arrive, he would get out of the car in somewhere like Clarecastle, and they'd put him up on a horse, practically, and he'd go in like the Lone Ranger,' he says, creasing with laughter. 'Hi ho, Silver. Away! And he'd go in to the [horse] show, and he'd pin this rosette on an animal of some sort – a horse or a bull or a heifer.

'The other big outing was, of course, the Sacred Heart Procession. That was a big thing ... the Men's Confraternity, the Women's Confraternity, children, First Communions, all up and down the village. "Hail Queen of Heaven, and the Feast of the Sacred Heart", and off we go. Oh, yes indeed,' he says, stifling a laugh. 'These were quite atmospheric. Then there were the missions, which came every now and again. There was a last day or two, having gone through the Mission Day, for delinquents, where they would have rounded up all the people who would have fallen away. There was always these Catholic repository stalls where you had everything from scapulars to rosary beads to statues ...'

'Was this merchandising?'

'Oh, merchandising outside, while the mission was on. Why not? Entrepreneurship, as you'd call it today. I remember there was one night where they would bless all the statues. There was a great story I heard once where a man who bought a statue of the Blessed Virgin – it missed the night of the blessing – and he brought it into the confessional with him, and as the priest pulled back the shutter, he held up this statue, and the poor priest nearly had a heart attack. I think he thought he was experiencing an apparition.'

In such a hotbed of Catholicism, Protestants were thin on the ground. He remembers three Protestant families in the area. 'There was Mrs Frost who used to sell poppies,' he says. 'People were very benevolent. They bought the odd poppy because she was such a nice woman, but I think that they probably dumped them the minute that her back was turned.'

He vividly recalls the sight of Catholic mourners refraining from entering the church near the graveyard at nearby Finlow for a Protestant funeral for fear of breaching a finer point of law from Rome – bringing to mind, he reflects, Austin Clarke's poem on Douglas Hyde's funeral, 'Burial of an Irish President' in which the Taoiseach of the day John A. Costello and his cabinet were left huddling outside the church for risk of 'eternal doom'.

Years later, Higgins found himself doing his bit in diverting many from doom whilst tutoring at Indiana University: 'When I was correcting papers in 1966–67, if you gave less than a C or if you didn't give a C+ to someone, you were changing their draft status, so you'd be sending them to Vietnam. I never gave less than a C; either that or I'd advise them to leave the country.'

University had seemingly set him on course for a life of teaching – and writing about – sociology and political science. Having left school at St Flannan's College, he worked for a couple of years: first at a factory in the Shannon Industrial Estate, and then as a grade-8 clerk in the ESB, before the kindness of a benefactor enabled him to take up a position in University College, Galway; the town has been his home ever since, apart from a couple of sabbaticals studying or teaching in Indiana and Illinois in the US, and Manchester in England.

He has twice served as mayor of Galway; he's a director of Galway United Football Club; and, as a measure of his local iconic status, he has inspired a song by The Saw Doctors – 'Michael D. Rocking in the Dáil'.

Despite the draw of academia, he was propelled into a career in politics – something he had in mind from very early on – in reaction to inequalities, particularly the lack of opportunity in housing, education and the infuriating repetition, he was witnessing, in the country's cycle of poverty; and, indeed, the sins visited on his father and his republican comrades. 'There was such a waste,' he decries. 'When I left secondary school, maybe the sons of about four or five teachers would go to university. I think maybe four out of St Flannan's. If you went to the Christian Brothers, you went to the missions; if you went to St Flannan's, you could have been lucky to be called for the diocese. God was very, very subtle. It was like picking the Clare hurling team.

'The business about going to university – very few people did. There was an enormous waste. That was my first point. The second thing was that I had been through the business of the housing shortage, and also I would have been very angry with myself for what I felt to be the betrayal of the good people who had fought [on the republican side in the civil war] – I don't regard what we have now as a republic. I regard now what we have as a betrayed republic. We wouldn't be having tribunals if we had people who believed in citizens. That's why I believe in universalism. That's why I believe in a single health system. It is the reason why I'm a socialist. My position is that I'm a republican socialist. I believe in the sense of it being a citizenry.

'That's why I find it so "God above in Heaven" when you have someone like the [former] Taoiseach [Bertie Ahern], suggesting that we need some kind of honours system so that you can give all the gombeens in the country a title. I can just see them all lining up. He'd be swamped. It's almost as pathetic as the auditions for *You're a Star*.'

His own star rose slowly but steadily within the Labour Party, being chairman from 1977 until 1987. He was first elected to the Seanad in 1973, serving a term until 1977; he returned there from 1982 to 1987. He first won a seat to the Dáil in 1981, holding it for only a few months. It was at a time – during the days of GUBU – when there were three elections in eighteen months. He won back his seat in 1987, and has held it since, despite, rather than because of, what is a noble but quite cavalier internationalist outlook – something that earned him the Seán MacBride Peace Prize from the International Peace Bureau in 1992, and has endeared him to many commentators. 'It's fantastic – we give out so much about the gobshites that our voters elect time and time again, and the bigger the gobshite, the greater the likelihood that he'll top the poll,' points out Stembridge. 'But it's a real tribute to the people of Galway [West] that they've consistently returned Michael D. to the Dáil, because I suspect he wouldn't be the greatest constituency politician – I could be wrong about that – but that he has his eye on the bigger picture, and very often in Ireland, politicians suffer because of that.'

It's something that Stokes puts into context: 'The thing is, you have this sense that Irish politics tended, historically, to be a real parish-pump kind of affair. People were incapable of looking beyond the borders of their constituency. The generalisation is flawed, but at the same time, broadly speaking, there is an absence of an interest in ideas, an absence of an interest in what was going on in the world at large. The focus tended to be very local. Politicians tended not to be interested in legislation. They tended to be interested in representing their own interests and the interests of their constituency in parliament, which is a problem with the Irish political system.

'But Michael D. is totally different in that respect. He's outward-looking. He's interested in foreign affairs. He's travelled widely. He's interested in intellectual ideas and political ideas and interested in bringing what you can learn from elsewhere to bear here [and vice versa]. Politics here is based entirely on pragmatism. There is very little space for idealism. He would have always wanted to carve out a greater space for ideas.'

Sometimes, his lust for political ideas – especially his socialism – has perhaps been too rigid. He has been Labour Party spokesperson for foreign affairs since 2000. 'He wouldn't be a realistic foreign-policy person,' argues Dr FitzGerald, a former Taoiseach as well as minister for foreign affairs from 1973–77. 'His foreign policy is based on ideals, but ignoring interests, and, of course, foreign policy has to be a mixture of ideals and interests. You have to balance both. I wouldn't think he has as much time for interests as he has for ideals.'

Inevitably, after thirty-five years in public life, Higgins has his detractors. (His friends kid that he's 'vain as a peacock'.) As well as being ideologically unyielding, he can be, it's argued, overly sensitive to criticism. One of the country's leading broadsheet columnists declined to comment on his public record, owing to a 'certain ambivalence' towards his career. The feelings of another, Kevin Myers – who coined the nickname Michael D. Norris – are more decisive. 'He thinks he is a national treasure; but he is actually a leftie windbag, and a posturing jackanapes to boot. Like David Norris, he is a great user of the "offensive" word, which is a key weapon of the politically correct. Cant is the term which comes to mind when I think about Higgins; but he is a pet of the media, because he articulates the moral laziness of many of the prating journalistic classes.

'For smugness and obviousness, he is Ireland's answer to Tony Benn. Benn gave Britain Concorde; Higgins gave us TnaG, which has achieved absolutely nothing for the Irish language, though it has given work to Irish-speaking television [programme] makers in Higgins' constituency.

'Higgins is one of the reasons why there has been no debate about immigration, because of his swiftness with the "racism" accusation.'

And, in the grubby business that is politics, Higgins has made compromises along the way. At a local level in Clare, campaigners against the proposed site for the Mullaghmore Interpretative Centre in the early 1990s recall that though he was the only senior politician to canvass with them initially, his support evaporated once he got into power, which cost them dearly.

He has certainly excited opinion in his travels. 'I remember when I was involved in one of the many referenda campaigns I did around the country – it was after the first divorce referendum [in 1986],' he recalls. 'There was a mission in Newmarket in which the priest said, "They have been defeated," he says, his voice rising thunderously, "but they're lurking in the bushes and one of them is from this parish and his name is Michael D. Higgins."

'I said to my sister-in-law – who was listening to this – afterwards, "What did you do when you heard this? Did you walk out?"

'"No," she said. "I was mortified."

'At any event, they went around the parish collecting money, and the good thing was that they didn't collect a penny in Ballycar. People have a sense of decency, you know.'

His finest hour, politically, came when he was appointed minister for arts, culture and the Gaeltacht in January 1993, holding on to the portfolio until the rainbow coalition came a cropper in the spring of 1997, having weathered the interim collapse of the Fianna Fáil/Labour Party government in 1994. During his tenure, he practically doubled the Arts Council's grant (which rose from £10.6 million in 1992 to £20.8 million in 1997).

He left a notable legacy of achievement from that period in office. As part of the Northern Ireland peace process, he scrapped Section 31 of the Broadcasting Act, which had prohibited the broadcasting of the voices of Sinn Féin or IRA members.

In the area of television and film, he re-established the Film Board; he bolstered Section 35 incentives for film production; and he created Telefís na Gaeilge, a move that has, despite Myers' contention, paid back cultural dividends for the country. 'I think probably one of the unsung achievements of Higgins' period as minister was the profound sense of ownership it gave to artists, arts organisations and arts audiences in the process of the government as it related to them. It felt, for the first time, that "one of ours" was there,' says Theo Dorgan, who was appointed to the Arts Council in 2003.

'He got as much as he could in terms of resources for the arts. I think he was probably occupied with laying the foundations for policies that could have a longer term, a larger impact, but as it happens – and he would be the first to appreciate it – the arts community in general has carried forward his agenda. The agenda is twofold – it's promoting excellence and promoting access. In governmental terms, those principles were nailed up to the mast as key aspirations during Higgins' reign.'

Many, such as the writer John Banville, would have despaired of the notion that art is anything other than a pursuit of excellence. It was to Higgins' credit that he railed against this elitist view, and helped inculcate a belief that arts should be more inclusive and embrace the wider community. 'It is a logical outcome of the view that we're all entitled to share arts equally,' says Niall Stokes. 'That there's no reason for people to feel excluded. If institutions make them feel excluded, it's not the fault of the people, it's the fault of the institutions. It's a bedrock socialist principle.'

There was nothing woolly about the aspiration. As part of the Access Programme during his time in office, there had been the establishment of Collins Barracks Museum, the Chester Beatty Library, and a total of eighteen theatres dotted around the country – from Tallaght and Blanchardstown in Dublin to Letterkenny, Sligo and Glór Theatre in Ennis.

He made no secret of his desire to run for the presidency of Ireland in 2004, but reluctant to gamble its election coffers, he was shafted by his own party hierarchy at the eleventh hour. Whether he would have unseated Mary McAleese is debatable. But there are few in public life in Ireland who inspires as much affection as well as admiration. There's his impressive intellect; the humanitarian spirit, embodied in his polemics and his pamphleteering; the rounded personality; the impish sense of humour; and he has those words at will, which keep those in his company wildly entertained and, on occasion, himself, too.

'I remember when the president of Nicaragua, Daniel Ortega, was over and there was a big bash at the Concert Hall,' says Senator Norris, snorting giddily at the recollection. 'He was to receive a cheque and say, "Thank you." I was the MC, in charge of the running order, and they decided – whoever was putting the programme together – to have the presentation of the cheque just before the interval. It was a huge mistake because Old Sandinista Man – in Latin America, they give awfully long speeches – he spoke for about forty-five minutes. And then Michael D. was overcome by emotion and spoke for another half an hour.

'The result was that the unions were trying to close the Concert Hall, and I was trying to keep the show going because the top-of-the-bill acts were in the second half. They were all furious. People were staying out at the bar. Oh God, it was a complete shambles; brain death, as far as I was concerned, but Michael D. was happily ensconced in the middle of it, burbling away about good socialism.'

KEITH WOOD

Dr James Robson has been the leading medic on the last four British and Irish Lions tours. A Scot, he's not given to melodramatic flourishes. During the video of the 2001 tour to Australia, there's a bring-out-your-dead scene where he goes diligently through the team's injury list after the second test. At the end of the pile, he arrives at the team's hooker. 'Keith Wood,' he says, gravely, 'has just got everything because he just tries so hard and lays his body on the line; and he needs total body therapy today.'

Few, indeed, tried as hard on a rugby pitch. By the end of that tour, an Irish photographer, scratching his head, said it was almost impossible to take a picture during the test matches without catching Wood in the frame. He was running everywhere and at everything, going for it bald-headed, as they say.

'The one thing I would say about Woodie,' says prop forward Marcus Horan – who played with him for both Munster and Ireland – 'is that he's not a big, big man, but, by God, he throws himself around with no regard for his safety.'

The result of that abandon is the stuff of rugby lore. He's had more operations than Joan Rivers – eight or nine on his shoulders alone. In rugby parlance, he is one tough hombre – his body, as writer Donald McRae intones, a 'battlefield of scars'.

'Oh, he got some desperate injuries,' says Mick Galwey, another old Munster and Ireland colleague, before smiling: 'You could say he was soft. He was a bit of a soft cock.'

Wood was born on 27 January 1972, the last of Gordon Wood's seven children. Gordon himself was capped in the front row for the Lions in 1959, although as a tight-head prop and with – unlike the iconic bald pate of his son Keith – 'the finest crop of hair you could see,' according to former Irish and Lions teammate, Niall Brophy. An old school mate of Richard Harris, Gordon Wood won twenty-nine caps for Ireland. He passed away in 1982 when Keith was only ten years of age.

A 'sports Billy' when growing up, Wood played under-age soccer and hurling for Clare, although, not surprisingly, contemporaries of his suggest it wasn't deft stick work that got him on representative teams: 'He would go through a lot of hurlers,' remembers his old Smith O'Briens and Ireland rugby teammate, Anthony Foley.

'The guy you'd like playing centre-forward – he broke a lot of ball,' adds James O'Connor, euphemistically, having played with him for the Clare under-16s.

At St Munchin's College, Keith drifted in and out of the rugby scene, failing to make his year's Munster Schools' Junior Cup-winning side (there is always hope, kids!), and played briefly at underage for Shannon and Bohemians before joining Garryowen, where he picked up two AIL medals in 1992 and 1994. 'Although Woodie mightn't admit it, he played in the centre for Shannon,' says Galwey, a former player and coach with Shannon. 'That'll tell you how much Shannon thought of him; having said that, he spent most of his time in the backs, so Shannon actually saw his true position. Garryowen stuck him in hooker, but he was really a winger or a centre.'

It wasn't until Wood had established himself as Garryowen's first-choice hooker that Galwey, an established international at the time, remembers first coming across him. 'It was a scrummaging session between Shannon and Garryowen – we used to do them back then – and I was looking at this young fella with a big head of curly hair, and he getting stuck in. "Who's this young buck?" That was the first time I saw him. Full of temper.'

Limerick's other All-Ireland League-conquering side at the time was Young Munster. Their totem forward, Peter Clohessy, has said that he remembers Wood as having a reputation of being a 'cocky little fucker' around Limerick at the time. But, of course, they grew to become firm friends. Having defeated France in 2000 – the first Irish win in Paris in twenty-eight years – The Claw said that Wood's smile alone was worth the pain of the game.

'He was confident – not cocky, but as outgoing as you'd get in a small, country town,' writes Anthony Foley in his autobiography *Axel*. 'He'd hold up his own whether it was up at Smith O'Briens GAA Club, at the top of the town or hanging around in Crowe's playing Pac-Man and pool.'

'He always gave the impression of being a bit fearless and a bit reckless,' remembers Paul Horan from their days at Munchin's and in the University of Limerick, where Wood studied before taking up a job at the Irish Permanent bank. 'I remember in college – of course, we met a whole new circle of friends – whether it was nervousness on Keith's part, but his way of greeting you at the time was to give you a dead arm: "How's it going?" Bumph. And I don't think he knew his own strength, so people used to be crumpled up in his wake.'

His former teammates used to characterise him as being good-humoured if a bit aloof, and, according to an interview with Rob Henderson – a good friend and guest at Wood's wedding – 'his humour is pretty dry and pretty abstract.'

Wood's tastes are certainly left-field and wide-ranging. He's a voracious reader, once citing Joseph Heller's *Catch-22* as his favourite book. 'Everything and anything,' he says. The day we meet, he's deep in a book called *Mismatch*, a study by two popular medical-science writers on genes and our environment; and although he's famous for his ability to belt out Irish ballads, he mentions he's 'a huge fan' of Leonard Cohen, the Grocer of Despair, and enthuses about a recent small-venue Aretha Franklin gig he attended; elsewhere, he's stated a penchant for music gods of the blues and rock 'n' roll firmament, such as the The Doors, The Rolling Stones and Lou Reed.

As a young man, these attributes – a rigorous mind, his outgoing manner allied to ambition and a stubborn streak – stood Wood in good stead as he blazed a trail during the nascent days of professionalism in the mid and late 1990s, much to the initial despair of the IRFU hierarchy, which was struggling to adapt to the demands of a new paradigm.

When the game turned professional in 1995, unlike the impressive provincial-based regime Ireland operates in 2008, the country's rugby union was hopelessly ill-equipped to deal with the transformation. It had no structures in place. It was haemorrhaging players to the UK – such as Wood, who left to join London club Harlequins in 1996 – and was turning out a national team that was stuck in a trough of poor form; as a barometer, Ireland's record to Scotland during the 1990s was: played ten, lost nine, drawn one.

By the autumn of 1998, Wood was billboard material. Singled out by Bob Dwyer (Australia's coach) on his debut against Australia in 1994 for future greatness, he was first made captain of the Irish team at twenty-four years of age, and as a hero on the triumphant 1997 Lions tour to South Africa, his ebullient persona and bullocking rugby style had endeared him to the nation – and to marketeers.

The IRFU sought to stifle his commercial potential by tying him to a contract that demanded he sign over his 'intellectual property rights', whereby any of the five main IRFU sponsors (including his old employer, Irish Permanent) could use his image without seeking his agreement or organising separate remuneration, and requiring that Wood seek IRFU approval before making his own individual promotional deals. While the other eighty-six players signed, Wood stood his ground, conducting a one-man strike before a World Cup qualifying game against Romania. It was a bold move, and the Mexican stand-off led to some harsh criticism – including jibes about the 'millionaire from Clare' – even though logic was on his side. 'The idea behind it was not necessarily wrong,' says Wood, 'but the law part of it was just rubbish ... I tried to make the more aggressive stance – and I did. I gave them an ultimatum: "Are you saying if I don't sign the contract I'm not to turn up for training?" and they said, "Absolutely", and I put out a press release – I'd it prepared just in case – two minutes later.'

'You were very young [twenty-six] to be at that caper – taking on the old blazers of the IRFU?'

'I was, to be totally honest, and it was a hard thing,' he says. 'It was applicable to me and not applicable at that time to virtually any of the other guys. They were saying, "All the other guys have signed it."

'"Well," I said, "all the other guys are in Ireland, earning a contract of £60,000, £70,000, £80,000; my contract was £5,000 for playing for Ireland so it was a very straight view, and the truth is I'd have played for Ireland for nothing, anyway."'

It is the truth. He donated that season's match fees (estimated, in a World Cup year, at £15,000) to a youth charity. Commendably, Wood has always been selfless and generous with his time. Often, for instance, he could be seen out on a pitch signing autographs half an hour after his teammates had departed the fray.

Interestingly, as a player, Wood always tried to treat Ireland–England battles as just another match that had to be won. 'I never wanted it to be different,' he says. 'Ultimately, when you look back on them, they're the ones that other people remember even more than you do yourself. My view was that those wins in 1993 and 1994 papered over the cracks, because we didn't really win a load of other matches, and people were happy with the fact that "Oh, we'd beaten England so that's a good Five Nations" and I wanted to beat everyone. That sounds a bit lofty or arrogant, but I just thought we were hung up about beating England.'

His try against them in the deferred 'Foot and Mouth' Six Nations international in autumn 2001 is one of the most memorable moments of recent Irish rugby history: a typically marauding break for the line by Wood, following a rehearsed move from a line-out that was used that day for the first time in a match, he reckons, in three years. The game is also remembered for some devilment at the line-out. 'I was standing by, and I was listening to the line-out calls, and I said, "I know those calls." And I'm trying to think because there are so many calls, and then Malcolm O'Kelly comes over to me and goes, "They're using the Lions calls."' Bingo. The advantage gained at the line-out helped with the Irish ploy, he says, of peppering English full-back Iain Balshaw – who was suffering from a 'knock in confidence' – with bombs from the sky, and in a dramatic game, the defining moment, he acknowledges, came with Peter Stringer's ankle-tap tackle on his Harlequins' teammate Dan Luger, who was almost in for a try.

The loss cost England a Grand Slam title, but they were missing three of their Lions players, one of them being the captain, Martin Johnson, whom Wood has huge regard for. Asked as to who was more important to England's triumph in the 2003 World Cup – their manager or their captain – Wood has no doubt. 'Johnson', he shoots back. 'In fairness to Woodward, his organisation was startling and he did an awful lot – he put structures in place to facilitate making it happen. I would have said he got too many plaudits out of it at the end of it. Johnson was a truly magnificent captain, and a guy you'd go through a brick wall for, which is hard for an Irishman to say for an Englishman, but I can with the greatest of comfort.

'He was a guy who had a very simple element of focus. The best part of his captaincy was that he always had four or five guys he could depend on. When Ireland beat England the following year [2004], I was sitting with him in the BBC box, and I was laughing at him because they were losing, and he was at a loss to explain it, and I said, "I can explain it incredibly easily: *you're* not on the field." I said, "You've got four guys out there who all think that they should be captain. They never thought that when you were there." You could see them bickering on the pitch, and they'd never done that when Johnson was playing.'

The respect is mutual. In Johnson's autobiography, the English colossus even wondered if Wood might have been a better captain of the unsuccessful 2001 Lions, given that Wood is 'always very positive' and that he was more obviously a 'people person'. It was an interesting admission. But no player is impervious to doubt, Wood points out. 'I think you question yourself all the time,' he says. 'People always talk about confidence players, and that's a bit of a misnomer actually because everybody is a confidence player. It's how people deal with the hard times [that] probably makes them better players, and [then] they're not so reliant on it [confidence], but everybody would have self-doubt a lot of the time.'

During his rugby career, Wood went through the horrors for a couple of years with his line-out throwing – that devilish art that calls on a hooker to stop in the middle of the maelstrom of a rugby match and pick out a point in the sky with the daintiness of a butterfly catcher. 'It was driving me absolutely mad. I'd the yips, effectively', he says.

Playing with injuries exacerbated the situation. He even went through a spell where he lost the ability to spin the ball. It was only two weeks later that he twigged the cause – his wrist was too heavily strapped. He'd been trying to cover for a knock he was carrying. How infuriating must that have been?

It seemed he'd finally cracked the problem during the World Cup in 1999 – it was a simple tic in his technique, which became pronounced in times of pressure. He devised a mental trick – 'an anchor that some spoon bender' alerted him to – that helped ground him when the heat came on. Against Australia in a bloody encounter – for Trevor Brennan, at least – at Lansdowne Road, the new technique held firm despite prodigious jumping from the Australian line-out. Four days later, Ireland travelled to Lens in France to play the Argentinians in a quarter-final play-off. 'I'd been practising and practising and practising this [technique]. I felt under so much pressure, and I threw the first line-out, and they took it and it nearly broke my heart,' he says. 'I actually went into free fall in the middle of the pitch and this was only five minutes into a game.

'[But] I remember using this mental tag to get it [right] and I got it. I think I won sixteen of the next sixteen line-outs, and from that time on I never actually felt under anywhere near as much pressure with my throwing. I didn't win all my line-outs from then on, either,' he says, laughing, 'but I didn't get stressed by it at all.'

Although the game marked a little mental triumph over something that had bedevilled him, he says the infamous loss was the lowest moment mentally he endured in the sport, though the experience wasn't without its lesson. 'We stopped off in Roscrea,' he says, as some of the Munster-based players made their way home. 'We went into a pub – myself, Claw, four or five of us – and it went quiet when we walked in. It was about four o'clock in the afternoon. I said, "You were reading us, lads, weren't you?"

'And they said, "We were. We were."

'I said, "Go on – get out with it."

'And the publican said, "Lads, what the hell were ye doing?"

'I said, "Look, I understand that we've let our family down and our country down and ourselves down. We tried to play as good as we could, and we just didn't perform … I have no excuse to offer. I think we played very, very badly. But I will apologise."

'And your man said, "That's the best answer you could possibly have given. Pints for these men."

'I'll tell ya, I learnt a lot from that, and, of course, the pub was full five minutes later – the whole town came in. The thing was that you need to face up to it as soon as you possibly can.'

Wood was always quick to make up for mistakes whenever any of his famous drop-kick attempts went awry, too, including one memorable effort in an Irish international. 'He always wanted to do it – score a drop goal for Ireland,' says Galwey. 'I remember, it was the "Foot and Mouth" year, 2001, and we were above playing against France. The next thing, Woodie gathers the ball in his usual out-half position, out in front of Rog [Ronan O'Gara], and he went for a drop goal. Trying a drop goal against France!' says Galwey in disbelief. 'By Jaysus, if it didn't go two feet off the ground – you'd get a better kick from a donkey – straight into the winger's hands, and you could see the winger flying down in front of the old West Stand. In fairness to Woodie, without even stopping to think, he realised he had made a mistake, and he chased down the winger, and I said to him after, "It was a good job you caught your man."

'He said, "Whatever about missing the drop goal, if your man had scored a try!"'

While at Harlequins, Wood and All Blacks international Zinzan Brooke – who landed a forty-metre drop-goal in a World Cup semi-final against England in 1995 – used to practise them after training, 'like two eejits', he says, and when it came to a £100 bet on who would score in a Premiership match first, Wood prevailed, popping one over two weeks later in a game against Northampton.

But when it comes to drop-kicks, the one Wood will be immortalised for was actually one he didn't score. In the second test for the Lions against the Springboks in 1997 – with the match locked at 15–15 – the tourists were soaking up drive after drive when Wood broke down the narrow side, kicked ahead, and somehow – with that trademark trundle of his – managed to chase the kick forty metres down the pitch, forcing a Lions put-in at the line-out. In the seventy-seventh minute of a gruelling test, it was a Herculean effort. The Lions gathered their line-out, and when Matt Dawson fed to Jeremy Guscott, he nailed a drop goal to win the series.

As to his memories of the tour, they're mainly ones of physical discomfort. 'I remember how tired I was – all the time,' he says. 'I remember how sore I was – all the time. We over-trained. We probably had to.'

Having injured his left shoulder against France in the Five Nations that season – doctor, another pin, please – he had been selected for the tour even though he wasn't fully fit. 'Oh, gee, we trained so hard out there,' he adds. 'I've looked at that video once since – *Living with the Lions* – and there's a scene inside where I'm with Tony Underwood and Tim Rodber, and we're in between training sessions, and we're nearly asleep having a conversation. We were absolutely shattered.'

Wood believes the Lions over-trained unnecessarily for the tour to Australia in 2001, which is borne out by the fact that the Lions failed to score in the last twenty minutes of each of the three tests. 'We had to [over-train] in 1997; in 2001, we didn't, and we were tired. We were tired before we went out. I think we had too many on the tour, and we'd too many matches, was my view. And yet, we still could have won it,' he says, before singling out the critical loss of flanker, Richard Hill. 'He was playing them off the park. I mean, Richard Hill for the first game and a half of that series was ridiculously good,' he enthuses, omitting to point out that Wood himself was awarded the Man of the Match award for the victorious first test in Brisbane.

Wood's quirky sense of humour came to the fore in a surreal series of events in the November following the 2001 Lions tour. Having left the Irish embassy in London – where he had been a guest with President Mary McAleese – Wood set off for Heathrow. On the way to the airport, he called his brother Gordon, wondering if he could pick him up at Shannon Airport. When his brother sounded a bit spaced on the phone, Wood quizzed him, only to discover he had just taken some valium a doctor had given him for a heart attack while they waited for an ambulance to arrive to take him to hospital. Wood began to frantically call his mother and siblings to alert them to the situation. Meanwhile, news broke in Dublin that Irish coach Warren Gatland's contract had not been renewed by the IRFU. Calls from some thirty journalists came raining in on Wood, the Irish captain, looking for a reaction. They were met with a 'can't talk – brother having heart attack;

bye' response. When Wood got to the hospital in Limerick, he fired out the news: 'Gordon, Gatty's gone and you wouldn't believe the crap you got me out of today.' It was enough to send the pair of brothers, one critically ill, into convulsions of laughter.

Unfortunately, the tragic postscript to this story is that his brother passed away ten months later after another heart attack. He was only forty-one years of age. In a case of the most extreme highs and lows imaginable, Wood's first child, Alexander, was born on the day of the funeral.

The fraught relationship that Wood had with Gatland at the end of the New Zealander's days in the Irish post has been well publicised. When *Sunday Times* journalist Peter O'Reilly asked Gatland how he rated the Irish hooker, he replied that 'he was a good Barbarians player' – and he was only half joking.

Wood believed that the team needed 'an Irish man for the Irish job' to understand and motivate the mercurial Irish psyche. Also, at a technical level, he had valid criticisms. For example, he found Gatland's delay in getting a defence coach infuriating. After Ireland lost a 21–7 lead against the All Blacks in Gatland's last international in charge, he has admitted this defeat nearly drove him into retirement. 'I've said it comfortably. I've said it to his face, too. I thought he did an excellent job with us in 1998 – consistency of selection, a lot of good things,' says Wood about the Kiwi's departure. 'I think when the team changed, he needed to change; he probably didn't change enough, really, and maybe took some things for granted; and then it was time for a change.'

As to what Wood has said to him when the pair met afterwards, Wood says: 'He was very upset and he was very hurt by it, you know? Yet, after it all, I think he learned an awful lot more out of it because he said joining Wasps was one of the best things he ever did.'

With Eddie O'Sullivan taking over the Ireland coach's job, Wood found a kindred spirit, and also a man who allowed him to have a greater influence on proceedings. 'Woodie's personality is such that no matter where he is or what he's doing, he sees himself as a dominant personality in a group situation, and he's very good in that, and a very good captain,' said a former teammate in an interview with the *Irish Times* in March 2008. 'In some ways it's like [Brian] O'Driscoll now. What they say, goes. Eddie was the coach, but with Fester [Wood] and with Drico, they basically dictated how we did things.'

Not every player warmed to his offbeat sense of humour and domineering leadership style though. 'I found Fester a funny character,' writes Trevor Brennan, a marginalised player on the Irish squad during Wood's playing days, in his autobiography, *Heart and Soul*. 'His greeting was usually along the lines of "You mad Irish bastard, how are you?!"

'"Yeah, how are you Fester?"

'"You're crazy. You're a looper, aren't you?"

'"Yeah, how are you going Fester, alright?"

'No matter whether it was breakfast, lunch or tea, that was how he greeted me. I was always a bit wary of him. I'd had a couple of run-ins with him at training sessions. I never felt comfortable around him. It wasn't that I took personal offence to the way he greeted me. That was good-natured, and he characterised nearly everybody in the way he said hello to them.

'That said, I thought there was something funny about the banter. I also felt that as captain he had too much influence on selection, so I didn't know whether to snuggle up to him or avoid him.'

One of the novel things Wood orchestrated as captain was to get Ranulph Fiennes along for a motivational speech before the team set off to Australia for the 2003 World Cup. It was only when Wood got through on the phone to Fiennes at his farm that he discovered the explorer had just had some medical difficulties. 'He said, "Well, you know I've had my little setback."

'I said, "No, what's your setback?"

'"Well, I had a bypass six weeks ago. They'd to re-start me fifteen times." This guy is fifty-nine, right. He said, "But I'm fine. That was just three months ago. I'm back training."

'I said, "Training? What are you training for?"

'"I'm doing this 7/7/7 challenge – seven marathons, on seven consecutive days, on the seven different continents." And he did it.'

'He came over to Dublin to a training camp, and I knew the guys didn't know who he was. I knew Eddie did because I'd given the books to Eddie. He came into the room and he's very bookish, very donnish. He's got the leather on the sleeves, and he's very English. He didn't try and play to the audience at all. He'd a slide show, and he went through it,' says Wood, smiling, 'and it literally was, "Oh my God"; suddenly the guys are fascinated. "Yeah, I lost a finger there. I couldn't get my glove on. This time we were there for three months in this little tent." In terms of mental strength, the guy is astonishing.'

Wood isn't far behind. A rampant All Blacks side arrived in Dublin in November 1997 to face an Irish team that had lost seven of its previous eight internationals, including defeats at Lansdowne Road to Western Samoa and Italy in their pre-Six Nations days. Wood's body was falling apart. Along with his problematical left shoulder, during the Lions' tests that summer, he tore ankle ligaments and his groin, and, worst of all, his back was at him. He was advised to take a break from the game, but flew to Dublin for the match regardless.

Ten minutes into the game, a double-hit by Zinzan Brooke and Andrew Blowers – who was keeping Josh Kronfeld out of the All Blacks side – caused him to rip his ankle ligaments again. Yet, defiantly, he played on, rumbling over for a try from a line-out and out-sprinting All Blacks winger Jeff Wilson for a second try. When the whistle blew for half-time, adrenaline subsided, he limped off the pitch, and had to be carried down the steps to the dressing-room and – as journalist Tom English remarks – 'into the folklore of Irish rugby'.

Remarkably, Wood says his body is doing well these days, with the exception of his back which gives him 'a bit of jip' from time to time. He retired from rugby after the 2003 World Cup, established as one of the giants of the game. Indeed, he won the inaugural World Player of the Year award in 2001.

These days, he can be seen by BBC television viewers in his capacity as a rugby analyst. He also writes a rugby column for the *Daily Telegraph*, although he says the game takes up 'less than ten per cent' of his time now, what with his array of business interests, including Touch Wood International, a property company, and Touch Wood PR, which looks after his corporate sponsorship and speaking deals.

It's no surprise he's using those talking skills of his to good effect. As president of the IRFU, Brophy remembers sitting beside Wood on the Irish team's flight back from the tour to South Africa in 1998. When quizzed about what he would do after he finished the game, the young Irish hooker said: 'I don't know, but one thing I love doing is talking.'

His quips during his playing career are legendary. During that tour, he took an unmerciful pasting from the South Africans.

'Before the first test in Bloemfontein,' writes Foley in his auto-biography, 'our bus was blocked at the gate of the stadium for what seemed like an age, with Bok supporters rocking it from side to side, pelting it with pebbles and shouting in Afrikaans – the only words we could recognise were "Keith Woods". Woody was virtually a hate figure in South Africa because of his part in the Lions success, and the Boks themselves seemed on a mission to take revenge, cheap-shotting him at every opportunity. He soaked it all up, kept answering back with lines about South Africa's record on human rights and then, after the second test in Pretoria, leading the entire squad in a defiant rendition of "From Clare to Here" at the post-match function.'

Two years later, after helping Harlequins to a Parker Pen Shield title, Wood was asked by a journalist what he thought the victory meant for English rugby: 'I don't care about English rugby,' he replied. 'I just care about Harlequins.'

Although, when his beloved Harlequins came to visit his old province, Munster, in 1997, he could only shake his head in bemusement at one particular exchange in the front row. 'We were playing Harlequins in Thomond Park,' recounts Galwey. 'Someone told

Claw that the prop up against him was from America. Claw was up against your man, anyway, and he kept saying, "Will you fuck off back to America you useless Yank."'

Wood couldn't make out what Clohessy was muttering to his teammate, Danny Rouse, but he quizzed him later that evening in the bar. 'Ah, I was tellin' him he was a Yankee prick,' said Clohessy.

Wood took a step back to get a good look at him. 'Claw,' he said, 'your man is from Fiji.'

SHARON SHANNON

'Her smile is as important as her music, isn't it?' says Liam Clancy, rhetorically. 'You know, it's that projection of pure joy.' Yes, it is. It's as familiar to us as Mick Jagger's pout or The Dubliners' row of shaggy beards – as much a part of her identity in the public's mind as the Castignari button accordion plugged to her hip.

Shannon is the cheerful, sexy face of traditional music. She is, as Maura O'Connell says, 'a gorgeous imp of pure music'. There's a revelry about her. Donal Lunny, a former boyfriend, once said that he composed his tune, 'Cavan Potholes' with her in mind because 'it's bouncy and bubbly like Sharon'.

The world seems softer around the edges in her company. Pixie-like at just over five-feet tall, she lives, for the most part, in Salthill, Galway in a terraced house; nondescript from the outside, but one that opens up at the end of a hallway into a huge kitchen and living area with light streaming in from the back yard. There's a lived-in, bohemian feel to it – not surprising since it hosts regular impromptu sessions late into the night, and is the living quarters for Shannon's battalion of cats and dogs – eight in total – overseen by Daisy, a big, placid, black-haired mongrel; a cross between a springer and a cocker, she lent her name to Shannon's record label, Daisy Discs. Founded by herself and her manager, John Dunford, it's a meeting house for many of her friends and collaborators, as it publishes an array of Ireland's leading musicians, including Lunny and Shannon, as well as Eleanor Shanley, Dessie O'Halloran and Pauline Scanlon. Given Shannon's warm, exuberant personality, she's always been a conduit and mentor to musicians.

'She's a kind of magnet,' says Donogh Hennessy, a guitarist in the Sharon Shannon Band for four or five years. 'If there's a gang of people there, and Sharon is in the room, you'll just end up doing crazy stuff. She encourages people to have a good laugh. People warm to her. She's like their best friend. She's all about fun and music and having *craic*, and that's what her attraction is, really.'

Shannon was born 12 November 1968 on a small dairy farm in the parish of Ruan, a mile and a half from the village, but, peculiarly, with a postal address in Corofin, where she spent all but her last year in primary school, as it was convenient for her father's commute to the creamery.

Shannon comes third among four siblings, the other three are all still living in Clare: Garry, the eldest and Majella and Mary, the youngest. Outside of school, and helping their father on the farm with the hay during summer and so on, they used to get up to your normal – or maybe not so normal – tomfoolery as kids. 'Big leafing,' explains Garry Shannon, matter-of-factly, like he's imparting the rudiments of an ancient Celtic pastime. 'You'd pick the biggest leaf on the tree and you'd crawl out to the edge of the furthest-out branch on the tree to get these leaves. We'd spend hours up trees. The other thing was we'd swing off branches – tag on trees. I remember Sharon fell off one of the trees and her hair got caught on the way down. She hung by the hair. We had to disentangle her.'

Sharon's obviously tough, like her father, I. J., who is still 'as hardy as ever' at eighty, she says. He always kept a string of Connemara ponies – as many as sixteen or seventeen. They were like 'pure pets,' says Sharon, and she's serious. As children, she explains, they used to bring them into the house, 'for *craic*, just to show them where we were livin'.'

Growing up, riding was 'as much, if not more, of a passion' as music. She would go on drag hunts, and, after school – with the run of the farmland – she would set about constructing her makeshift show-jumping arena with tar barrels, old car wheels and tyres, moving them around every day to prevent the land from getting scorched. At weekends, she was able compete for proper. 'Everyone would have to go whether we liked it or not,' says Garry, 'to horse shows and gymkhanas all over the country, and if we had a girlfriend to meet on a Sunday, either you didn't meet her or she'd have to come to the bloody horse show, too. Unless you were involved or unless you were riding, they were mind-numbingly boring.

'Sharon started off with one pony, and then we'd have two ponies going. She was tough and strong – fearless. It kind of indicated the fecklessness which is important in choosing the life that she did, [showing a] disregard for conservative values or for security. You know, *carpe diem* – live for the day. This fearlessness on horses was the same as going away and living a life which was very unstable.'

All four of the Shannons are musicians: Sharon plays the two-row button accordion; Garry, the concert flute; Majella, the fiddle, and Mary – who has her own band, The Bumblebees – the banjo. In fact, the family quartet played a couple of gigs together in 2007 – for the first time in fifteen years – as part of the Corofin Trad Festival and one in Ennis' Glór Theatre.

They were mostly self-taught, Sharon says, with a bit of direction from Garry and encouragement from their parents, who would often get up and dance to their music. Practice came as easy as breathing in the air. 'We ate and drank and dreamt music,' she says. Frank Custy, the noted local fiddle player and teacher, once remarked that whether he phoned the Shannon house at nine in the morning or nine at night, he could hear an accordion belting away in the background.

Custy used to organise *céilís* in Tuna every Friday night with 'huge, big pots of tea,' remembers Shannon, and music and dancing for all ages in the vicinity. She joined a band called Disert Tola at fourteen years of age, along with other of Custy's pupils, which involved tours – 'an insurer's nightmare,' as Garry Shannon points out – to the UK and the United States, coordinated by Gearóid O'Halloran.

'She was so committed at the time,' says Garry. 'She would have recorded musicians and tunes at sessions played in Boston and New York – people like Séamus Connolly. I remember once she was very, very annoyed with me – I don't know if she ever forgave me – [when] we met a legendary figure in New York called Martin Wynne who was a great composer of Irish music from the 1930s and 1940s. We were so excited meeting Martin Wynne, and Gearóid, being the scholar, had to record this conversation with Martin Wynne to capture for posterity the pearls of wisdom that might roll from his tongue. Sharon's tape recorder was the only one close to hand so she was strong-armed into giving it for recording this interview. Of course, when the tape ran out, we turned it over. She was absolutely apoplectic. All her tunes had started on the other side, and a huge welt of tunes got recorded over. She didn't speak to us for days, and passed the very accurate remark about the recorded footage of Martin Wynne: "That auld fella, ye'll never use it and ye'll never listen to it again, and all my tunes gone." And she was right.'

Having finished secondary school at Coláiste Mhuire in Ennis, she went to Cork, where she was 'supposed to be' studying for an arts degree. Every weekend and summers were at this stage being passed in Doolin, where she spent a spell living in a mobile home at the back of Susan O'Connor's house. She'd be playing nine, ten gigs a week, 'loving every second of it' even though the clientele may have listened but weren't always watching the musicians. 'Most of the time during the summer, the pubs were so packed,' she says. 'We'd no amplification or anything. Four of us used to be sitting down. There'd be a table in front of us, and in front of the table were just all arses. Everyone used to have their back to us, talking – no one was listening, but we didn't give a damn because we were just buzzin' ourselves.'

One patron who had his ears cocked was P. J. Curtis, the music producer and writer. He remembers first coming across her in McGann's pub in 1988. 'I first heard Sharon in Doolin,' he says. 'She was like a beacon inside in the middle of a session – like a light, like a burning light. Her whole demeanour, her personality, her playing, she just kind of leaped out of the circle, and that right away tells you something about the personality, and the music, then, of course. There's a purity about her. There's no guile.'

Disillusioned with college and to please her mother, she took a secretarial course in Limerick, which lasted a year. Much as she loved Doolin, she moved to Galway in 1988. Having met the poet Maura Hughes one night at a session, she moved in with her into a house on Henry Street, not far from the Róisín Dubh pub; it became home for four years.

After a spell with traditional group Arcady – which included musicians such as Frances Black, Seán Keane and Cathal Hayden – Shannon began work on a solo album. It was co-ordinated by Dunford – the soundman for The Waterboys at the time – and Philip King. As Shannon was nervous about recording in a studio, they recorded in Winkle's pub in Kinvara. A group of fine musicians joined in – Lunny, Steve Cooney, her sister Mary, and one of the members of U2. 'Philip King had just started his *Bringing it All Back Home* television series at the time,' explains Shannon. 'He had asked Adam Clayton to be involved in it, and Adam was saying, "Ah, I don't really know much about this kind of music."

'Philip said, "Come down to Kinvara – I'll show you what it's all about!"'

Mike Scott from The Waterboys showed up as well. He had seen Shannon at a gig with Arcady in the Purty Loft in Dún Laoghaire, and, liking what he heard, asked her if she'd come along with The Waterboys for a few gigs. Shannon agreed, playing on the main stage at Glastonbury the following week.

It was the start of a magical, meandering stint with the band. She loved it – 'a real, mad adventure, and just really, really good vibes' – but the long-haul travelling was wearying. 'I just remember constant delays at airports – hours and hours and hours, missing connection flights. We'd always have these amazing sessions at airports and on planes,' she says, bringing new meaning to the notion of in-flight entertainment. 'Steve Earle would have his fiddle out, and Anto [Thistlethwaite] always had the mandolin; everyone always had a little instrument at hand.'

'And the flight attendants, they'd let ye off?'

'Yeah, they were delighted – most of the time.'

She cut loose after eighteen months. 'It was just way too much touring for me,' she says. 'We'd be away for five- or six-week tours. We might only be home for a week or two weeks, and then we'd have another one. I was just missing home so much. Even though we were having a great time, I was missing my friends, the sessions we'd have in Naughton's, and I was missing the horses and missing going off riding. We'd spend six hours in an airport and I'd go, "I wish I was out galloping on a horse on a field," thinking, "Oh God, this is such a waste of time."'

After work for a spell with Christy Moore on an uncompleted album, she decided to go back and harvest the material from the Winkle's sessions, but also to brave the studio this time round. The result was staggering. She released the *Sharon Shannon* album in 1991, and it became the biggest-selling traditional album of all time. The phone hopped. Often, she wouldn't answer. 'I found that I was always ringing up John Dunford for advice,' she says. 'I'd say, "John, what'll I do now? This one is after ringing asking me to do this." Then I said to John, "How would you feel about managing [me] instead of this one or that one or the other one doing it?"'

'And John said, "Oh, I've never done anything like that before," but I think for a manager, all you need is somebody that you can trust.'

After a couple of days chewing it over, Dunford agreed to make the arrangement formal. It was a stroke of good fortune for her. 'She's very well managed,' says Garry Shannon. 'Her manager is very much in her corner, and looks after her very well – genuinely believes in her and genuinely wants the best for her; and hasn't spread himself too thinly.'

Shannon, for her part, has spread her tentacles far and wide. She has released eleven solo albums, each one a new departure, and has a hunger for reinventing herself and for absorbing different influences, from bluegrass and Cajun tunes to roots and gospel. 'One of the great things about her – like Davy Spillane, like Martin Hayes – is that she came from such a rooted tradition,' says P. J. Curtis. 'That's what gave her the roots of a strong tree, if you like, but she had the will and the mind to be able to stretch out and not be confined. She was able to say, "I can sit in with The Waterboys; I can sit in with a country musician like Steve Earle; I can sit in and be comfortable because it's all music, and it's all good music."'

'Okay, you've got the traditional which will always be pure, but she can come back and play with the local musicians here in a flash,' Curtis continues, clicking his fingers. 'She can now also step up and play with reggae, and she's done it all. I really think that what she has done has been a phenomenal journey. That young girl I met in a caravan [in Doolin] could never in a million years imagine that she could go and play with reggae and rock, but she had the open heart and the soul to embrace it.'

Interestingly, for all Shannon's experimentation, she still doesn't read formal music. There is something wondrous, something inexplicable about her talent. 'She's got an incredible rhythm,' says Donogh Hennessy. 'I transcribed all of Sharon's best-known tunes – writing out the notes for about five or six sets from each of her albums. I wrote them out in a book for her. So I had to go through every tune, note for note, and write each one down exactly as she played it. If you write the notes down the way they're played, they're really straight, but the amount of rhythm Sharon puts in – the emphasis on each note – is very unusual. She has her own little internal rhythm going on in the tune.

'You can't say that there's anybody who sounds like her, except a couple of people who have tried to copy her. She just has something very, very special. She's very skilled and has great technique, but there's something else going on, an X factor. There is something there that's a little spark of magic.'

'It's interesting,' adds Colm Ó Snodaigh – a flutist and guitar player with Kila; 'we played with her in Switzerland about five years ago. There's a very different feel to her music. There's a very different lilt. There's a different swing. We described it as west-of-the-Shannon sound.'

Back across Ireland's great river, Shannon leads a very inconspicuous, everyday life, popping into local pubs where her friends congregate, and taking in long, daily walks. 'I'm not really on the telly every day of the week,' she laughs. 'My face isn't that recognisable. Most of the time when I'm out walking the dogs, I have wellies on, and dirty auld clothes.'

Her private, low-key existence was fractured briefly when the media got hold of a botched drink-driving charge in which she was involved, following an accident at Taylor's Hill in Galway on the way home from a party at the Crane traditional music bar in September 2001. Shannon, over the drink-driving limit, told the gardaí when they arrived on the scene that she was driving the car, in order to protect a friend – who wasn't insured to drive her car – but when the case came to court, she admitted that she wasn't driving. Judge Mary Fahy disregarded Shannon's claim, maintaining Shannon and her friends had told the court 'outright lies'. As a result, Shannon received a fine and driving ban for two years. On appeal, the case was thrown out of court on a technicality, which – after the ordeal of a two-and-a-half-year court saga played out intermittently in the press – was a relief, but it never allowed her to properly state her case. 'It was really, really stressful,' she admits. 'It was awful. The judge didn't believe us, and I wouldn't blame the judge for not believing us because it was really badly handled, but we were completely telling the truth.' It was an unfortunate incident for someone so retiring to have to endure.

Sadly, her long-term partner, Leo Healy passed away, aged just 46, in his sleep in May 2008, the very month in which Shannon's latest album, *The Galway Girl – The Best of Sharon Shannon* reached No. 1 in the Irish Charts. Remarkably, as a result of nervousness, Shannon – one of the most recognisable faces in Irish music – has only ever given one TV interview: recently, on RTÉ's daytime show, *Seoige & O'Shea*. In fact, when Gay Byrne hosted a tribute *Late Late Show* towards the end of 1992 in her honour, she wasn't interviewed for it. Her music, as they say, did the talking for her. 'We were contacted about it – John and myself,' she explains about the invitation. 'It was really daunting: "Oh my God, this is just a massive thing to be offered." It was really scary. We were thinking, "God, it could be a disaster – I'm so bad at interviews." We were kind of considering maybe we shouldn't do it because it could be the ruination of us,' she says melodramatically, before collapsing in laughter.

'But then we had a good talk with Bridget Ruane, the woman who was researching it. She was lovely – really, really nice. She came down to visit my parents. She spent time with my family and where I grew up, and really got to know us. She was really sound. She was saying, "Don't worry, you don't have to talk." And she was asking who would ye like on it,' says Shannon, making a warble sound with her tongue to convey the excitement. 'So once we decided to do it, we said we'd do it right. Everything was timed down to the last second. We put an awful lot of work into it, and it was very nerve-wracking, but it was well worth it.'

Her humility and lack of pretence is very disarming. It's remarkable how indifferent she is to her success. There's nothing forced about it or her personality. It seems as if the success has happened as a by-product of a simple immersion in the music. As she remarked once after a session, 'You just play till the tunes stop chasing you.' She keeps churning them out, often oblivious to where they travel, as was the case with two instrumental tracks that she lent to the 'diddle-eye girl-power' movement. 'I don't really take much notice about what's going on with the business,' she says. 'I just let John look after everything because I totally trust him and he's such a good friend. I was down in Dingle one day, and I heard that track, "Only a Woman's Heart". The woman in the pub had it on a CD. [I said] "That's lovely. I never heard that before."

'She said, "That's an album called *A Woman's Heart*, and you're on it!"'

ANTHONY DALY

On a balmy June bank holiday weekend in 2001, Clare played Tipperary in Cork's Páirc Uí Chaoimh. It was Cyril Lyons' first championship game in charge of the Clare team. Before the players went out onto the pitch, he asked Anthony Daly – who was a sub in his final season as an inter-county player – to say a few words. No better man. Daly set the dressing-room on fire. 'I just remember I was ballin' my eyes out, running out,' says Seán McMahon, laughing now at the memory of it. 'It literally didn't matter where the door was – you'd have gone straight out through the wall.'

Four years previously, when Tipperary was also the opposition – again in Cork – Daly used a different tack. Before the two counties clashed in the Munster final, a team meeting was held. The mood in the room was grim, given their recent history, including Nicky English's unfortunate grin in 1993 and a filthy league game earlier that season in 1997 – the 'toughest match', former manager, Ger Loughnane ever saw, according to his book, *Raising the Banner*.

'It was: "Jaysus, we'll go and get these and do this and that,"' explains Ollie Baker, 'and Daly was there – "No, we're Clare. We'll play to our own strengths. Don't personalise this. We want to beat them not because they're Tipp but because we're Clare."'

His appeal to self-belief worked – Clare won in a stylistic encounter that afforded him his chance to air the famous 'We're no longer the whipping boys of Munster' speech, the one that unsettled Tipp PRO, Liz Howard. Did he overstep the mark? 'I don't think he did,' states RTÉ radio commentator, Micheál Ó Muircheartaigh, 'because he was only stating a fact.'

Daly was the consummate captain – a position he inherited in May 1992 at the tender age of twenty-two – and he went on to captain two All-Ireland-winning teams. Beyond the Churchillian flourishes, he was an exceptional hurler in his own right, having garnered three All-Stars during his career. 'He was a great reader of the game,' says former Kilkenny star, D. J. Carey. 'One of the best parts of his game was coming in around the back of Seánie McMahon and sweeping up. He was a great player at sweeping.'

'The funny thing about Daly was that he was unhookable,' adds one of his former Clare teammates. 'Whatever way he swung the hurley, and it actually used to look big and slow and awkward, but I can't ever remember him being hooked even though he wasn't fast, but he'd be clever enough to shorten the grip or whatever. Fellas would often be talking about it in training.'

To meet and chat with Daly is to be whipped up in a whirlwind of stories, the eyes straining out of their sockets, as he hops from side to side in his chair like a boxer jabbing away, story connecting after story, peppered with a wicked turn of phrase and a facility for mimicry. 'When he's out, people want to be over listening to his stories,' says Baker.

During days under Loughnane in the 1990s, recounts physio Colum Flynn, the management would often be huddled together in a hotel or hostelry, and if a burst of laughter broke out amongst an adjoining group of players, Loughnane would go, 'I bet Daly is in the middle of them.'

Both friend and foe seem to regard him highly. 'I'd be happy to share Anthony Daly's company any place, any time. He's a man of his word,' enthuses former Tipperary manager, Babs Keating.

His ability to appeal to a broad spectrum made him the ideal leader. 'It didn't matter whether you were a nuclear physicist or a block layer,' remarked James O'Connor in Denis Walsh's book, *Hurling: The Revolution Years*. 'Daly had the ability to relate to you on your level … When things got tough in Crusheen, or on the hill in Shannon, he could say something that would make people laugh. He could always say the right thing at the right time, and he said what he thought. You know, he's a confident guy. He's not afraid to stick out his chest.'

Or to confront an issue head-on. In 1999, for example, Clare played Tipp in the semi-final of the Munster hurling championship in Cork. The game was a draw, and re-scheduled for six days later. Five or six of the players, including Daly and Baker, were staying in Jury's Hotel with their partners, and met up after the game for drinks and a debrief, and then toddled off to bed around 11.30 p.m. The following evening, they gathered for training. 'I was met at the door by the management,' says Baker, 'and was asked, "Were you out drinking last night?" I said I was. I told them exactly what happened, and they asked me did I think that [Tipp player] Tommy Dunne was out last night? And I said, "I don't know what Tommy Dunne was at. I can only take care of myself."

'And I went away into training and I met Dalo inside, and I said, "Have the boys a problem with us staying down in Cork last night?"

'He said, "No, no. No one came to me at all."

'I said, "Jaysus, I'm after bein' stopped outside at the gate … that I was drinking last night."

'He goes, "They never said anything to us, and we were all together."

'So up on his heels anyway, and he went in to meet the management and he said, "Have ye a problem with what happened last night?"

'And the boys said, "Well, actually we do" – and I had come into the room at this stage. "That man there was out drinking last night after drawing a match, and he only after coming on and he out injured. Do you think this is the best way to act – getting drunk and falling around the place in Cork?"

'Daly cut in, "Hold on a second," and recounted what had transpired … "and I know that's what happened," he said, "because I was there and I had five pints" – and he named all the people that were there – "and we all drank, and if you've a problem with him, you've a problem with all of us. This isn't a problem: that's what we've always done and what we'll always do."

'Then it was thrown back: "Do you think the Tipperary team were doing that?"

'To which he goes: "I don't know what the Tipperary team were doing and I don't care what the Tipperary team were doing. I know what we were doing and I know what I'm going to do next Saturday."

'It was a real power-play moment, and I was just in the background with my eyes opened, jaw dropping. It was him against them, and he argued his case and they backed down. He stood up for me, stood up for the other guys that were there, and then at the end of it: "By the way it won't be affecting our performance next Saturday." Game over after that. And next Saturday we all lined out.

'Daly just saw trouble coming down the line and cut it off. In a way, he was after dragging both of us – the management and the players – behind him.' It was a master class in conflict resolution.

Daly grew up in Clarecastle, 'sleeping with a hurley in his hand'. He was one of four boys and four girls. His father, Pat Joe – who had represented the Clare hurlers in the late 1940s and early 1950s – passed away when he was only eight years of age.

'He was very thin, stringy. He wasn't very strong,' says Bishop Willie Walsh, who trained young Anthony on the 1987 Dr Harty Cup-winning team, arguably St Flannan's finest-ever hurling team. Daly was corner-back on that team. 'I was always a corner-back in my own head,' he says, even though Loughnane later had the foresight to convert him to wing-back.

Having repeated the Leaving Certificate, and disillusioned with a course in what is now Limerick Institute of Technology, he landed back in St Flannan's after Christmas for a third crack. 'Jeez, you must be fair thick?' one of his classmates goaded, as he took up a seat at the back of a history class.

'It was the hardest thing, I ever did,' admits Daly, with an inhalation of breath. The ordeal only lasted about four days, though, as he nabbed a job in Ennis with the Trustee Savings Bank, which he subsequently gave up, when fame came knocking, to open a sports shop. He still runs it, along with a pub that he took over in 1999: Murty Browne's, located halfway between Ennis and Kilrush.

He was appointed to the Clare senior hurling panel in 1989, making his championship debut the following year. Of course, they were dark days. The arrival of Len Gaynor as coach in 1990 marked a pivotal moment in Daly's career. Gaynor had been a wing-back on the all-conquering Tipp team of the mid 1960s. While a Clare selector in 1989 daring to dream about getting out of Division 2, Gaynor, as the new manager, spoke about winning Munster titles. But more than just his ambition for Clare, something in Gaynor's personal story and earthy philosophy resonated with Daly. 'He told us about himself. He was sent off to Flannan's as a boarder. The only way he could prove himself as a man was on the hurling field. He talked that sort of stuff – go out and live it. A great one was, "Do your livin' best." That's something that I took with me through life.

'When I'd go off the rails as a young fella – "Are ya doin' your livin' best?" I'd ask myself. "You're doin' your best to kill yourself, you eejit," and I'd say, "Get back on track!", and I'd get back on track. He was a huge influence.

'He changed training as well. Back to basics – hardy, hip-to-hip stuff. The one [ex-Clare teammate, Fergie] Tuohy always remembers – "splinters of ash flyin' up into the stand, lads". That's the way he wanted it, you know.

'Poor old Tony Kelly was the manager the previous year – I've great time for T. K., you know,' he says, breaking into the precise, afternoon-tea-and-cucumber-sandwiches diction of the schoolmaster:

'"The highest hurley wins possession." Gaynor was on about: "Break his hand if he puts it up. He's sacrificed …" you know what I mean?'

Daly played in some ferocious encounters through the 1990s – none more so than ties with Limerick at a period when the two counties shared five Munster titles in a row, and winter league clashes has people talking around the fireplace. In the autumn of 1994 a twenty-man barney broke out between both sides; the titanic drawn game in March 1997 drew a staggering 20,000 people, there on the promise of some 'schelping'.

'I remember that one. I remember distinctly [Mike] Houlihan like a lunatic 'cause [Liam] Doyle hit him with his open palm, and the ref couldn't really put off Doyle for slapin' him,' he laughs. 'It was the ultimate insult to Houlihan – that Doyle had hit him like you'd hit a girl. Slapped him rather than hit him. That's a low blow. If Doyle hit him a belt of a fist and knocked him out, Houlihan would have had no problem with him. Ah, they were great matches and there was plenty of jawin'.'

Nobody liked to banter on a pitch as much as Daly. Some of the exchanges he had are part of the game's lore. The verbal exchanges with Tipp's John Leahy, in particular, are the stuff of high farce, though not to all hurling supporters' taste, it seems. 'I have good time for Anthony Daly, yet at the same time he's an unusual character,' maintains one former All-Ireland-winning hurling manager. 'The word on the ground was that he was a dreadful slagger, and I hate that. I don't agree with that. I don't like it. I think it diminishes the man, and I think there's no sweeter thing in victory than having done it fairly, in a fair fight.'

'I was as good as any of them,' admits Daly, but adds in defence: 'I always say, "I never started it." On my father's grave, I never started it. Tommy Dunne and myself never had a word – ever – in our lives, and we marked each other ten times in club and inter-county. We'd leather each other. Myself and Johnny Dooley never had a word either, I'd say.

'[Cork's Seánie] McGrath obviously I had a bit of a go at [in a 1998 Munster championship match] in a nice way. "Right, we'll do a wager, Seánie." I says, "You don't get more than two points, you're buying the pints."

"'That'll do," he says. I thought maybe it was taking him off his game.

'There wasn't a word between [Waterford's Dan] Shanahan and myself [until] Shanahan scored a third point off me in the drawn [Munster final] game in 1998. I was playing off this big young fella that had never been heard of. "You're not marking Seánie McGrath today, boy," says Daly, mimicking him like a bloke with a mouthful of gobstoppers.

'I says, "You're definitely bigger anyway. Hang on till I have a look at ya, and a good bit uglier." He laughed at that. After the game, there was no bother. Shanahan and myself are good buddies; he's a nice fella.'

One Waterford player did, however, overstep the mark that day by calling Daly a 'wife-beater'. Moving from the realm of harmless schoolyard braggadocio to downright character defamation, this incident most certainly 'diminished the man'. The slur was the high-water mark, in public circles at least, of an ugly swirl of rumours that circulated around Daly, the victim of a very Irish trait of feasting on its own. Envy and jealousy may be universal emotions, noted historian Joe Lee, but it is only the Irish that have managed to coin a term for the resultant personality type: the 'begrudger'.

'It just got out of hand for a small while,' says Daly. 'Ah, sure, we booked the wedding for the weekend after the [1997] All-Ireland because we'd notions of winning the All-Ireland, you know? Some people saw that – within the county – as cockiness, the cosy yoke booking his wedding for the following Saturday. Maybe now, but I wouldn't see it that way. I don't know where it came from. Obviously, some malicious fella said that I was beating her up. It just went like wildfire.'

There were several incidents in which family members overheard the rumours in public, at hairdressers, in the workplace, for example, and after a few tears and a correction, the encounters would be relayed back to Daly. 'The only worst thing you could be called is a child molester,' says Daly. 'I mean, all over the country as well. But you know what? All you can do is ride it out, stay married, have a few children, be seen going to funerals and weddings together,' he adds philosophically.

Even today, 'the daily spite of this unmannerly town', as W. B. Yeats put it, occasionally surfaces, but not in such a targeted, malicious fashion; now, it's just the baleful odour of age-old, small-town bitterness at the success of a neighbour, all the more unfortunate given he's a soulful, humble bloke with simple tastes. 'You know, I often heard, "Who does he think he is opening up a sports shop?" You know? That kind of thing goes around. "Who the hell's he on television [as an analyst on *The Sunday Game*]? He came out of Madden's Terrace. They survived on a widow's pension."

'But when you reach thirty-eight, you start saying, "Who gives a damn about them?" [Former Clare selector, Tony] Considine used always have a great saying: "Feck the begrudgers. Dazzle them with success." He was right. I'd dazzle no one with my old country pub and small sports shop, but money isn't a motivator for me, either. If I've the price of an old Yankee on a Saturday, the price of a few pints, and be able to drive around in something that's reasonably comfortable, and the kids don't want for anything ... what more do you want?'

Another hurling All-Ireland title would do nicely. Daly couldn't resist the call once they came looking for him to manage the team after Clare had suffered a tame exit from the championship in 2003. Even though he had only finished training with the panel as a player eighteen months beforehand, he was the players' irresistible choice. Three senior players made a petition. He hunted them, but once the County Board came back with an official offer, his interest was piqued. 'The first man I rang was him [Loughnane],' says Daly in conspiratorial tones, bent over in his seat. 'I said, "The boys were on to me."

'He said, "All right, that's one thing." (Never one to be swayed by sentiment, Mr Loughnane.) "Look, Dalo, there's feck all left in them fellas. But there might be one last kick. You might be the man to get it out of them. Go for it. But only take it for one year. Get in and get out."'

Daly took the job. Initially, the buzz was good in the camp. Training put a premium on freshness. Clare's late surge in form in the league was noted. Galway rolled over Waterford in the National League final a week before Waterford's first-round Munster championship encounter with Clare. And besides, the Déise in the championship had never been a problem for Clare lately. It argued well, as Larry Tompkins would say.

Not so. In poker, they call it a bad beat. Clare were soundly beaten like old times. A nineteen-point defeat. It was a thrashing that ranked down there with any of the historic leatherings: Cork in 1972; Tipp in 1987 and 1993. But thank God for the qualifiers, and the season closed out with a thundering display against Kilkenny in the quarter-final, when Clare were unfortunate not to catch the Cats napping.

Still, there was a lot of criticism, not least from Loughnane, whose lacerations came booming from the balcony like Statler and Waldorf. In each of Daly's three seasons in charge, Clare were dumped out of the Munster championship in the first round. Perhaps he was too close to his old comrades, it was suggested. The decision to start Brian Lohan in the replay against Kilkenny in 2004, when he wasn't fit, was a case in point. 'I mean, to be fair, he took us all off,' argues Seán McMahon. 'He took Ollie [Baker] off [Waterford, 2004], me off [Wexford, 2006], Brian Lohan off [Kilkenny, 2004]. People label that at him. But I think he did whatever had to be done [though] it would have been difficult for him. Brian Quinn was another one who didn't play in his last year, and he left him as a sub. He didn't start Jamesie too much, either. He did make the calls, but I'd say none of the players fell out with him on it because of the respect that was there for him. We knew at the end of the day that his interest was Clare.'

116

For this interest, he left bits of himself behind on the sideline during games. 'Whenever we were on the line, there was a vast difference between his style of management and my dynamic on the line,' notes former Cork manager John Allen. 'Jeez, should I be saying more because this man is shouting and roaring and driving on fellas, and I'm saying nothing?' he wondered. 'But then we were winning the games, I suppose,' he quickly qualifies.

Daly met a more overtly feisty counterpart when Clare clashed – literally – with Waterford in the league in April 2005, eleven long months after the championship annihilation. When, at one stage during the match, Waterford manager Justin McCarthy went to remonstrate with the linesman, Dickie Murphy, Daly blocked his way, and the pair collided like two wild stags. 'There was a bit of a remark or something, and a bit of pushing and shoving,' explains McCarthy. 'You know the way on the sideline – everyone gets a bit excited. It was one of these things. Fellas would be trying to size you up a bit, too … and psyche you out of it, but I've been on the line a long time. It wouldn't worry me one bit. You know, I'm still there and I was there before him, and I'll be there after him,' he says, chuckling, ironically a couple of months before he was ousted as manager by a players' revolt.

Daly makes no bones about his desire to manage the Clare senior hurling team again; once some of his peers from the 1990s have had their chance. After his reign, he left Clare 'an established Top 4 team' in the words of *Irish Times* hurling critic, Seán Moran.

It had been a worthy effort, given the curate's egg he had to make his omelettes with. Each year, he had to draw from an ageing pool of talent. Notably, the Clare team that played Kilkenny in his last championship match – the 2006 All-Ireland semi-final – included six players who had started in the same tie nine years beforehand; no one on the Kilkenny side re-featured.

Shorn of the luck that swept his greyhound, Murty's Gang, to an Irish Derby title in 2002, Daly had brought to management the same qualities he paraded as captain a decade beforehand: forthrightness, pride, infectious enthusiasm, and his defining trait: what Loughnane described in *Raising the Banner* as his 'unbelievable, unwavering self-confidence'.

'I remember after we had played Galway in 1999 – the drawn game,' says a former Clare player. 'Loughnane was telling Brian Lohan and David Forde to throw off the shackles. The boys weren't playing well. They were going around as if the weight of the world was on their shoulders and he was there: "Up the pressure. Throw off the shackles. Look at Daly. He miss-hits a clearance, gifts Joe Rabbite a point. What does Daly do? He won the next three balls. He didn't give a rat's ass." That's the type of guy Daly was. I don't know did the guy ever get nervous.'

'I was always nervous until I'd meet the boys,' says Daly. 'The bus would collect us in Clarecastle – whether we were going to Dublin or we were going to Thurles. The strength of the wolf is in the pack, ya know? I'd look at Lohan's puss and Baker's puss. What'll stop us?' he says, snarling. 'We'd often run with our arms around us, doing the warm-up. Finishing off, I'd say, "Come on, we'll burst into a sprint." I always remember going up into the top corner of Cashel before we'd go into Thurles, and I'd say, "Feel the power, lads, Feel the power. What is going to stop this machine? We don't give a damn if we're ten down, we will grind them down,"' he says, the blood boiling at the recollection.

'The Munster Final in 1995 was the defining moment. That was the monkey. I hadn't a nerve that was ever known in the All-Ireland final in 1995,' he adds, with an are-you-mad? expression. 'I hadn't a nerve. I took in the whole week. I did the Captains' Table the previous week with [Offaly captain, Johnny] Pilkington. "Will you drink a glass of wine, Ant-knee?" This is maybe eight days before the final.

'"By Jaysus, I will, Johnny. Not a problem."

'"Here [*Sunday Tribune* journalist, Enda] McEvoy, get us a bottle of red wine, there. Myself and Ant-knee, we'll have a bottle," says Daly in a thick Midlands accent.

'That'd be Pilkington anyway. A beagle. He thought he probably had me – "This eejit from Clare". Because Pilkington would be laid back, he probably thought, "Your man is only bluffin'." It was like poker. I drank about three glasses. He got about a glass and a half, and McEvoy maybe two.

"Jeez, that's lovely stuff. Will we get another bottle, Johnny?"

"We better not," he says.'

TONY GRIFFIN

All-Star hurler Tony Griffin's road to Calvary began on 2 May 2007. For seven bloody weeks, through swirling winds and belting showers of rain, he pedalled across the second biggest country in the world.

He's not the first person to have cycled across Canada. Hundreds of people do it every year. But Griffin's journey was different. It was no saunter. Propelled by the memory of his father's death from lung cancer in December 2005, Griffin, aged twenty-six, was cycling to raise a million dollars for cancer research. And he was doing it against the clock. He had targets to meet, as his route was dotted every five days with fund-raisers, culminating with a transatlantic flight to Ireland for the last leg of his campaign from Dublin to Ennis, arriving in his home townland on 1 July.

The distance he was travelling across Canada – from the Pacific Ocean in Vancouver to Halifax, Nova Scotia on the eastern seaboard – was 6,650 kilometres. According to his itinerary, it would take him fifty-one days. The most gruelling sporting event on the planet, the Tour de France, covers just over half that distance, approximately 3,600 kilometres, in twenty-three days. A fair enough trade, you would hazard. Not quite.

First, Griffin was a novice cyclist. Beyond mucking about on a bike as a kid, he'd never cycled properly before. Sure, during an intensive four-month training regime, he re-sculptured his body, shifting to his legs the muscle repository he'd built up in his upper body from years of weights work in the gym. 'How much have they grown this week?' his college roommates would kid. But no one can acquire the technique of a professional cyclist in a few months.

In his prime, seven-time Tour de France winner Lance Armstrong used to spin his pedals a hundred times a minute while ascending a slope – faster than any other competitor. It gave him a keen edge, but to perfect these cadences took years of application, in consultation with his coach, Chris Carmichael, and Johan Bruyneel, the director of the United States Postal Service Pro Cycling Team. It's frightening to imagine the energy Griffin must have needlessly wasted through his uncultured cycling style, horsing through the countryside, his body flailing from side to side unwittingly.

Second, and more crucially, Griffin was cycling alone. Although accompanied by a three-man support crew of mates in an RV – who cycled patches of it alongside him, socially – he didn't have the luxury of a *peloton*, the 'platoon' that makes up the pack of riders on the Tour de France. Each morning, Griffin's road crew belted fifty kilometres up the road, attending to media and food provisions while leaving him to cycle on his own. This meant he was at the mercy of the blasted winds he encountered. A change of wind, Griffin gauged, would alter his speed from an average of thirty kilometres an hour, reaching forty kilometres an hour one minute, down to eleven an hour the next.

There are studies that put this plight into perspective. Several years ago, a professor of exercise metabolism at the University of Birmingham, Asker Jeukendrup, attached power meters to cyclists in the Tour de France that measured the watts they generated with every turn of their wheels. His calculations told him that cyclists riding for six hours at forty kilometres an hour in the middle of the *peloton* – shielded from the wind – save as much as forty per cent of their energy compared to what a cyclist like Griffin would expend over that distance riding on his own.

Physical pain was his only constant companion. Every day was about 'eating bitter', as the Shaolin monks would say. 'Just getting used to going to bed sore, waking up sore, thighs sore, wanting to sleep a lot,' he concedes. 'Also, you've no teammates – if the ball's down at the other side of the field, you might get a chance to take your breath. If you do that on a bike, you stop moving.'

His IT bands – the strips of tissue that run from the hip to the knee – were so tight on the first couple of days that he thought he'd have to pull out. 'They were excruciatingly tight,' he says. 'I thought to myself, "I must be corroding some part of my knee here." Okay, if I am, I was thinking, "Who do I know?" If I can get to the end of this, I was thinking of Bill Standish, a knee surgeon – surely he could give me [an operation]. That's the way I was thinking. That was what I needed to do to get there. If my knees needed to be replaced, we'd replace them. Then Rob's [Rob Book, friend and member of his road crew] girlfriend – a masseuse – stripped the daylights out of them, just worked through them. It loosened up and disappeared. That was a big mountain to climb: "Okay, we're getting stronger here."'

It was a constant battle with his wits. Often, his mind would play tricks – thinking he'd done fifteen kilometres, he'd look down at his speedometer to discover he'd only done three. The monotony was crushing; the grinding out of revolution after revolution, click after click, a kind of Chinese water torture, and it nearly drove him mad. He was 'a prisoner of the road', as cyclists put it. 'There were times,' he confides, 'when I thought to myself, "I'm going to go crazy out here. I am actually going to break here and I'm going to be insane." In some small ways, I think I might have, both for good and otherwise. I broke down in tears so many times [when] maybe miserable or wet or I'd biked maybe seven hours and I realised that I had another two or, in some cases, three to do.'

Left to his own devices, he'd replay old matches in his head; he'd talk to himself, he'd shout at bison in the fields or ducks in lakes he would pass, and he thought about his dad, all he did for him, and the values he imparted. 'I was fourteen years of age, broke and bored during the summer,' he wrote in his cycle diaries. 'I advertised in Quinnsworth with a sign that said I would do any job that was offered. The one I received entailed barrowing three loads of topsoil from the front to the back of a house. In my naivety, I told the house owner it would take me two days. We agreed on £30 regardless of the time it took to finish the task.

'Three days later, I was regretting the agreement. The end of the fourth day came and there was no light at the end of the tunnel. My father came on his way home from work to check progress. Progress was slow. He grabbed a barrow and more than doubled my efforts for four hours and we finished it together. That was my father.'

Whipped by ferocious winds and rain that made it difficult to see beyond his handlebars, he hovered over Ground Zero one day in the Prairies, the terrain in which they say – as he remarks in his diary – 'you can watch your dog run away for days'. Several people stopped and offered him lifts. One lady asked where he was going, and he just grunted, 'Ennis'.

She said, 'I think you're lost.'

He said, 'You could be very right,' and trundled on.

The other extreme saw him hit speeds of ninety kilometres an hour on descents, resting precariously on a Trek Madone bike that would have weighed about fifteen pounds. Disaster arrived on day fourteen when he met gravel for the second time on his journey, this spill causing a dislocation of his collarbone. The pain was blinding, but he saw the injury as 'a challenge' – as you do if you've got his talent for pain and endurance – and ploughed on.

There were also moments of unadulterated bliss triggered by daily endorphin releases from the exercise: winding past an avalanche on the road; exchanges from a close distance with wild animals such as moose and prancing deer; and, of course, the jaw-dropping scenery in the Rockies and Canadian Shield – in his words, 'the rawest natural beauty imaginable'.

His route was peppered with well-wishers and cancer sufferers and survivors. A Mayo man decked out in a Clare jersey, whose daughter had died from suicide three months earlier, met him on his bike forty kilometres outside Saskatoon. Hearing their stories, being touched by so many 'angelic strangers', drawing from their goodwill, has been a life-affirming experience.

'I definitely developed an awful affinity for people during it. I met so many good people. Matt [Bethune, his college roommate] said to me one day on the road – it was so true – "Do you know, Griff, the biggest challenge from this will be going back to normal life and keeping what we've learnt." Which was pulling in to a gas station and someone fills up our tank for us, buys all our food and won't accept payment, or getting complete strangers taking us into their house. To try to hold on to that sense that it's not about me, it's about what you give out to the world.'

Griffin's mission began in November 2006. While in his apartment in Halifax, he received an email from his roommate Bethune that showed footage of Dick Hoyt, the American dad who has completed over sixty marathons and six 'Ironman' triathlons with his son Rick, who is paralysed from the neck down. Griffin was stung. It was almost a year since his father Jerome had passed away, and a gnawing sense – 'a rumbling feeling' – that there was something he needed to do, got him thinking. The idea for a short charity cycle snowballed. Within six months, Griffin had marshalled a sixty-strong team of volunteers, and was ready to hit the road. He'd also enlisted the services of Armstrong, one of the world's most famous cancer survivors. On a visit to his home in Texas, Griffin presented him with a bespoke hurley from Dowlings in Kilkenny, and enjoyed a private tour of the room in which Armstrong's framed yellow jerseys from the Tour de France hang.

Griffin found Armstrong to be cagey when they met, but he used Irish sports journalist David Walsh to disarm him. (Walsh has plagued

Armstrong with a book, *Lance to Landis*, examining allegations that Armstrong was a dope fiend during his cycling career.) 'He's not warm,' says Griffin. 'He sizes you up. I think he was a small bit taken aback because I tried to be as relaxed as I could with him. I was saying, "You're going to have to come to Dublin."

'And he said, "Ahhh, maybe."

'I said, "Sure, look, we can put David Walsh down on the road and you can cycle over him." He just turned around and looked at me, and started laughing.'

Griffin had made his impression. Later, Armstrong felt comfortable enough to try and mimic Seán Kelly's famous mumble, referring to his friend as King Kelly. The pair cycled out together, and Armstrong helped with promotional and fund-raising work. He signed the bike that Griffin used to complete the cycle which was sold for €15,500. In fact, the Lance Armstrong Foundation is one of three charities into which Griffin has been funnelling his funds. The other two are the Irish Cancer Society and Ovarian Cancer Canada.

Griffin, as you can imagine, is an irrepressibly optimistic person, and quotes happily from the likes of Gandhi and Sun Tzu's *The Art of War*. He's never lacked for enthusiasm. When he first made the Clare hurling panel, as a gangly nineteen-year-old in Ger Loughnane's last season in charge, panel members would look askew at him as he wrestled with weights that 'the Incredible Hulk wouldn't manage'.

His no-is-yes, have-a-great-day attitude is refreshing, but in a land that likes its heroes to be brooding like Roy Keane, or rogues like Richard Harris, his personality type is closer to the kind revered in Boston, Massachusetts than in the parish of Boston near Corofin, County Clare. *Sunday Tribune* GAA correspondent, Kieran Shannon – a friend of Griffin's – has written incisively on what he describes as the 'Oprahisation of a country lad from Ballyea'. He uses the parable of the rich, successful neighbour to illustrate the problems that Griffin has faced. 'It's like the one Bono tells,' says Shannon. 'In the States, a guy goes, "See that bastard up on the hill? One day, I'm gonna be like him." Whereas the Irish guy goes, "See that bastard up on the hill? One day, I'm gonna get him.'"

Admirably, the whispered cynicism doesn't faze Griffin. He sees the bigger picture. 'There were times when I was saying to myself, "What do people think that I know when I say: Tony Griffin Foundation?" Who is this guy? Then I thought, "Best of luck to anyone who says or thinks that." My thought pattern was if we raise one dollar that makes a difference to someone, that's our job done.'

Griffin is a sharp guy. He's got enough of the joker in him to lend him street cred with his peers in the bear pit of a hurling dressing-room. 'Griffin is a great fella to have around,' says Seán McMahon, who played with him on the Clare hurling panel for seven seasons. 'He'd always talk positively … "We can do it", you know, but an intelligent fella, and a fella then that would have the *craic* with anyone as well. Fellas would listen to him and wouldn't just say, "Who's your man, Mr Positive, over there?"'

Also, although full of an easy, old-world politeness in company, he's no Mother Theresa. He's got the hard streak running through him that all top athletes in contact sport need. 'He's a dirty bastard,' laughs McMahon, who marked him a lot in training. 'He'd be hard, like. He'd pull a stroke as quick as anything. I used to hate marking him. He pulled some dirty strokes on me. He'd maintain that I was giving it to him, but I reckon I wasn't. He's very competitive, like. He'd be temperamental; I wouldn't say he'd lose his head, but he could be fiery. If he thought he could take the law into his own hands, he would, but you need a bit of that.'

He's certainly fond of being in control, and has always had an ascetic, focused streak that makes him the perfect vessel for life as an elite sportsman. Distractions off the pitch have never, it seems, been a problem. Nor has the sacrifice required to be a top-class athlete. 'I never saw it as a sacrifice,' he says decisively. 'I never saw … maybe when I was a teenager – fifteen, sixteen – my friends were starting to go out a bit more, but I always just saw that I was going to play for Clare and that was my vision.'

Comfort zones are briefly visited regions for him. A couple of years out of college, following an economics degree in UCG, he was established on the Clare hurling team and working as a sales rep for a medical company, when he moved to take up a position at the renowned sports academy, Dalhousie University, in Nova Scotia, to study for a degree in human kinetics. He became known as the 'guy with the big stick' on campus. 'Hey dude, what are you doing with that stick?' he'd be asked as he set off on his solo training sessions, hiking up Citadel Hill for stamina work, knee-deep in snow during winter, his gums aching from pain in temperatures that could drop to as low as -40°C.

In such an ecumenical environment, he worshipped lavishly at the different altars available to him: doing a bit of sparring in the boxing ring, and track and field to hone his speed off the mark; while he repaid the favours elsewhere, helping out as a consultant sports psychologist for the basketball team, proselytising to homeboys from Toronto 'covered in tattoos' about the wonders of hurling.

In his first academic year, he commuted back to Ireland – a twenty-hour door-to-door journey – nine times to turn out for the Clare hurlers. One time, due to snow, he was in danger of missing his flight, so he blagged his way onto the plane by saying he had to get back to Ireland to propose to his girlfriend, producing an engagement ring he was actually bringing back to Ireland for Ennis-based chiropractor Travis McDonagh, his great friend and mentor.

In the post-Loughnane era, when most of his teammates' form ebbed and flowed, Griffin ended each season in credit with a steady graph of progression. He burst onto the Munster-championship scene with six points from seven shots against Tipperary in 2002, arriving at the All-Ireland final that September having scored seventeen points from play. Though dogged by a pursuit of excellence, his memory of the final is tinged with a sense that at the time he was still an unfinished article. 'The first half, there was a really strong wind, and I remember Colin Lynch shouting at me, "Come on! Come on!" I think we were about four or five points down at the time, and for the first time all year I remember thinking, "I'm not at this level. I'm not at the level I need to be at." I remember just thinking, "You've got work to do." I didn't have experience yet. Experience like everything else is earned,' he says in typically analytical fashion.

In 2003 he dragged his club, Ballyea – a minnow – to its first and only county final, scoring 1–7 – his side's entire score – in the semi-final win over neighbouring club, Éire Óg. In 2004 and 2005 he was in the top-five scorers from play in the All-Ireland championship, and in 2006 he bagged an All-Star award. A year later, when Anthony Daly was asked for his highlight on the TV *Sporting Review of the Year*, he said it was Tony Griffin's Ride for the Cure across Canada. It was a common sentiment for many, although there is a lingering impression – heightened by some patchy performances in 2008 – that Griffin has underachieved on the hurling pitch. 'He's never consistently done it, but he's a very complex personality,' argues hurling analyst Liam Griffin. 'He's a busy mind, so his focus and attention is not just hurling. That's not a criticism. It's a fact. He's riding across Canada; he's doing his studies and his various qualifications, so he's never applied himself in the same way as Lohan or Seánie Mac or Anthony Daly. He pursues different things.

'I believe he's never fully realised his full potential. He's certainly shown glimpses of it over time. He's never stayed consistently at the game with the same element of focus that others would. He's not as driven on the hurling field as the others are, so I think potentially we never saw the best of Tony Griffin. Well, we haven't seen it so far. We only saw glimpses of the greatness of Tony Griffin.'

It may be true. We've probably only seen glimpses of his greatness as a hurler – he might not yet have scaled the heights of peers like John Gardiner and Tipp's Eoin Kelly – but one gets the sense that, in life, there's a lot more to come from this inspiring young man.

Who dares speak of '98? Clare manager Ger Loughnane leaves the Limerick Inn following a showdown with the Munster Council. Minutes earlier, it had handed out a three-month suspension – which three priests and Loughnane had prophesied – to Clare hurler, Colin Lynch. (Pic: Séamus O'Reilly, *Clare County Express*)

Former President of Ireland, Mary Robinson with Fr Bernard Lynch at Áras an Uachtaráin 28 November 1995. (Pic: Fr Bernard Lynch)

Six-time British Champion Jockey Kieren Fallon in his natural habitat, 14 February 2004. (Pic: John Kelly/*Clare Champion*)

Michael D. Higgins (right) accepts the nomination from Labour Party Leader, Frank Cluskey to run in the Connaught/Ulster constituency for the European Parliament elections in 1979.

Keith Wood, right, in action against England, with team-mates Peter Clohessy, centre, and Neil Francis, left, January 1995. (Pic: Brendan Moran/Sportsfile)

'Hold him thus.' Anthony Daly with his manager's hat on while Clare play Kilkenny at Croke Park in the 2004 All-Ireland hurling quarter-final. (Pic: John Kelly/*Clare Champion*)

Sharon Shannon with her beloved Castignari button accordion. (Pic: Peter Shaughnessy)

Come Fly with Me. Tony Griffin contests a *sliotar* with Kilkenny's Peter Barry in the All-Ireland hurling final in 2002.   (Pic: John Kelly/*Clare Champion*)

YMCA (left to right): Ger Loughnane, Fr Harry Bohan (Manager), Jackie O'Gorman, Colm Honan and Gus Lohan (father of Clare hurlers, Brian and Frank) parade the National League hurling title in 1977. (Pic: Philip Brennan)

'Are you for real?' Anthony Foley, who has captained Ireland, fields an inane question at an Irish rugby team conference. (Pic: *Clare People*)

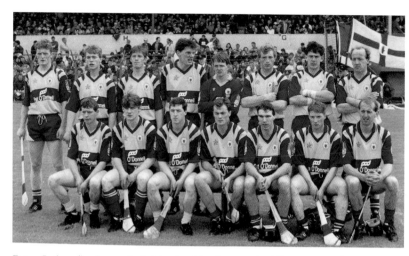

Brian Lohan (back row, far left) takes his place on the Clare team to face Limerick at Cusack Park in 1993. It was his first Munster senior championship hurling game. The team was captained by Anthony Daly (front row, fourth from right) and also included James O'Connor (front row, second from right), another player making his championship debut that day. (Pic: Séamus O'Reilly/*Clare County Express*)

'The owner told me this had been schooled.' Martin Brassil rides Jane Nightingale's *Shear Success* in the Nenagh Point-to-Point in 1987. (Pic: Brendan Conerney)

The East Clare Brigade (left to right): Keith Wood with his Munster rugby teammates, Marcus Horan and Anthony Foley in 1999. All three grew up within a few miles of each other.   (Pic: Séamus O'Reilly/*Clare County Express*)

Marcus Horan (left) in his Ireland Schools rugby gear in 1995.
           (Pic: Paul Horan)

'I feel very comfortable on the stage. I always tell my son Jesse, "I sing for free, I travel for money." I love it, and I just can't help it. I'm a hound. I'm a big, old folk diva so I am.'

(Pic: Sherry Rayn Barnett Photography)

Des Lynam, cool as a cat.   (Pic: Jane Morgan Management)

CLARE INTER-COUNTY FOOTBALL TEAM.

Top Row—MICHAEL SMYTH, (Ennis); P. O'BRIEN, (Castlefare); P. MALONE, (Ennis); JOHN CLANCY (Miltown); JIM CLOHESSY, (Ennis); FRED McMAHON, (Ennis)
Middle Row—DAN CLANCY (Miltown); PADDY HENNESSY (Miltown); TOM CLOHESSY (Ennis); CORNEY MacDONNELL (Kilrush); JACK KELLY (Ejo); ML. CARMODY (Ennis)
Lower Row—FRANK FOLEA (Kilrush); JOHN GRIFFY (Ennis); PAUL HAYES (Ennis); JACK TALTY (Kilrush); PADDY KENNY (Ennis), (Capt).

Des Lynam's grandfather, Packo Malone (back row, third from left) lines out amongst his teammates on the Clare football team which lost to Kerry in the 1912 Munster Gaelic football final by 0-3 to 0-1 at the Ennis Showgrounds. (Pic: *Clare People*)

Kevin Sheedy (right) relaxes with former Irish soccer international teammates, Kevin Moran (left) and Paul McGrath (centre). The three met up an Italia '90 reunion bash at the Guinness Storehouse building, St James Gate, Dublin, 23 July 2001.

(Pic: David Maher/Sportsfile)

Mick O'Dea painting in a studio in Paris in 2006.   (Pic: Amelia Stein)

Above: Three Kings (left to right). John Doyle, Christy Ring and Jimmy Smyth share a cup of tea beside Ruan National School, County Clare, at the re-opening of Ruan's hurling field, 6 June 1971. (Pic: *Clare Champion*)

Sharon Shannon squeezes in between Steve Earle (left) and Mundy (right) at the Cambridge Folk Festival in 2007, some months before their single *Galway Girl* became, as they say in the business, a smash hit. (Pic: Daisy Discs)

'Do you wanna dance?' James O'Connor makes a point to his Clare teammate, Brian Lohan during a county club hurling championship quarter-final match at Cusack Park in 2004. (Pic: John Kelly/*Clare Champion*)

James O'Connor in full flight against Tipperary in the 1997 Munster hurling championship final at Páirc Uí Chaoimh. (Pic: John D. Kelly/*Tipperary Nationalist*)

Tom Morrissey reaches highest in this aerial encounter during the Munster Gaelic football championship final between Clare and Kerry, 19 July 1992. (Pic: *Clare People*)

FR HARRY BOHAN

Fr Harry Bohan was born in Feakle in 1938. Feakle is a small village, like hundreds around the country, the little communities that give Ireland its heartbeat and its character. It has a post office, a church, a school and a sprinkling of pubs, one of them in which Fr Bohan grew up.

He remembers, one day, seeing a girl from his class standing at the bridge in the middle of the village with her suitcase. She was waiting for a bus. The bus would take her to Limerick, then to Cobh, where she would catch a boat to the United States.

He never saw that girl again. There were others who disappeared, too – lost to the scourge of emigration. In the 1950s Ireland was dying on its feet. Each year, more people emigrated than were born in the country.

But people didn't need to read the statistics. They could see with their own eyes. Of the fourteen kids in Harry Bohan's class, nine emigrated. Indeed, within a few years of leaving school, all his class had left the village; a whole generation gone, leaving a trail of heartbreak and dismembered families in its wake.

Harry Bohan made a promise to himself the day he last saw that forlorn girl. 'Even at that time,' he says, 'I pledged I would do whatever I could to help people stay where they wanted to be. Change enforced like that was savage, and this, more than anything else, inspired me to do something about it.'

By God, he was true to his word. Infused with a belief in the importance of the family and the community to our well-being, his life's work has been a struggle to preserve these two great civilising forces.

Having studied at St Flannan's College, he attended Maynooth College, where he was ordained in 1963 – the year, it is said, the 1960s really began. It was a decade in which the Western world experienced social change at a rate it had never encountered before.

In Ireland, the arrival of televisions into homes opened the imagination to glamorous new worlds. For the first time, the availability of free education gave the country's youth the confidence and awareness to dream of a better world. Economic changes ushered in by Seán Lemass and Ken Whitaker meant the industrial revolution was finally arriving in Ireland in earnest, perhaps a hundred years later than others, argues Fr Bohan, but he wasn't complaining.

As a young cleric, the Church's new social encyclicals, particularly Pope John XXIII's, were intoxicating for him. 'It was as if it was written for Ireland,' he says. 'It just identified clearly with my native place – and with what I was thinking – even though it was a document for the wide world.'

They were heady times, and the great social flux he was witnessing, he feels, helped inform his world view. Having finished at the seminary, he was despatched to the University of Wales in Cardiff to study sociology – chiefly the understanding of community development. 'A huge experience – going from Maynooth to a secular university; my best friend, who was studying for a PhD, used to describe himself as an atheist,' he says, half-marvelling at the incongruity of it.

'I did a little study on an old Irish community in the docks in Cardiff,' he says. 'They were descendents of the Famine Irish. There were about 700 of them locked away from the rest of the city – a hugely intriguing little group. They were mostly dockers. In fact, when I was there, the first young fella was going to the university even though there had been free education from years before.

'They had a little church. The stories that were handed down were stories from Ireland. They talked about places in Ireland even though they had never seen the sky over Ireland. When Ireland played Wales in the Arms Park [in rugby], which was just up the road from them, they would cheer for Ireland against Wales.

'There's a great message,' he says, inviting you into his confidence. 'In urban renewal, their area was demolished because they were very old and that community were scattered. I believe that's a dreadful thing to do to a community. It broke their hearts. I actually believe that we need to be extremely careful in Ireland that we don't do something similar on a way bigger scale. The bonds that were created there – with generations of people that grew up together – there's a massive power in that. I know you could say they got very introverted; maybe so. But there's a huge power in it, too.'

Fr Bohan completed his MA thesis, entitled 'The Effects of Industrialisation on the Settlement Patterns of Britain', paying particular attention to the alienation and social decay engendered from living in tower blocks in the North and Midland regions, a housing strategy that was reversed within twenty-five years.

After five years in the UK, which included a stint in Birmingham, he came home, taking up a post under the aegis of the diocese as a sociologist with Shannon Development. Around him, he viewed the Irish government's residential-housing construction policy – 'planning for houses not communities' – in dismay.

'I came back to Ireland and saw all that repeated. I saw the Moyrosses, the South Hills, the Ballymuns, which I really railed against, and said, "They are destructive. People are never intended to live in these kinds of places." Imagine trying to rear young children, six, eight, ten storeys up into the sky? Crazy – it's unnatural.'

If families in Irish cities were being penned in the time, they were being splintered out in the countryside areas. After a night back in west Clare, listening to people despair about the haemorrhaging of youth from their region, Fr Bohan had an idea. Maybe they wouldn't get a factory in Feakle, but what about building a score of houses there, and giving young couples a start in life. Surely people would realise that it was better to commute twenty miles along a country boreen from a village like Feakle to jobs in Limerick or Shannon, than crawl, dispiritedly, through three miles of Dublin traffic. Something had to be done. For instance, in Feakle at the time, there were 120 people in the village; only three of these were between the ages of twenty and forty. The village was disintegrating, along with hundreds like it around the country.

'I absolutely dreamed that I'd be able to do something for the part of Ireland that I knew and loved, which would be symbolised by the place I was born and reared in,' he says.

No faulting his earnestness, but people looked awry when he aired his plan for a rural housing-development scheme. 'I wouldn't have been able to drive a nail,' he adds, almost alarmed at his own foolishness, 'and going into a bank manager and asking him for a loan, being told by a county manager, "This is stone mad."'

But it came to pass. 'I remember,' says journalist Nell McCafferty, 'John Healy saying: "Isn't it great to see the lights going on in Clare when you look out of a dark night? When there used to be nothing, now the lights are back on."'

Having founded the Rural Housing Organisation in 1972, a necklace of distinctive, dormer-shaped houses sprung up in rural pockets around the country. Many of their inhabitants still refer to them as the Fr Harry Bohan houses. The revival it stimulated – which was supplemented in 1983 by the establishment of a work-oriented support body, the Rural Resource Organisation – is something he cherishes. 'We started building houses in small villages and we finished up, from a small, voluntary group, building 2,500 houses in 120 villages from Cavan down to Cork. Everyone that time told me it couldn't work, but yet the people with their feet said, "We want to live in the community."

'For example, we built those first houses in Feakle, and the chairman of the [GAA] club told me that of the under-12 team, ten of them came out of those houses. All that age group were gone out of other villages. They in turn started little businesses, the school got an extra teacher, and that whole community regenerated.'

A generation later, in a country bloated from the excesses of the Celtic Tiger economy and seemingly bereft spiritually, Fr Bohan's time – outside of his diocesan duties – is spent grappling with a more abstract challenge. Irish society, he argues, is struggling to cope with the rapid change that has resulted from what Roy Foster has described in *Luck and the Irish: A Brief History of Change, 1970–2000* as an 'astonishing transformation ... a leap into modernity from an archaic base'. Almost overnight, the country – as has been well chronicled – became, for a spell, the fastest-growing economy in the world.

Forced emigration, Fr Bohan thanks God, is no more. 'Any of us who had lived through the 1950s were delighted with this,' he says. 'This was terrific. This was the best Ireland that any of us had ever lived in, and we now had the chance to make choices.'

But many have found the variety of choices bewildering. Although jobs are aplenty, alas, we've a job being happy, it appears. While wonderful advances in communications technology – namely the Internet and the mobile phone – have helped to keep us connected, we have, as a community, become disconnected. So in order to understand and to adapt to the sudden changes that the country was experiencing – economically, technologically, socially – Fr Bohan helped found in 1998 a think tank, the Céifin Centre. The name derives from Céibhfhionn, the Celtic goddess of inspiration.

'Basically,' he explains, 'we set up the Céifin Centre a) to identify these changes and b) to try and understand what values were shaping us and how we need to look at the direction Irish society was taking, and that has taken off. We have run ten conferences. This year will be our eleventh. We've published all the books – the conference papers – they've gone into universities, students have been using them for post-graduate degrees; they have gone into communities where people discuss them. This year, we're doing one on the family.

'The debate so far has indicated to us that the greatest revolution that has taken place in Irish society is in the whole area of relationships and especially within family life. In a short period of time, the family went from the extended family to the nuclear family, for the first time, to all kinds of definition of family.'

Fr Harry adds that this year figures from the Central Statistics Office would indicate that only twenty per cent of housing units in the Dublin area will be taken up by traditional families – by 'man, wife and children' family units. 'This is one of the things,' he says, 'that has emerged out of one of our conferences: adolescents now spend less than five per cent of their time with parents and two per cent with other adults. That means that there is a generation of young people in Ireland growing up alone, and then we're surprised,' he says – allowing you to conjure up the ghastly consequences.

'That's the first thing; the second thing is: when I see a society hand over so many of its children to be reared by somebody else other than the parents, and hand over their elderly to a nursing home, I'd be seriously bothered by what we call civilisation. That bucks nature. Once we allow the market value to override us so badly as to allow that to happen, we're in trouble.'

As a notable intellectual – he has published several spiritual and sociological books – Fr Harry is an informed cautionary voice; and, unfortunately, his anxiety is well founded. There is evidence to suggest that we are becoming less compassionate as a society. While, paradoxically, Ireland surged ahead for a decade as one of the world's richest economies, it has left many of its disadvantaged people behind. For instance, homelessness – the great pockmark, the visible barometer of our level of compassion as a society – has, according to a Focus Ireland study in September 2007, doubled in the last sixteen years.

'[The economist Ernst Friedrich] Schumacher,' quotes Fr Bohan, 'once said, "It's not preachers and teachers who will get the message across; it's events." And the events are out there. They're screaming at us. Sometimes, I wonder if we have become deaf to the sound of alarm bells ringing.'

To illustrate, he points to three indicators in particular: the persistent carnage on the roads; ballooning homicide rates (ten times as many in the country in 2007 compared to 1960); and high rates of suicide (although low by EU standards). For example, in 2007 there were seventeen suicides in County Clare, sixteen of them males – up marginally from the previous year. 'It's obscene when the old bury the young,' he states, quoting Rose Kennedy.

Among the high-profile speakers – including war journalist John Pilger and social philosopher Charles Handy – that the Céifin Centre has attracted to its conferences has been one of Fr Bohan's intellectual brothers-in-arms, Robert Putnam, author of *Bowling Alone*, a landmark treatise on the atomisation of American society. A Harvard-based professor who had the ear of Presidents Bill Clinton and George W. Bush, and, indeed, former Taoiseach Bertie Ahern, he stresses the importance of what he calls social capital, which accrues from having a network of friends and neighbours, and from having a feeling of trust in them. The more integrated we are within our communities, Putnam's research illustrates, the less likely we are to experience colds, heart attacks, strokes, cancer, depression and premature deaths of all sorts. The evidence of these protective effects has been confirmed for close family ties, for participation in social events, and for affiliation with religious and civic associations such as Fr Bohan's beloved GAA. It would seem that the old Irish *seanfocal, Ar scáth a chéile a mhaireann na daoine* (everybody needs everybody else), has never been truer.

'What we're saying in the Céifin Centre,' says Fr Bohan, 'is the debate in itself is vital; otherwise, we lose the language of values, we lose the language of relationships, and we buy into the language of the marketplace and the commercial world, and lose that whole language to do with relationship and people connecting; otherwise, the family and community would be seriously undermined.

'I believe we've a marvellous opportunity. We've so many young people now living in the country. We've a great opportunity to build a society, learning from the mistakes of the past, including our own mistakes. The other thing that was being brought home to us in [our] debates,' he stresses, 'was that the second half of the twentieth century was about the material, and rightly so, because the effects of the Famine were still in the Irish psyche up to the late 1950s, so jobs and the economic and the material were vital to this country. But it was pointed out to us several times that the twenty-first century would be about the spiritual. Like, go into any bookshop and see all the stuff that's written about spirituality. [Also], there's a massive growth in prayer groups. That's a clear indication that there's a need.'

'I would be on both sides of the argument,' cautions *Irish Times* columnist John Waters, who spoke at Céifin's 2007 conference. 'In a strange way, you have to be. The conference can be in danger of just becoming a talking shop, of issuing pieties into the ether, denouncing the incoming tide. I was making my point not just about Céifin but about the Catholic church and the churches in general, and the extent to which, in putting out critiques of modernity, they announce that religion and belief have no place in the modern world. They basically ask people to choose between modernity and values, and people at a certain point will say, "Okay: values? Modernity? Well, values seems to be saying that I have to go into an eternal loop of self-denial and not enjoy myself and be sitting around like it was in the 1950s. You know, I think I'll go with the auld modernity." They think that it's enough to say things were better back then and we've lost something [in] some vague way, and we should forgo all this modernity and money and sex and drugs. Nobody's convinced.

'[But] Céifin is an important element, and it's good that they're there. They're asking the questions, and I think gradually they're moving towards some kind of point of clarity, but it's not there yet.'

No doubting Fr Bohan will persevere. Winner of a Rehab People of the Year award in 1982, the man is an incurable optimist, and draws on a deep well of stamina to get through a prodigious workload, managing to balance his work with Céifin with his duties as a parish priest to Sixmilebridge and his post as director of pastoral planning for the Killaloe diocese.

'He certainly carries a very big workload, but then he's driven,' chuckles Bishop Willie Walsh, who oversees him in the Killaloe diocese. 'He has great energy. The same thing – he went back into the Clare hurling team in 2004, and he was as enthusiastic about that when he went back into it as he was back in the 1980s.'

Fr Bohan has been at the hub of several waves of Clare hurling teams since he was first appointed manager in the autumn of 1973. In an era when teams were picked by a selection committee, himself and Kevin Heffernan were the country's first designated inter-county managers. He always had a *grá* for hurling, being a hurling captain at Maynooth at a time when the seminary was overrun with inter-county stars and was a fellow with 'a do-or-die spirit', remarked the *Clare Champion* when he helped Feakle to a county final in 1958.

Sometimes, word of his obsession went before him. When he arrived in Birmingham in the mid 1960s, a delegation from John Mitchel's waited for him to finish Confession on his first day's ministry to persuade him to turn out for their club. The following evening, playing centre-back, he was laid out after shipping a hurl 'from a fella who was half-drunk'. On noticing his stitched lip, the local canon made known his disapproval that one of his charges played 'that barbarian game', relieving him of his duty to say that particular evening's mass. Not that it put a stop to Fr Bohan's hurling.

When he first became manager of the Clare hurling team, his self-belief and left-field ideas – including 7 a.m. training sessions – were lapped up. He even got in guest speakers for motivation. Briefing Dr Tony O'Neill – who had arrived down from UCD – he suggested, 'Drink isn't a big problem for us, Tony, but you might just mention what it does to a fella.'

Where the inter-county team had been Balkanised by internecine local club rivalries, he sought to foster harmony and a group ethic, and brooked no mindless denigration from outside the camp. When a well-known 'supporter' wrote to him to criticise the team, Fr Harry tracked down his phone number and called him at four in the morning to confront him.

'Harry was this anti-establishment type of person at that time, a different type of priest, a different type of individual. He had this kind of madness,' says All-Star hurler, Johnny Callinan. 'When he came along and started talking about winning All-Irelands, "Whoa, this is new," we said, but we were ready for him as a group. We knew we could hold our own. A very good man manager – that was his greatest strength, and Harry was prepared to break moulds, and what he didn't necessarily know, technically, about hurling or physical training, he was quite prepared to bring in the experts to do that in Colum Flynn and Justin McCarthy.'

Not that intimacy with the intricacies of the game – or 'how to drive a nail' – was going to be a stumbling block for him. Having lost a Munster final to Cork in the late 1970s, Christy Ring, a selector for Cork, went to commiserate with him. 'He came down and shook my hands after one of the matches. "You're young," he said, "but stay with them. You're a good man and you're going the right direction." I said to him, "Sure Christy, I don't know a lot about it." And he said, "I don't either." So I often remind people who know all about hurling: Christy Ring told me one time he didn't know a lot about it.'

For all his apparent lack of expertise, Fr Bohan helped Clare to two National League titles, the county's first notable silverware since 1946. And he shared the heartbreak – either as manager or selector – of losing out on five Munster finals in 1974, 1977, 1978, 1981 and

1986, and experienced those All-Ireland semi-final defeats in 2005 and 2006.

The Munster final defeat in 1977 was particularly dispiriting. They had been 'seriously unlucky' to lose, he felt. Critically, fullback Jim Power – 'the cleanest man we had on the team' – had been sent off just before half-time, reducing Clare to fourteen men. But he hoped the excitement that the league victories engendered, the sight of thousands of Clare people filing into Thurles, might fire the imagination of children around the county and lead to minor All-Ireland glory a decade later. The dream never materialised. But a little later, something better happened, when his great friend Anthony Daly – who has a picture of the 1977 National League-winning team in the office over his sport's shop in Ennis – captained Clare to a first Munster title in sixty-three years and an All-Ireland title shortly afterwards.

Watching the Clare team cross over the bridge in Feakle on a sunny July afternoon in 1995 – as part of a week-long parade of the parishes with the Munster title – must have been a nourishing experience for Fr Harry Bohan.

For a man who rightly sees the GAA as being a key, enriching constituent in the fabric of Irish society, a cornerstone for small communities around the country, this kind of moment would pay dividends for generations. In its way, almost as good as a row of new houses would be to the village. Almost.

ANTHONY FOLEY

On a blustery New Year's Eve in 2005, Munster played Leinster at the RDS in the Celtic League. Munster were at sea. Late in the second half, Leinster's Felipe Contepomi gathered his own chip ahead to saunter in for a try under the posts to put the game beyond doubt. Then came his celebration, as he carried on running towards Munster's fans with his hands behind his ears as if to say, 'What have you got to say about that?' Oh the joy. The South Dublin faithful nearly choked in their scarves with the excitement.

'So that was noted,' says Anthony Foley, laconically. When it mattered, four months later, in the biggest domestic rugby game in the country's history, Munster reddened Leinster at Lansdowne Road, beating them by 30–6 to book a place in the Heineken Cup final.

Foley wouldn't have let himself get carried away with the semi-final win. Having already lost two European Cup finals, the win over Leinster would mean nothing unless Munster won their most coveted piece of silverware. He was a professional athlete. It was about winning week in, week out. But the motivation to put one over Leinster would have appealed to him greatly. It was an old tribal joust, a throwback to a bygone era of interpros and persistent slighting of working-class Limerick-based players by the national selectors. 'This is a day for men,' he said, gravely, to his Munster teammates the day of the match.

His rugby philosophy, he says, has always been founded on two principles – perfectly enshrined in that sunny late-April afternoon clash – bitterness and pride. The soccer-style celebration by Contepomi would have been deposited in the bitter bank; pride, on the day, to be absorbed from the sea of red that draped the ground, as the Munster fan-base, like a good back-row forward, got their hands, by hook or by crook, on two-thirds of the match tickets. In Leinster's backyard.

He retired from the Munster scene after fourteen years of service, and is still the most capped player in European Cup history, and the competition's second-highest try scorer. For a forward, this is an incredible statistic. It's worth noting that of the top twenty-five all-time international try scorers, every one of them are backs. In a province that uses the word as a term of endearment, Foley is, indeed, a 'legend'. But it is the esteem in which he is held by his peers that rings loudest. Ronan O'Gara – forgiven for indulging in the rugby man's penchant for warlike hyperbole – once remarked that he could probably count on one hand the guys he'd be prepared to die for, Foley being one of them.

'Fellas like him don't come along very often. He's just a hard, hard man,' says Munster player, Mick O'Driscoll, rolling slowly over the word 'hard' – like Marcellus Wallace in *Pulp Fiction*. At six-foot-three, Foley has landed some memorable hits in his time. Early in the game against France at Lansdowne Road in 2001, he knocked over the French enforcer, Fabien Pelous, with a thundering tackle to set the tone for an Irish victory. And then there was a game-defining hit in the 2006 European Cup final. Three minutes into the second half, John Hayes got a hold of Damien Traille in the middle of the pitch. A fraction of a second later, Foley came steaming into the fêted French centre to turn over possession. 'If you're looking for moments in matches and you remember O'Connell and Chabal, how about that – Foley and the Munster pack send Traille back,' screeched RTÉ commentator Ryle Nugent.

Five minutes later, Foley smashed into Jean-Baptiste Gobelet, again in the middle of the park. The ball was recycled, went cross field and back again in Biarritz's fifth phase of play. Harinordoquy took it forward, but who was there to send him tumbling backwards? Foley. It's like he has a sixth sense.

'Foley [is] one of the smartest players I played with,' remarked Keith Wood, a friend of his from days growing up together in Killaloe. 'There's a line called the Fat Man Track – the shortest distance between any two points, where the ball is or where it might end up. Foley instinctively knew that line and was there. Even though he wasn't faster than the other guys, he would beat them to the ball, and once he got there, he was incredibly effective.'

'He's got a very good understanding of the game, which isn't learned from books,' adds Alan Gaffney, who appointed him Munster captain in 2004. 'Some people have got it; most don't. He just has this feel for the game and this brain that works in advance of where things are going to happen, and whereas some people will run a full marathon in a game, Axel will run a half-marathon.'

Foley was born on 30 October 1973. A day after his fifth birthday, his father Brendan – who won eleven caps for Ireland – turned out for Munster in the second row the day the All Blacks were resoundingly beaten 12-0. Foley used to go along to Thomond Park with his dad to Shannon games, carrying his father's gear bag and slinking around the dressing-room while the players togged out. This day, because of the crowds, his mother wouldn't allow him go. 'It was just another game for me that I was missing out. Obviously, I was a bit upset about it, but you get over that and move on,' he says, chuckling. 'I'm probably one of the only ones saying I wasn't there.'

Given his genes – his sister Rosie used to play for the Irish ladies' rugby team – it was no surprise that Foley was a rugby prodigy, though he also enjoyed a truncated under-age hurling career that included a game for the Clare minors against Galway in Tubber.

For three years, he played on the Munster schools' rugby team, and for two on the Irish schools', losing out, famously, to an injury-time penalty by Jeff Wilson against their New Zealand counterparts. A certain Jonah Lomu was opposite him at number eight that day.

More heartbreak came in a Munster Schools' Senior Cup final loss to Pres in Cork. 'They had a crafty bastard as their coach,' pleads Foley, acknowledging the role played by his future Munster boss, Declan Kidney.

With Shannon, it was all about winning. He captained the club in 1998 – their AIL four-in-a-row season – and, testament to his durability, he played in all forty-eight games over those seasons. Remarkably, by the time Munster played in the European Cup final in 2006, Foley had played in seventy-five out of seventy-six of the province's appearances in the tournament since its inauguration eleven years beforehand.

Foley was called to play for Ireland for the first time in January 1995. In those amateur days, it was customary for the newly capped player to rest on the Saturday before the international, but Foley insisted on turning out for Shannon in a table-top league clash with Blackrock in Stradbrook, probably making him the first player to do so, points out Mick Galwey, who lined out with him the following Saturday against England and later stood in as best man at his wedding in July 1999.

'The build up to the game you're so nervous, you're vomiting,' says Foley, recalling his first cap. 'You get out onto the pitch and you get the anthem and whatever, you're so nervous. Kick off happens, and you try and hit the first fella you see. I was fortunate enough – Tim Rodber ran across me, so I managed to hit him. You just get into it. Then suddenly, bang, it's all over; you're in the changing-rooms after the game.'

The game wasn't without incident. Ireland were well beaten by a score of 20–8, but Foley scored a consolation try late in the match. He also took on one of the giants of the English game. 'I had a run-in with Dean Richards. He threw an elbow across a line-out, and I went for him, but I was twenty-one,' he says, laughing at the naivety of it. 'He was telling me to "Calm down, young man".'

He kept his place for the remainder of what was then the Five Nations, but ran aground in a warm-up game against Italy for that year's World Cup. 'We had all sorts of shenanigans going on beforehand – the bus didn't turn up to bring us to the game,' he says, smiling at the memory. 'You know, we're all there waiting to play an international match, standing on the side of the road. Noel Murphy, our manager, in fairness, was out trying to flag down taxis with lira hanging out, like this: "Stop! Stop! Stop!" Then we get to the ground late, and the Italians wouldn't put the game back half an hour, and, basically, we rush a warm-up, rush out onto the pitch – a lovely warm summer's day in Treviso – and suddenly we're getting absolutely hosed.'

The embarrassing 22–12 defeat cost himself and Shannon teammate Eddie Halvey their places in the back row for Ireland's first-choice side in the World Cup. What Foley describes as 'complacency and indiscipline' in his autobiography, *Axel*, was at the root of the problem. On the Tuesday before Ireland played the All Blacks in the tournament, along with a few other players, he broke curfew to go drinking. He was caught by Murphy, the team manager, when he arrived back in the hotel. 'You're slurring your words, Anthony,' said Murphy. 'I always slur my words, Noel,' replied Foley, whose nickname is 'Slurpy', owing to a lisp he has. Suddenly, having picked up six caps in his first international season, Foley found himself in the wilderness, as he could only muster three more appearances over the following four years.

Although Foley played in a Munster team full of unselected players that beat Ireland in a warm-up game in Musgrave Park before the 1999 World Cup, he had to watch the tournament on television.

An ignominious exit from the competition by the Irish team to the Argentinians at Lens, and Munster's impressive showing in the pool stages of the ensuing European Cup – including epic back-to-back wins against Saracens and a first away win on French soil – helped to get Foley back into the Irish side. But it wasn't going to be an easy ride. A 50–18 pummelling by England at Twickenham put his place in jeopardy again. On the Monday before the next game against Scotland in the Six Nations, the panel convened for a training session in Greystones in which their disgruntled New Zealand coach called an impromptu trial game. 'In fairness to Warren Gatland,' says Galwey, 'you can see how he can be successful – he said, "All bets are off. Nobody's guaranteed their place next weekend. More importantly," he said, "there are places up for grabs."

'The following weekend,' he says, giggling, 'the team read: Claw, Woodie, Hayes, Galwey – who was the other second row, Malcolm O'Kelly, probably – and the back row would have been … ah …' he says, starting to giggle again, 'Foley, Easterby and Kieran Dawson. You know, I don't think anything even had to be said. It was a nod and a wink: "Lads, get stuck in here now and make sure that we stand by each other; there's a few of us [Munster players] getting on this Irish team." I think it was the last fifteen left standing got picked,' adds Foley. 'It was a muddy night, awful conditions and we just went out and went hell for leather. A lot of fellas put their mark in and said, "Look, we want to be selected", and it happened, you know? Gatland just let it off. That's what he was good at. It was one of those moments that made that side for the next couple of years.'

Foley was on a roll, making the Irish number eight position his own and captaining the side on a couple of occasions before arriving at the 2003 World Cup. By the time the Irish team was set to play France in the quarter-final, Foley had played in thirty-eight out of Ireland's previous forty-six tests, but Irish coach Eddie O'Sullivan chose Victor Costello instead of him. 'This is, in effect, the first time he's been dropped in four years,' wrote Gerry Thornley in the *Irish Times*. 'And for the biggest game in four years at that. It'll be eating away inside.'

'He took it so badly,' says Galwey, who holds the record, he states, for being dropped the most times from the Irish rugby team. 'Victor Costello was a good player but I just felt Anthony was playing well at the time. I know he came back and got a few caps after, but that was a bad blow to Anthony. We all have had them. Nobody saw it coming, including Anthony. I remember being out with him that night, and we had a few pints and he got over it, like, but it takes its bit out of you all right.'

'Maybe World Cups aren't meant for me,' says Foley. 'It was a hard thing to swallow at the time, but you put it away at the back of your mind and get on with it.'

'How do you deal with it?' I asked.

'You get down,' he says, 'but there's two things – fellas will see if you're not disappointed to be dropped, they'll say you don't care: "Ah, it didn't bother him anyway. Fuck him." You have to be disappointed at being left out or being dropped, but then you have to get over that quickly because the bigger picture is the game, and you have to flip over and help the boys get ready. It's a hard place to be.'

In his autobiography, Foley describes arriving back to his hotel room having received the news from O'Sullivan that he'd been dropped. His roommate, Paul O'Connell, was sprawled on his bed reading. Foley told him the news, letting rip about his manager 'with a fair few expletives' thrown in. O'Connell commiserated, but then couldn't help himself: 'Sure, play a few holes of golf with him. He's a grand fella,' he said, collapsing in laughter. It was a line Foley used – having played golf with O'Sullivan and Wood in Portumna before the World Cup – when other squad players complained that their manager was a bit distant.

Foley had plenty of time to play golf in the summer of 2005 when he was overlooked – as he had been in 2001 – for the Lions. Harshly so, according to many from the rugby fraternity. He's also endured a lot of criticism over his career, not least from some journalistic quarters, those unsatisfied with his lack of pace and by the fact that he didn't serve up the conspicuous, rampaging Chabal-like charges in open play that delight the crowds; far simpler to listen for those roars than to pick laboriously through the video analysis of a game for tackle counts and work around the rucks. Although Foley had an uncanny rugby brain and prodigious stamina, to many in the press he was an 'unfashionable' number eight.

'Just watch all the matches he played in the teams [that] won,' says Munster hooker, Frankie Sheahan, emphatically. It's true. Foley had a 60% win record with Ireland and a 72% success rate with Munster. 'At times, people get carried away with what individuals do,' adds Sheahan. 'I'm a professional athlete, and I'm playing and training every single day at it, and I'd watch a live match and I might only have a fair idea what went on. I'd need to watch that match another one or two times to really comment on exactly what happened, you know? It's why it would piss you off at times – there's fellas writing up their reports just after watching a live match, they're chatting, there are distractions … "Who did that?" they're asking each other. The flip side – I've played some of the best games, I'd say I've ever played, and there hasn't been a word on it, not a mention in the paper. Then the opposite – I wouldn't be playing my best game by a long shot, and I'd get a mention in the paper because I'd one break.

'From that respect – now, he still scored a phenomenal amount of tries – a perception just grew a couple of years ago that Foley was sort of over the top. The media has an awful lot to do with it, too. Some guys would have fierce PR machines behind them. Foley wasn't going away pushing himself on the media. He felt he'd nothing to prove.'

'You just ignore it, to be honest,' says Foley.

'Would it spur you on?'

'You try to ignore it. If a renowned international rugby player came out and said bang, bang, bang about you, you'd sit up and take notice, but [not] if it's a reporter who's working off opinions of other reporters, or whatever. You'd have people that you trust that you can talk to. You talk to your coaches and get a proper, informed opinion. The worst thing would be to work off what people are saying who don't know what's going on out on the pitch.'

After the 2003 World Cup, Foley notched up a further fifteen caps, finishing with sixty-two, which included his fiftieth in March 2004 – an improbable afternoon that saw Ireland defeat England, the newly crowned World Cup champions, and put an end to their twenty-two-match unbeaten run at Fortress Twickenham. The win also set Ireland up for their first Triple Crown title in almost twenty years.

Meanwhile, there was still unfinished business with Munster. 'We were like a dog with a bone to chew,' he says. Each year threw up gallant victories – the semi-final win over Toulouse in 2000, a personal favourite; the quarter-final defeat of Stade Français in 2002; the slaying of Leicester in their backyard in 2003; 'miracle matches' against Gloucester in 2003 and 2004 – set against perennial near-miss stories, of legitimate tries scored but not allowed, and tries on the cusp of being scored but denied – it was lamented – by old bloody English chicanery.

There were lighter days, too, including one free-scoring day in the 2001 quarter-final game. 'Brian McGoey [owner of the Dominos franchise in Limerick] had told somebody – Foley heard it, of course – that the first player to score a hat trick in a Heineken Cup match, right, would get free pizzas for life,' says Galwey, adding the topping to the story. 'So we were playing against Biarritz in Thomond Park, and who stayed out on the wing for three tries? Foley. Foley scored three tries that day, and it was only after the game was over that we realised that he was going to get free pizzas for life. Now, a lot of people said that Foley doesn't need free pizzas for life, but that's beside the point.'

The final defeats in 2000 and 2002 left their marks, though. 'We got too emotional the night before the game,' says Foley, looking over the corpse of the agonisingly close defeat to Northampton in Munster's first final. 'When it came to the game, then, we were drained. A team meeting over-spilled. Fellas got too emotional. We kinda played the game the night before, I suppose.' He goes on to say that a re-viewing of the video of the match would suggest that they were 'desperately unlucky' in the end to lose by 9–8, but concedes that they were 'outplayed' in the 2002 final defeat to Leicester.

Three minutes into the final against Biarritz in 2006, and a contentious try by winger Philippe Bidabe made us wonder if more despair lay in store. But Munster regrouped, and twice, having won kickable penalties in the twelfth and fourteenth minutes, Foley, the Munster captain, forsook points on the board to kick into the corner. This wasn't percentages stuff. 'They were a bit shell-shocked that we weren't taking our kicks at goal,' said Munster wing-forward Alan Quinlan in the commemorative DVD, *Munster: The Brave and the Faithful*. 'Anthony made up his mind himself that we wanted to go for it, and we weren't gonna sit back, and everyone rowed in behind him.'

'He just always seems to do the right thing on the pitch, and seems to know what the right thing to do is, not only for himself but for the team,' maintains O'Driscoll, who finished out the final as Munster captain. 'He's an amazing leader and an amazing captain. Having him around is almost like having a guiding hand – someone you'd put full faith in knowing that whatever decision he makes will be the right one.'

Taking that line was a bold move, but after stubborn defence by Biarritz, it paid off subsequently with tries by Trevor Halstead and Peter Stringer in the sixteenth and thirty-first minutes, respectively. It showed balls and presence of mind by the captain, but then he's got lots of presence.

The Tongan islander Lifeimi Mafi, marvelling at Foley in the Munster dressing-room, suggests that he has *mana*. 'It means,' he says, 'that he has presence; that he commands respect; that he has substance.'

And as for Foley's most memorable day on a rugby pitch – amidst stirring victories over World Cup holders Australia in 2002, and a number of great wins over the English – nothing, he says sweetly, compared to that 2006 European Cup triumph. There was a day of pride.

BRIAN LOHAN

Bono once said that, compared to Johnny Cash, every man is a cissy.
Bono must never have seen Brian Lohan hurl. Three minutes before
half-time in the 1997 All-Ireland hurling final, Lohan had shortened
his hurley to make a clearance when Tipperary's John Leahy came
across and hacked him on the pelvic bone. 'Anyone will tell you that
ever got a belt there – it's paralysing,' says Colum Flynn, Clare team
physio that day. 'It's the worst pain possible. There's no muscle there.
The bone is subcutaneous – there's nothing between it and the skin,
and the main nerve to the quadriceps passes down there. If it starts to
bleed in there, you're goosed – you can't move the leg at all.'

Having been carried up to the dressing-room, Flynn got Lohan
in as comfortable a position as possible, and worked some ice-packs
around the offending area. Lohan was 'giddy'. Flynn reminded him
about Leahy, and told him some fairy tales about the wonders of the
body's hormone system. 'I know when you stand up it's going to be
as bad as it was when you came in,' he said, 'but when the adrenaline
starts to pump again, you won't even feel it.'

Before the team went back out for the second half, they were called
in for a huddle. 'We were coming in for a clinch and I grabbed Lohan by

the ribs,' says Ollie Baker. 'He nearly hit the roof. I said, "What's wrong with ya?" He just shook his head at me. No way – he wouldn't say it.'

Flynn watched Lohan leave for the second half. 'He actually hobbled. He was going from leg to leg, like an auld fella with a bad hip.'

Can you imagine the teeth-grinding?

'I talked to him afterwards,' says Baker. 'I said, "What happened you?"'

'Lohan said, "I got a belt in the first half and I was in serious fuckin' pain and I didn't need you hittin' me either at half-time."'

'"How did you manage the second half?" I asked.

'"I couldn't lift my hand. I couldn't raise it. I just had your man [by a clump of jersey] and there was no way he was going to get away from me."'

His man, Eugene O'Neill, did get away from him. Twice. He scored 1–1, but the goal had nothing to do with his marker. It resulted from a fortuitous rebound off the crossbar. For his efforts in the company of Lohan, O'Neill received a Young Player of the Year award.

'Any mere mortal would have sidelined himself. He would have come off,' adds Baker in disbelief. 'But unless it's in a casket, that's the only way Lohan'd be taken off.' 'Tis mental strength to blank pain out like that; he's just awesome.'

Two years previously, after the All-Ireland hurling semi-final against Galway, Lohan had to be carried off the field with a torn hamstring. After daily sessions of physio and dips in the therapeutic waters of the Atlantic Ocean in Lahinch, he was told that the first time he could sprint again was when he ran out onto the pitch for the final against Offaly. With twenty minutes to go in that match, it snapped again. He signalled to the bench, but manager Ger Loughnane just turned away and gave instructions that he was to see out the game. Lohan shrugged and resumed his sentry on the edge of the square. A few minutes later, the Offaly full-forward John Troy picked up a loose ball under the Nally Stand. As he did so, Lohan let out a roar that would dislodge paint from a wall. It was enough to encourage Troy to move the *sliotar* on to one of the Dooleys.

After the final, Lohan was dispatched to Ger Hartmann's physical-therapy clinic in Florida to sort out his injury. The day after his assessment, Hartmann phoned Flynn. 'He said, "I don't know how he kept himself going for the last four months. He has thirty-three per cent capacity in the right hamstring." Thirty three per cent,' repeats Flynn incredulously. 'I mean, you're looking for ninety to one hundred per cent at all times. He'd a third of the capacity. It wasn't there at all. It was barely hanging in. He shouldn't have been even training.'

He's that peculiar beast who does not brook defeat: restless, surly, with an almost pathological desire to win. We know their kind from a distance: Keane in soccer; O'Connell in rugby; and Lohan in hurling. The kind of men Shackelton would have favoured. Or, in local vernacular, 'a bunch of men', as Lohan's old trainer, Mike McNamara would say.

Failure is not a term of reference. It disgusts Lohan; it's invariably the product of ill-discipline, laziness and a lack of ambition. 'He wouldn't like to lose a toss,' says former teammate, Fergie Tuohy.

'It was the lost causes he used chase,' remarked Liam Doyle in an interview about Lohan, his former teammate. 'You would see him going after balls that he had no right to get, and so often he would come away with it.'

'I don't think any man ever approached a *sliotar* in search of possession as determined as Brian Lohan,' says RTÉ radio commentator, Micheál Ó Muircheartaigh. 'I remember talking to [referee] Dickie Murphy the way you'd be talking about different players, and I mentioned one time, "Now what do you think of Brian Lohan?"'

'And he said, "He's the most intimidating player I ever refereed."

'I said, "In what way?"

'"This way," he says. "You're watching him. He's after making this ferocious drive and he'll get it," he says, "and he has put so much into it, you'd feel a bit guilty if you blew him after taking five steps … He put so much into it that the very actions and effort he put into it hardly merited being blown for a thing like that." And, you know,' adds Ó Muircheartaigh mischievously, 'I'm convinced that he took an odd *sliotar* off the grass as well.'

'You'd always be advising players to get ahead of him, but he was a great man to attack the ball,' says Justin McCarthy, who advised several Waterford full-forwards over the years on how to cope with him. 'He was a risk-taker, too. Full-backs play safe and play behind their men. They wouldn't be attacking the ball, but Brian Lohan could go out and attack the ball. He could go right across his goal,' he says, allowing himself a laugh, 'and across the goal again with the ball on his hurley. Back in the 1950s, 1960s, 1970s, 1980s, if you did that, you'd be taken off.'

Loughnane has spoken about the 'poison' in Lohan's veins. 'He hates every forward that comes near him. He hates every county,' he said of him, with evident relish.

'He'd bury ya,' adds Baker. 'If he thought that you were scared of him, you were finished. He'd crawl over ya – he'd live in your shirt.'

Because Lohan was so driven, the onset of that aggressive battle mindset, the nurturing of it, would envelop him earlier than others. He admitted in an interview with Seán Moran of the *Irish Times* in 2006 – Lohan's last season – that he would be 'hard to live with the week of a match'; and, famously, on the day of a game, he was a no-go area.

'You knew coming up to a match, the "DO NOT DISTURB" sign would go up,' says one former player. 'He'd just be going around with a growl on him, a scowl. I remember going down to play one game in Thurles, and one of the guys was passing a paper around. It was being passed through the hands and arrived at Lohan, and he just caught it and scrunched it up and threw it up on top. As in, don't be annoyin' me, like, with that rubbish. You could almost see it in him on match days that he was like a dangerous bear.'

For management staff, his moods were a weather vane for the team's fortunes. 'I always liked to see him grumpy on the day of a game,' said former selector, Tony Considine, in a Kieran Shannon interview in 2002. 'We might be getting onto the bus and Ger [Loughnane] would say, "Well, how is he today?" And I'd say, "He's grand. He's growling." I remember one time in 1998 – Lohan had always roomed with Michael O'Halloran up to then; in fact, last year [2001], he was Michael's best man. Lohan comes up to me and says, "Tony. Is Hallo playing?" I said he wasn't. Lohan went, "I want to be in a room with someone who is." So I went to Ger, "We better get someone else in with Lohan."'

'Brian had to be the winner. End of story,' says Ollie Baker. 'We'd be doing sprints [and] be it going up the hill [in Shannon] or long stamina runs … at the end you could put any money you want on it, but Brian Lohan would be the winner. However he does it? Obviously in his own mind, he has said, "I'm going to win." Everyone would be trying to beat him, like. Jamesie was a speed merchant … Barry Murphy, Gilly [Niall Gilligan], P. J. O'Connell – speed merchants, but no one could get near him. Going up that hill, I was as good as any man, but the last sprint, Lohan would beat you. That's the way he is – I'm going to win and put ye all behind me. That's how intense he was.'

The fact that he might be a right-side/wrong-side-of-the-bed kind of person heightened this intensity. 'I'd ring Lohan up, and I'd know within two seconds whether I'd be on the phone for fifteen minutes or whether I'd be on the phone for two minutes. That's just the way the guy is,' says another former teammate.

Fergie Tuohy used to tog out beside him at training and on match days. 'A lot of people say, "It's very hard to know Brian – he's so serious." But he's serious because he wants to do the right thing by himself. He wants to be the best. Do the best.'

Given this perfectionist streak, it's no surprise that the days when things went awry stick out a bit more than days of triumph. When it was right, he'd move on; when it was wrong, he'd be perturbed, he'd question. 'You remember more about the one you lost than you would about the ones you won. I suppose that's progression of time as well,' he admits. 'I thought when we went in for the All-Ireland final in 2002 … we took a wrong turn going in. You know, we got lost going in,' he says in that slow, deliberate style of his. No drama. It's left for you to come to your own understanding of how much of an imbecile that driver must have been.

'There was a fellow behind me,' continues Lohan. 'He was on his mobile … well, he'd borrowed somebody else's mobile phone to ring back to the hotel to ask somebody at the hotel to see if they could find his mobile phone. He left it in the room. Not a member of the team or the panel but somebody associated with the panel.'

'Eventually, I just had to turn around and asked him, could he hold off and make that phone call inside in Croke Park,' he says, his voice rising almost imperceptibly, 'when we're gone from the bus? You know, it's …' – this next adjective is delivered with oomph – 'stupid things like that that you remember, that you'd have forgotten about, I suppose, if we won, but when you lost, you remember those things. D'ya know how the f-f … how could you be right going in there?'

Indeed.

'The morning of the All-Ireland, there was rooms booked, but whatever happened, the room – I was sharing with Gerry Quinn – that we were supposed to be in, myself and Gerry, that room was double-booked, so we had to go down and get another room, and then they had no other rooms, and then eventually, you know, you're supposed to go to bed for an hour but we didn't get to bed for an hour.

'We got in late to the actual dressing-rooms; we didn't get a proper warm-up done. All stuff, the logistics … it's very important at that level – you have to have everything right. You don't wanna be dealing with it. It's just stress that you can do without.'

With all the stories of the famous Lohan cocoon, you'd imagine he was some kind of glowering ogre, but in the second half of his career, he forsook the routine of a nap the morning of a game – like he used to have when rooming with O'Halloran – and instead roomed happily with Quinn, who, from Lohan's account, seems to have been like a teenager on a school trip, spending the time yapping away on his phone or watching TV and DVDs. 'But it used work. It used work well,' he says, laughing at the abandon of it.

Lohan is part of Clare's most famous hurling dynasty. Along with his brother Frank and his father Gus – who played inter-county for both Galway and Clare – the Lohans recently surpassed the Whelahans as the family to have played the most hurling championship matches in history.

Gus Lohan was a tough, hardy, no-nonsense hurler. 'There was no reverse gear in Gus, and I would see that Brian inherited that,' says hurling analyst Liam Griffin, who played with Gus Lohan for both Newmarket-on-Fergus and Clare while studying at Shannon's Hotel Management School in the late 1960s.

His son Brian had an undistinguished under-age career. He was a mainstay on club teams, but failed to get on the Clare minor hurling team in 1989 – in which his father Gus was a selector – that reached an All-Ireland final. He had better fortune with the big ball, although by his own admission he was 'no good' at Gaelic football. 'I was no good at kicking,' he points out. He was still good enough to be called up for the county minor football panel, but it was a disillusioning experience.

When his club-mate, Paul Lee – that year's Clare minor hurling captain – said he wouldn't play because he had to study for his Leaving Certificate, the manager tried to reassure the rest of the squad: 'Don't worry about the Leaving, lads – the GAA looks after its own!'

Lohan disregarded this advice and went along to University of Limerick to take business studies. In a Fitzgibbon team that included Clare's Seánie McMahon and Waterford's Fergal Hartley, UL won the tournament in 1994, winning each round of their three matches in extra time. Lohan won the Player of the Tournament award, 'playing a lot of hurling' for a corner-back, says McMahon.

'At the time you think it's better than what it actually is, but you're certainly experiencing hurling at a level that's completely different to what you're used to,' says Lohan about the standard. 'I hadn't played inter-county at minor. It was a big step up for me. All I'd experienced was club, and when you're playing corner-back with the club, you're not marking the best hurlers. In a lot of cases, you wouldn't even be marking the second tier down. When we won that Fitzgibbon in 1994, P. J. Delaney was corner-forward [for Waterford IT], and he was an All-Star at the time. He was after winning an All-Ireland with Kilkenny in 1993, so you're up against a different standard of player.'

'I haven't spoken to Lohan about it, but I think that's where he made his mind up that there was no one better than "you",' argues O'Halloran. 'That's the kernel of Brian Lohan and his success: "Just because I'm from Clare and you're from Cork – you're not better than me. I am better than you because I have worked harder than you." That's the essential Brian Lohan. He wouldn't be happy if he didn't have the work done, but once he had the work done, that he knew he had prepared properly, then that was it – he was going to be better than you on the given day.'

Loughnane concurs with this assessment. 'Most of what Brian Lohan achieved was through really hard work,' he says. 'His ability to perform under pressure came from the fact that he had worked so hard, that he knew nobody had worked harder than himself.'

'The tougher it was, the better,' adds O'Halloran, 'because that was upping the stakes and the test even more. That was his outlook: "I'm going to be the one left standing at the end", and that's the way it panned out. It was sheer will. It wasn't any dirt – and he had a gammy hamstring as well – but he had what he had, and obviously great concentration. He was beatin' fellas out to the ball. He wasn't afraid of it.'

By the time Lohan finished university, he had established himself on the Clare senior hurling team, having experienced a torrid afternoon in the infamous thrashing by Tipperary at Limerick's Gaelic Grounds in July 1993. The joke around the UL campus was that he knew every one of Pat Fox's studs because he was looking at them all day. There were other ropey days, too – most famously when Tipp's Micheál

Webster gave him the run-around in 2005 – but mere blemishes when balanced against so many imperious days.

Against Limerick in 1996, he flailed all that came before him, earning one of his four All-Stars on the back of a single championship outing that season. In the autumn of that year, observers say that, almost singled-handed, he kept Waterford's Ballygunner at bay to help Wolfe Tones to a Munster club title by a single point.

And great, great days in Croke Park: against Galway in 1995; a Man of the Match performance against Waterford in the All-Ireland semi-final in 2002; and, of course, Cork in 2005, when he settled an old score with Brian Corcoran. Clare had played Cork in Cusack Park behind closed doors on 12 June 2004, and Corcoran – recently lured out of retirement and converted to full-forward – ran amok. But Lohan's mind, he insists, had been elsewhere. The throw-in for the match was at midday in Cusack Park in Ennis. After the game, Lohan had to make a train at 3 p.m. with the hope of making it to see his beloved Pixies [an American band] on stage at 6.30 p.m. in Dublin's Phoenix Park.

'We were playing Cork in this challenge, right,' says Lohan, 'and all I was thinking about was getting up to see the Pixies. Played it; wasn't tuned into the game, and was marking Corcoran, and he got three goals.'

'Brian Corcoran we felt had it over Brian Lohan from that day forward,' says John Allen, who was a Cork selector that day.

Twelve months later, Clare were waiting in the long grass for Cork – the reigning champions – in that year's All-Ireland semi-final. Before the game, Lohan rang his old college buddy for some information. 'I got on to [Fergal] Hartley. He had marked him in the Munster final that year. He said, "Listen, they're all blaming me down in Waterford but eleven balls came in that day, and I cleared eight of them, and he scored 1–2. He was lucky." Hartley reckoned that I'd roast him.

'I was asking how to handle [Cork's] Joe Deane as well. Basically, what Waterford did was that they put Eoin Murphy out in front of

Joe Deane, and if ball broke behind Eoin Murphy, it was up to the full-back to clear it. That was the way that we said we'd play them as well. That [Clare's] Gerry O'Grady was to come out to every ball in front, and if a ball broke behind O'Grady, it was up to me to clear it, and that was part of my job for the day.'

Lohan lorded it, showing flashes of his majestic best, resulting in Corcoran – one of the giants of the modern era – being hauled ashore after fifty minutes. Writing a report for the following morning's *Irish Times*, Tom Humphries – fearing it might be Lohan's last day in Croke Park – suggested: 'if it transpires to be so, the famous red helmet should be transported under guard to a museum.'

'Brian Lohan came back that day,' chuckles Allen – manager this time for Cork. 'He was excellent and was too good for Brian Corcoran; we had to replace him and put on Neil Ronan. Brian Lohan had won his duel with Corcoran.'

Lohan played his last campaign in 2006, helping Clare to the All-Ireland semi-final, but that day in August 2005 – going toe-to-toe with Corcoran – provided Clare supporters with one last, great opportunity to indulge in the communal primal scream that used accompany those big, booming clearances of his.

'I remember being at the second Clare–Offaly game in 1998,' says *Sunday Times* journalist Christy O'Connor, 'and I was sitting near his sister – obviously I don't know her and she doesn't know me; except to see maybe – and he came out one time and cleared the ball … the cheer went up, and I saw her, and she was just laughing, shaking her head, like, "This is hilarious."'

'I never really noticed it while I was playing,' says Lohan, with a nervous titter. 'Or I didn't notice it to an extent. Ah, I never paid too much attention to it,' he says, growing quiet.

'If you're walking up O'Connell Street [Ennis, where one of his two financial advisory offices is based], you don't ever hear the roar go up?'

'If I'm going for lunch or something,' he admits, 'and there's a couple of lads, but it's always students that start roarin' at me … at one o'clock or whatever it is, you're just going for your lunch, and you'd see a couple of them, and there'd always be one that would start roarin'.'

'What? "G'wan Lohan!"'

'Somethin' like that,' he laughs.

An interview normally takes between one and two hours. It's quite rare one goes for more than two hours. Three hours after being ushered into Lohan's house, we're stood outside in the driveway on a bitter Sunday evening in early March as Lohan chats away frivolously about the Munster rugby team. There's actually a tear streaming down his face from the cold. Not that he would feel the cold. Jeez, you think, what a decent skin – a sound, friendly bloke. What about the distant, intimidating Lohan of yore, the one like Keyser Söze who, if called on, would butcher his wife and children? He's even mentioned retiring from the club scene – that he's 'gone pure soft'. What's wrong with the world?

Former teammate Brian Quinn has said that the great thing about Lohan is that 'he's very loyal. He'll always back you up.' No doubt. Still wouldn't like to have him mark you, though.

Twenty minutes into the first half of the 2001 National League hurling final between Clare and Tipperary, a Tipp corner-forward – debutant Lar Corbett – followed a ball into the corner of Semple Stadium's pitch. 'The boy Corbett chases the ball out over near the end-line,' reported Ó Muircheartaigh on the radio before switching pitch to tenor, and rattling car dashboards across the country: 'The maaaan Lohan comes away with the ball!'

MARTIN BRASSIL

Red Rum, three-time winner of the Aintree Grand National, was BBC's Sports Personality of the Year in 1977. It seems almost comical that a horse could scoop this prestigious award, but it's a measure of the place that the National holds in the public's popular imagination.

Martin Brassil, born in August 1956, added another chapter to the race's storied 170-year history in 2006 when he saddled the winner, *Numbersixvalverde*. Remarkably, it was Brassil's first time entering the race as a trainer; he had ridden at Aintree as an amateur in one of the chases in 1982, the year that *Ben Nevis* stormed home in the National. *Numbersix*'s triumph was fairy-tale stuff.

Brassil grew up, he says, on a 'very small farm holding' in Newmarket-on-Fergus, County Clare. The family is consumed with racing. One brother, John, is an established trainer; Michael, his other brother, has campaigned successfully on the point-to-point field; while his sisters and their spouses have had the kind of stock in 'legs' of horses that only a mafia family would rival.

Brassil got the bug early. While at school, he mucked about first on his brother John's pony, and then on his neighbour's pony, *Caesar*, who, incidentally, was owned by the father of international show-jumper, Shane Carey. Michael Brassil – Martin's older brother by nine years – recalls the day Martin and *Caesar* first met. 'I remember meeting

Shane's father one day, and he said, "Do you know anyone who'd ride a hardy pony for me?"

'And I said, "What height is he?"

'He said, "14.2hh. This fella's a tough divil. You'd want a hardy lad."

'I said, "Martin's riding well at the moment. Give him a chance on him."

'So he said, "Bring him down tomorrow evening to Bunratty."

'Martin was twelve at the time. So I went down anyway, and this pony was pulled out, and he'd a step on him like a horse. Jesus – the head above in the air and he prancing around the place. So we brought him down to this field anyway. There were two brothers, Pat and Seán – the father of the show-jumping lad. So Seán led him and Pat brought a ladder, a big long timber ladder; neither of them was letting on what this ladder was for. There was a gap below in the field – there was no gate in it – so Pat put the ladder across the two piers. He gave Martin a leg up and said, "Try and pop him over that." Pop it? It was higher than the top of the mirror,' he says, still in disbelief, as he points at a huge mirror resting over his fireplace. I thought it was a film I was watching. The pony turned, took one look at it, three strides and up over it like a bullet. He turned him back and up over it again. "Jaysus," I said, "This is a serious pony."'

Brassil was hooked after that. For three years, himself and *Caesar* paraded around the country, Sunday to Sunday, competing in show-jumping gymkhanas – sometimes two competitions a day, and remaining unbeaten.

He was enchanted with the horse-racing game, but his brother John – a professional jockey – broke his neck while Martin was at school in St Flannan's College, which meant 'the last thing' that his parents wanted was for him to follow in his footsteps. Instead, he was press-ganged into doing hotel management. Peter Malone – Martin's brother-in-law and future chief executive of Jury's Hotel Group – was given the task of cajoling him into the trade. It worked, but only for a short spell. On Christmas Eve 1975, while working at the Shelbourne

Hotel, Brassil called his brother John – who was in Cork, working for Mick Neville – looking for an exit strategy. 'When I had a year and a quarter down in hotel management, I rang him and told him I was getting out, and could he fix me up with a job, and thankfully he did,' he says.

He had a year at Neville's yard before moving to a job at Mick O'Toole's. He has great affection for O'Toole, who trained several Cheltenham winners, including the 1977 Gold Cup winner, *Davy Lad*. Brassil spent ten years under his tutelage, being responsible for O'Toole's only classic winner, *Dickens Hill*, who won the Irish 2000 Guineas, the Eclipse, and also finished second in two Derbys. 'He was a very flamboyant sort of man, great to be around. A great man to take a chance,' he says, drawing attention to a picture that rests on the piano in his sitting-room of himself and O'Toole at a function. Brassil was particularly taken with O'Toole's perfectionism. 'He was very thorough and very professional. He'd leave nothing to chance,' he says. It's something those close to Brassil see in him, too.

Full of *bonhomie*, Ennisman Bernard Carroll – a property developer – is the owner of *Numbersixvalverde*, and has known Brassil for nearly twenty years; in fact, Brassil once rode a winner, *How's the Boss*, for him in 1990. Trivia fans might be interested to know that he named *Numbersix* after his holiday home in Quinta Do Lago on the Algarve, and that he decks him in the colours of Palmerstown Rugby Club. When prompted about what makes Brassil tick, Carroll quickly cites his exactness. 'He's a very patient guy. He's meticulously into detail. I would call him conservative. That's just the facts as I would see it. He won't take any risks. It can be frustrating to be an owner with him. That would be an opinion others would have given me as well. His being meticulous can lead you then to missing smaller days but getting the big one.'

Ted Walsh concurs. He has known Brassil since the Clareman was sixteen and attended his wedding. 'We talk every day,' he says. 'We're friends right through. Martin is a very quiet, soft-spoken fella, like most of the family. His father and mother were gentle people. He's a real grafter, first of all. He's very meticulous about preparing a horse, a very dedicated fella, really conscientious about doing it right.

'He'd be a serious fella. He wouldn't be the greatest fella in the world to sell himself. He's a quiet fella. If you'd loads of money, you wouldn't want anyone on your side except Martin Brassil. He'd be trustworthy and do the job to a tee. Anywhere Martin was, anyone would have nothing but the highest praise for him.'

'His biggest trait is that he has fierce patience and he gives horses an amount of time,' adds Michael Brassil. 'He's unbelievable for detail. He leaves nothing to chance. He's unreal about legs and feeding and giving them time and not rushing them.'

Brassil himself will joke that he 'has a head like a sieve', but in conversation has an historian's grasp of dates, and easily calls out phone numbers from memory. One detail he paid particular attention to at O'Toole's was that he surrounded himself with good people. 'What I noticed was that he'd a brilliant staff there the whole time,' says Brassil. 'It's the secret to any successful yard – you can't do everything yourself,' he suggests.

Brassil has five staff on the books at his modern yard, Dunmurray Hall, near Rathangan, County Kildare. The family home is a short canter away, where he lives with his wife Deirdre – a psychiatric nurse – and their four kids.

He had a dozen horses under his charge when *Numbersix* won the Irish Grand National in March 2005 – a figure that doubled within a year. He has around twenty-five horses on his books at present; he wants to keep it at that number as he feels individual attention – or 'quality' – will suffer if he grows much further.

'Martin wouldn't ever be into huge numbers like a hundred horses or anything because he wouldn't be a socialiser,' adds Ted Walsh. 'He'd get it on his ability, which is a great thing rather than being able to cultivate people, working people and [doing] PR. Martin is a family man. He'd be going out for a drink with Deirdre and his own pals. He wouldn't be going on the social scene to grab horses. Basically, to be a huge success, that's what you have to do – to be a Paul Nicholls or a Noel Meade, you have to be able to put yourself about and let people know you're there.'

Brassil beams while showing off *Nickname*, another illustrious racer in his stables, who he picked up that summer after *Numbersix*'s win at Fairyhouse in the Irish National. Having been a high-class juvenile hurdler in France, *Nickname* sustained an injury that was so serious, a panel of vets in Switzerland reckoned he might never race again. Rejuvenated under Brassil's charge, he 'campaigned him very, very cleverly,' says Donn McClean, racing correspondent for the *Sunday Times*. A horse that needs soft ground, he kept running him in Ireland but only on soft ground. He had clocked up five wins that season by the time he kicked up at the Cheltenham Festival in 2007 with a view to entering the Queen Mother Champion Chase. 'He didn't run him, which was fair play to him, I thought,' says McClean, 'because the easy thing then was to allow him run: "Ah, sure, we're here and let him run." But he walked the track in the morning and just thought it wasn't safe or he wasn't happy for him on it, so he took him out, which was a hard thing to do. He obviously has the horse's interest at heart.'

Having ridden about forty winners, Brassil's jockeying career came to an end in April 1991 when he damaged his ankle at a race in Punchestown. Typically for a jockey, he dismisses the gravity of the injury, which took a number of operations to sort out. 'Ah sure, look – when you're riding horses … like, I would have broken collar bones, shoulder blades, fingers. You can fix bones,' he says.

'To this day, if he drove for an hour and got out of the car, he wouldn't be able to walk, he'd be so stiff,' says Michael Brassil. 'He shattered bones all over. There's bits of bone they could never really put back together.'

The day he smashed his ankle, the foundations for his house were being poured. 'I hadn't given it to a builder – I was doing it direct labour, so I found myself in an old battered-up Datsun and a trailer, getting fellas to do different bits and pieces. It probably kept me very occupied. Then in September 1993 I cast around to see who'd support me if I started training. I started off with four or five horses,' he says.

His first runner was in January of the following year. The mare – owned by Miss World runner-up, Siobhán McClafferty – was called *Aberedw*. Later, as it happened, she became the dam of *Hedgehunter*. His first winner came a few months later – in May 1994 – in a maiden hurdle in Killarney with *Nordic Thorn*, who won six races in total for him, although one was a week later than it possibly should have been. Brassil laughs at the memory. He discovered on the Saturday before a race that the rules for declaring had changed – you had to declare on a Friday for a race on a Sunday. '"What am I going to do?"' he said to himself, anxious not to unsettle its owners unnecessarily. '"I better look first at what's coming up next." There was a big hurdle race in Gowran Park. "There's a nicer race for that fella next Sunday," I said.' He duly won.

'The day before I had another winner,' he says. 'It was called *Practice Run*. I'd been down to Bolger's that September, and Jim would always let you ride a horse to see if you liked him, and he said, "Go on down the gallop and let him come up there with Anthony."

'Two of us rode down, and this young fella was talking and telling me he was after breaking his leg through the winter, and he was getting heavy, and he was probably going to have to ride over jumps, and if I had any rides going, would I give him a shout.

'So Anthony Powell rode *Nordic Thorn* when he won his first hurdle race, then he won in Gowran that day, but I'd a horse in the previous day – a two-day meeting there in June – and I rang Bolger's and I booked this young fella, Anthony McCoy. He went to England the following few weeks. I remember Bolger ringing me. He says: "You *ring* him. Tell him he's too young. Tell him he needs another year."

'I says: "I will not tell him. He's after getting a good job." He went over to Toby Balding. He rode seventy-three winners conditional, and he only started halfway through the season. Champion ever since.'

Indeed, although McCoy has yet to ride an Aintree Grand National winner. 'Nobody plans to win the Grand National unless you're J. P. McManus,' says Brassil in consideration of the feat.

Brassil rides *Numbersix* out most days. Although *Numbersix* didn't win in any of his first five bumpers, Brassil was unfazed, feeling he would come into his own once he went chasing, which would play to his key attributes. 'He's a very active horse. He doesn't like to be crowded when he's out in a string of horses. He makes unbelievable use of himself. When you see him out loose in a field or that, you'd think that he was a ballet dancer. You wouldn't think his feet were touching the ground. He's not quite that way when you're riding him. I always felt that, as a horse, whatever he gave you, he always had plenty more to give. The big occasion of those races always brought out the best in a horse like him. He has unlimited stamina. He has a great method of jumping.

'For a horse to be a National horse, you can't be really extravagant. *Nickname* could fall at the first in the National because he'd go down and he'd just let fly, not realising there's a five-foot drop the far side. Whereas *Numbersix* would weigh up everything. He could spot a horse making a mistake in front of him – he'd have it weighed up to avoid him.

'Even the day Ruby [Walsh] rode him in the Irish National – Niall Madden [who partnered the horse at Aintree] rode a horse for Noel Meade in it, and he fell at around the sixth, and he fell almost under his feet, and Ruby went to pull him right, and he shot left, like that,' he says, darting his hands for effect. 'Ruby said he nearly fell off him. He had his mind made up where he was going. He's very quick, very nimble on his feet.'

He beat *Jack High* by a whisker that day.

'Much as I was delighted for Martin winning,' says Ted Walsh wearily, 'it was mixed a bit because I had the second horse.'

It was a tangled web. Walsh's horse, *Jack High* – partnered by Garret Cotter – was pipped at the post by a horse trained by his close friend and ridden by his son Ruby. It was a 'weird' feeling, Ruby remarked afterwards.

The victory – which had come a couple of months after *Numbersix* had won the Thyestes Chase by beating *Kymandjen* by a short head and becoming the first horse since 1976 to complete the double – set up a trip to Aintree the following year (2006). Brassil remembers the crossing to Liverpool vividly. He went over on the Wednesday. 'I brought the horse over myself on the trailer. He travelled well. It was one of the concerns I had – how he would travel – because he goes everywhere in the trailer here. Once or twice, I sent him in a lorry to the racetrack. He didn't enjoy it at all. He sweated a lot.'

The journey went smoothly except for some navigation hiccups on the home stretch, which required him to stop and ask for directions once he got near Aintree. 'I wouldn't have a great sense of direction when it comes to roads, but at least the horse hasn't the same problem,' he quipped after the race to Sue Barker, BBC TV's anchor.

On the morning of the race, he walked the track, glad of the six millimetres of rainfall the night before. He didn't take much notice of the commotion of race day. 'You'd be caught up in your own little world, doing what you have to do,' he explains, adding with trademark coolness, 'It's not something that I was overawed with.'

He says he didn't give much advice to the jockey, Niall 'Slippers' Madden – a twenty-year-old riding in his first National, and the son of Clareman 'Boots' Madden and brother of 'Socks' Madden. 'I just said go out and enjoy yourself,' he says. 'Don't have him going any faster than he wants for the first circuit. Jump off a handy position and make sure he's up there and sees the first three fences, anyway. If the race is going too fast for him, go along at his own pace. If they're going too fast on the first circuit, his stamina will come into play on the second one, which it did.'

Brassil was hardly able to watch the race. 'I went to watch it with the binoculars, but, sure, I'd to put them down [his hands were shaking so much]. I couldn't see him on the [TV] screens. When he came back around in front of the stands and jumped the water, I spotted where he was, about twentieth. Next thing, he was about eighth or ninth, and I could pick him out from there. I was happy to see that he was in the first half a dozen. With four [jumps] out, I said if he jumps the last few at least he's run a good race.'

Numbersix wasn't settling for that. His stamina pulled him past the two leaders – Ruby Walsh on *Hedgehunter* and Anthony McCoy on *Clan Royal* – in a pulsating finish, managing to win the four-and-a-half-mile bruiser by six lengths. Nina Carberry piloting *Forest Gunner* was the last home of only nine finishers.

Strains of 'Spancil Hill' and 'From Clare to Here' rang out in the winners' enclosure. 'There was a huge Clare crowd there – Noel Glynn, Pat Quinn, Donal Carey,' says Carroll. 'We all got together then. There was three hours of singsong and drinking champagne in the Owners and Trainers' [area]. We led that place a merry dance. It was great *craic*.'

When Brassil woke up the following morning, he had seventy-four text messages waiting. The celebrations went on for weeks afterwards; indeed, the impact of the win is still reverberating. 'It's the one race you're not allowed forget,' says Brassil. 'You could win a Derby; the following week it's the Eclipse. There's always another race to take its place. With the National, it's not that way at all. Everyone would recognise you now that you've won a National. It's the one race that people that wouldn't watch racing would have a bet in.'

The win has made life easier in a way, he suggests, and harder in another sense – the workload having increased. But the quiet satisfaction that it has brought to this incredibly unassuming man – see, for example, the simple announcement on the plaque that adorns his yard: '*Numbersixvalverde* was trained at Dunmurry Hall by Martin Brassil' – is the stuff that dreams are made of.

'We all walked the track, amazed to be there,' recalls Ted Walsh about the day himself and Brassil were at Aintree in 1982. 'At that stage, Martin was saying, "I'd love to have a ride in the National." In his wildest dreams, he couldn't have thought he was going to go back there twenty-four years later and train the winner. Most fellas going to a concert, to a famous stage, would say, whether it's Carnegie Hall or the Grand Ole Opry, "Wouldn't it be great to play here?" Not to be the main act!

'It's like a young fella,' he says, warming to his theme, 'walking around Croke Park and saying, "Jeez, this is a great place. I'd love to play here some day." But you wouldn't say to yourself, "I'd like to play in the All-Ireland and be getting the Liam McCarthy handed down to me."

'It's the same achievement as Anthony Daly to come out of all the young Clare fellas to win an All-Ireland when you consider ye hadn't won any kind of fuckin' All-Ireland. It wouldn't be as much if it was Cork – 'cause they win All-Irelands – or Kerry, but a Clare fella?

'For Martin Brassil to go and win the English National was gigantic. Gigantic. No Clareman had ever trained the winner of the National. Here he was, coming to win the most famous steeplechase in the world, the *crème de la crème* of jump racing. It's of the same proportions as Pádraig Harrington winning the British Open.'

MARCUS HORAN

Prop forwards aren't your average species. They spend their Saturday afternoons as a point in a battering contest between two 130-stone packs of men. They revel in the brutal, arcane combat of scrummaging; an area where few rugby fans and fewer referees understand what goes on. Recent law changes mean that they spend a lot of their down-time from scrums lifting twenty-stone second-rowers at the lineout. The rest, by and large, is spent hitting rucks, driving off the side of them, or tackling.

To be a prop, you'd almost want a screw loose. Some of them actually have. Or *had*. The French prop Armand Vaquerin – capped twenty-six times – killed himself playing Russian roulette in 1993.

You can spot props easily as they shuffle into position for a national anthem before international matches. Wide as they are tall. Square-jawed, they rarely have discernable necks. And they're usually hairy, cranky-looking buggers. Then there's Marcus Horan.

'Fresh-faced, clean-cut, all the things you don't expect a prop forward to be,' laughs Alan Gaffney, who trained Horan as coach of Munster for three seasons and is presently working with him on the Irish squad. 'Marcus is a bit different because Marcus is not your big, lumbering, eighteen-stone prop. Marcus has gone out there on a constant basis and played against guys with two and three and four stone on him, but Marcus will give as good as he gets.

'He's a rough and tough boy. He's not this person that goes out for deliberate to-dos, but he's tough. He'll give and take, and he's got by because he's got a good technique. Apart from the fact that he's a dogged scrummager, he's very, very quick for a prop, and he's got exceptionally good skills.'

Given his physique and preponderance for conspicuous athleticism, Horan has received a lot of stick over the years for a perceived weakness in scrummaging or as rugby's technical experts put it 'his arse isn't big enough'. Energy expended – the traditionalists tut-tut – in forty-yard bursts with the ball is energy lost to scrum time. Indeed, after Horan and his Munster and Irish colleague John Hayes had an admittedly tough evening against Leicester in January 2007 – the day Thomond Park was breached in a Heineken Cup game for the first time in eleven years – the Welsh coach, Gareth Jenkins, rejigged his front row for the Wales–Ireland encounter in the belief that Gethin Jenkins and Chris Horsman would go to town on the Shannon pair. The plan backfired woefully. The Irish scrum overturned the Welsh unit, helping Ireland to eke out a win in Cardiff's Millennium Stadium.

Still the sceptics muttered darkly. A slew of English 'experts' – in a bout of uninformed punditry – decried the fact that English coach Brian Ashton had left out Leicester's Julian White for the historic February 2007 Croke Park fixture between Ireland and England, suggesting Ashton 'was missing a trick in not bringing in White to try and terrorise Marcus Horan and the Irish scrum as he terrorised Horan and the Munster scrum in the Heineken Cup.'

Referencing the announcement of the English team, another journalist suggested that if White was picked, 'Horan would already have endured a dreadful five days of doubt.' Again, Horan trumped his critics. Overturning an old nemesis – the English captain, Phil Vickery – Horan scored eight out of ten from Robert Kitson, the *Guardian*'s rugby correspondent. 'Against England, he has probably never had a better day at the scrummaging coalface,' gushed Gerry Thornley in the *Irish Times*.

'One thing about Marcus Horan scrummaging is that he mightn't be the strongest, but if you let off on him at all, he'll go to town on you. There's a fella who scrummages for the first eighty minutes,' says Mick Galwey, who used to pack down on his side for both Munster and Shannon. 'Traditionally, scrummagers would take it easy after a while, but I can guarantee Marcus will be going as hard in the last scrum as he will in the first scrum. The guy would never give up. That's the one thing I noticed about him. You'd have to work all day with Marcus. There's no such thing as lying in and taking it handy.'

The political reverberations in the run-in to that game against England – the first by an English team in Croke Park, nearly eigthy-seven years after the butchery of Bloody Sunday – made for an emotional afternoon. 'The proudest moment for us, funnily enough, would have been the English national anthem and the reaction from the supporters. I just thought it was amazing. That silence then between their national anthem … you could feel the build-up,' says Horan, almost helping to summon up the hairs-on-the-back-of-your-neck feeling … 'Guys were just welling up, like. Then, we just belted it out.

'It was an amazing day. That feeling then, from the flipside of depressing a nation the previous Monday [a fortnight before, after narrowly losing to France] compared to the elation that was there the following day after the England game was unreal.'

Horan was born in September 1977, growing up in Clonlara, County Clare. He's one of six siblings. Rugby was an acquired taste for the four boys. 'Certainly, there was no drive from the parents,' says his eldest brother Paul. 'My father [from Tipperary] used to be bored out of his tree watching rugby matches. He had a complete GAA background. He'd go because we needed a lift. He said it was like watching milk go sour. That was his opinion on it.'

Younger brother Marcus has vague memories of watching Irish Triple Crown triumphs on TV, but he got the rugby bug in earnest having been hauled along as a ten-year-old to the 1987 Munster Schools' Junior Cup final to watch his brother Paul playing for St Munchin's College at Thomond Park. 'It was a run-down old shack with barbed wire over the walls,' says Marcus of his first memory of visiting the hallowed ground. 'It was before the stand was done up. I remember passing it for years and wondering what the hell was in there, you know? It was a weird place. I remember when the final whistle blew – as was tradition, everyone jumped the wall and ran in. Myself and my brother [Philip] were only young fellas. We were running towards our brother, and he roared at us to get back out in case we got crushed.'

The experience was enough to get him scampering around the garden at home with a football doubling as a rugby ball. All that was needed was for him to figure out a position to take up. Prop seemed a good fit.

'He was kinda chunky,' says Paul. 'In some of the interviews he did before, he mentioned that I used to have him propping down the hall at home. I guess that was my thinking of it at the time – that he was chunky, that he'd fit into that position fairly handy; though what I was doing trying to teach him to prop I've no idea. I couldn't do what I was supposed to do myself.'

Once he arrived at St Munchin's, Horan was swept away by the game. Hurling – in which he used to play mostly centre-forward for Clonlara – began to take second place, though it remains a passion. Indeed, the 2007 Clare hurling manager, Tony Considine, presented Horan with a signed jersey from the Clare hurling team in the run-up to the Irish rugby team's first game at GAA headquarters.

As a first year in secondary school, he remembers the towering presence of Anthony Foley – the school's rugby captain – and the intoxicating feeling that year of jumping on board one of the ten or eleven buses down to Cork – awash with colours and singing – for a Munster Senior Schools' semi-final win over Christians. Horan later helped the school to a Junior Cup victory in 1993 against a Presentation Brothers College team that included Peter Stringer and Mick O'Driscoll.

Watching from a distance as Keith Wood's career took off further emboldened Horan's ambition. A regular visitor to the house, Wood had been a classmate of his brother Paul. Horan's ascension up the ranks was textbook, passing each stage post along Ireland's circuit for elite under-age rugby players: Munster Schools', Irish Schools', Munster under-20s, as well as playing on an Ireland under-21 Triple Crown-winning side alongside O'Driscoll, Ronan O'Gara, David Wallace and Frankie Sheahan.

He couldn't have learned the art of forward play at a better academy than Shannon; he tips his hat, in passing, at the influence of Niall O'Donovan. Horan was the youngest member of the club's historic All-Ireland League four-in-a-row winning team in 1998 – a team whose pack included grizzly gauchos like Hayes, Galwey, Foley, Eddie Halvey and Alan Quinlan. For a loose-head prop, his boyish looks raised a few eyebrows initially.

'I'll always remember we were playing a match above in Bective,' says Galwey, 'and the next thing, this young pup – to this day, I still call him the pup, Puppy – this young fella comes on with a baby face on him, which he still has, and I was saying to myself, "Who's this little muppet?" because he looked like he was fifteen, you know? But, fair dues to him, from the off, what a player.'

After Shannon, came Munster. He couldn't have received his ticket aboard the Munster train at a better time, securing his first professional contract in the autumn of 1999 while a student of electronics at LIT. He says he nearly threw his college books into the Shannon after getting the offer from Declan Kidney. A few weeks later, in Munster's away pool game to French side, Colomiers in the European Cup, a catalogue of disasters turned their front row into a sick bay. 'Before the match, that other soft cock [Peter] Clohessy cried off, which meant

Marcus was getting his first cap. Then, twenty minutes into the game, John Hayes pulled out, so Ian Murray from Cork came in, and, in fairness, Ian Murray gave it everything, and with about five minutes to go, Ian Murray went down,' says Galwey, allowing himself a chuckle. 'So we had to put Woody in propping, which meant we had Marcus, Frankie Sheahan and Woody in the front row.'

It was an incredible night. Munster won and Horan scored a try into the bargain. Coming after the win away to Saracens, it was another notable early scalp in what has become Munster's never-ending European odyssey. 'I remember after the game,' says Horan, 'there must have been about twenty supporters on the far side. That's all that travelled – they were the early days. There was such emotion. This was the first time that an Irish team had won on French soil in this competition. It only started sinking in when we jogged across the field, and we clapped and waved to our supporters, and then when you think of how that just rocketed into the crowds we had at Twickenham the same year.'

Horan topped off a fairy-tale season by winning his first cap for Ireland in a game against the US in the summer of 2000, but was hit by 'second-album syndrome' as he found his path blocked for the following two seasons – in what he admits was a frustrating time for a young buck in a hurry – by that old 'soft cock' Clohessy. There was no arms-around-the-shoulder pep talks from the legendary Young Munster prop to his apprentice during that time – which, in effect, was a compliment to Horan. 'He's a quiet guy,' says Horan about The Claw. 'He's a real messer, like, but he wouldn't be the kind of guy that would purposefully come over and give you advice. But he's a guy that I felt I learned an awful lot from, anyway, just from watching the way he played. I think it was more out of respect that he maybe felt that I was a threat that he wasn't giving me advice.

'A man of few words,' he adds. 'He would never have said anything to me personally but I think the one thing I would draw from him is how much Munster and the area meant to him. For a man that people felt was so tough, it would be rare that he would be in a dressing-room without a tear in his eye going out onto the pitch, and that would inspire any man, you know? Gallimh [Mick Galwey] would have been the same, and you think, "Jeez, this means the world to them."'

Horan speaks convincingly about the parish feel that the Munster camp engenders, and the advantage that their camaraderie gives them over more vaunted teams they encounter; teams, for example, such as Stade Toulousain or ASM Clermont Auvergne, both with access to five, six times Munster's annual budget. It's an *esprit de corps* that helps to explain the province's phenomenal record in Europe over the last decade. 'For us, when you're in a dressing-room, you can see it in a guy's face how much it means to them. It's one thing the new guys that we got [in 2007–08] noticed. They've seen it. They've seen guys – Ronan O'Gara, Anthony Foley – talking in the dressing-room … "God, this really means something to them." They row in with it. John Langford was one guy that really embraced the whole Munster thing. Jim Williams was another man … Shaun Payne – they know what it's like because they come from similar backgrounds, you know? They realise what this means to us, and then you'll get the odd guy that comes over and they're just there to better their career. Off with them.

'You can see with teams that are put under pressure. Big-name teams – and it's happened so many times when they've come to Thomond Park – when they're put under pressure, they fold, because they don't know what the guy beside them is like. Is he going to back them up? We've been in situations where the shit hits the fan and you know that the guy beside you is going to back you to the hilt. You can't buy that. You just can't.'

Horan has savoured many of the great days at Thomond Park. Interestingly, he points out that the mosh-pit atmosphere there doesn't just materialise from the ether. 'A thing Gallimh always said to us, even when we were playing with Shannon: "The supporters aren't gonna win the game for you. They don't just come out and start shouting. You've gotta give them something to shout about." It's a great point in the sense that they're a knowledgeable crowd, they know their rugby, and they're not just gonna come out and make the atmosphere for you. I think that's one of the key things if you look back at any of the games. There have always been great moments. I think Paul's [O'Connell] hit on [Sale player, Sébastien] Chabal [in the 2006 European Cup] would be a big one. Moments like that would lift the crowd.'

Horan has given Munster fans a thing or two to cheer about in his days there: two tries against Gloucester in 2004 and a try against Stade Français – a personal favourite – in the quarter-final later that spring. The try was more like what you'd expect to see from a French three-quarter than an Irish prop, as he jinked his way through their defence to score at a time in the game when Munster were struggling.

Of course, Horan has a bit of a reputation for eye-catching tries. In the 2008 Six Nations encounter between Ireland and Scotland, he had the audacity to turn up on the wing to gather a trademark O'Gara cross-field lob and spill over for a try. In fact, in fifty-eight games for Ireland, he's notched up six tries; not bad going considering the revered Irish prop Phil Orr – one-time world-record holder for caps as a prop forward – never scored an international try in fifty-eight appearances. Or that six tries is also the try-scoring haul for Irish and Lions players, Rob Henderson and Tyrone Howe. And both of them were backs.

Horan nearly missed out on Munster's historic win in the 2006 European Cup. He popped a calf during a scrummaging session on the Tuesday after the team's quarter-final win over Perpignan. Missing the semi-final game over Leinster was the toughest eighty minutes he had to endure in a rugby ground, but he made the starting fifteen for the final, despite not being fully match fit. 'I had all the work done,' he says, putting his condition in context. 'My fitness base was pretty good before that, and the fact that it's a European Cup final would give you an extra twenty per cent from somewhere, definitely. Obviously, you wouldn't finish the game, and I didn't finish the game, but I remember hitting the first scrum and just felt, "This is good; this feels good." From then on, you're buzzin'.'

The European Cup win two years later was a lot more fulfilling – the majesty of the controlled manner in which the Munster pack closed out the game. Pick and go. Pick and go like an assembly line. Henry Ford would have enjoyed the symmetry of it, and, of course, there was the satisfaction of being part of a more mature, professional outfit doing the business.

'Everyone felt a bit more confident than in 2006," says Horan. "We were a bit more relaxed. I felt myself, personally, I was. I think it kinda showed, too, after the game. A lot of the guys, myself included, we seemed to enjoy the celebrations way more. There wasn't the tension there of 2006, the "God if we lose again, it'll be three finals". That was gone this year. We had got the monkey off our back. It was just go out there and enjoy it, enjoy the occasion. Looking back on it now, the celebrations afterwards, it was such a way better feeling the second time around. Obviously that we were relaxed but Jesus, we'd done it a second time, you know? It was not just a flash-in-the-pan-sort of thing.'

The 2007 World Cup was the low point in his career, he admits. 'Personally, I felt I wasn't playing well, anyway,' he says. 'We're a bunch of guys there that take things to heart. You try and do everything right. The work ethic had been superb that year … The most frustrating thing was that no one could put their finger on what happened.

'I think the hardest thing is that everyone has to live with this, now. That it's a black mark, I suppose, on your career, and you can never take it back. For a couple of guys there, they know they're not going to make the next one. You can never fix that, you know?'

Horan always maintains a keen sense of *omertà* around the teams he is part of – a trait that was tested to the limit during and after the World Cup failure, given the high expectations that announced the team's arrival at the tournament. 'He would be pig-headed in some respects in terms of being very hard to talk to about the goings-on inside the camp at the World Cup, for example,' confides his brother Paul. 'He's very single-minded about the job, and I'm sure they have respect for the coaches. He wouldn't go around blabbing about what goes on internally.'

The consternation that enveloped the Irish camp during the pool stages left Horan with a queasy feeling, not least because of what he sees as the abdication of the Irish press's responsibilities regarding the rumours saga. 'One day, coming back from training, one of the boys started listing out all these rumours,' he says. 'I actually thought they'd made them up for the *craic*, but these were actually genuine rumours. They got an email. Some of them were crazy, unbelievable. Some of them you can laugh at, but some of them were fairly hurtful.

'I think it was the one thing that you learnt from the World Cup – that once the comments in the paper go beyond rugby, it's wrong. It hurt a lot of guys. It's very hard to concentrate on rugby when there are other things happening, when you've got to worry about your personal life as well.

'I was disappointed with the Irish press that they didn't support and row in behind us. They should have been close enough to the team to know that there was nothing going on. They ask you a question at the end of the day, and you say, "Nothing", and they didn't buy it: "No, no, you're not telling us the truth." That's disappointing.'

When prompted about the players he admired in his days soldiering on a rugby field, Horan cites Foley – 'one of our own' – Martin Johnson and Jason Leonard, whom, he suggests, was a real throwback to the *bonhomie* of the amateur era. They exchanged jerseys after the Grand Slam decider at Lansdowne Road in March 2003, and after the game, Leonard burst into the Irish dressing-room with a six-pack of beers, which he shared with Horan, Hayes and hooker, Shane Byrne.

Not surprisingly, he has less fond memories of the Frenchmen he's scrummaged against. 'The toughest guys I've come across would be some of the French guys,' he says about troublesome opponents. 'That's their bread and butter. There are certain teams that put all their efforts into certain things, and the scrums would be their big thing. For the All Blacks, it would be more of an open game. The Springboks, then, are just big men, so they can get away with not working on it so much. You always get one or two guys who are pretty tough, and you relish it more when you can get through these games.'

One of those games, undoubtedly, was the 'Miracle Match' in January 2003. It was Horan's first full season in the Munster loose-head jersey. Gloucester came to town with a formidable front row – Rodrigo Roncero, Olivier Azam, and that man Vickery again, the 2001 British and Irish Lions tight-head test prop. 'They had an all-international front row, and they were beating up teams every weekend over in England,' says Sheahan – Munster hooker that day. 'It was a massive game for us. We said, "Jesus, we'll be up against it." Marcus was outstanding. He not only held his own, but he shunted Vickery off a few of their balls. Not only did it set a platform, but it really set a marker down, to let them know that we weren't giving an inch; in fact, we were going the other way and they wouldn't get a sniff for the whole day.'

Another auspicious day for the not-so-average prop forward from Clonlara.

JAMES O'CONNOR

There's a picture hanging in the kitchen of James O'Connor's parents' house of him on the run, slightly arched, amid the shadows of the Hogan Stand, flashing over the winning point for Clare against Tipperary in the 1997 All-Ireland hurling final. It captures the moment that every young hurler dreams about; the one practised against the gable-end of houses up and down the country every dry evening for generations.

It was the culmination of an incredible year for O'Connor, garlanded with a Hurler of the Year award. Just turned twenty-five years of age, at the peak of his powers, he had helped Clare to a second All-Ireland title in three years. After the bedlam of 1995, when the hurling world was overrun with *bodhráns* for the first time, 1997 'was very much about business,' he says. Whereas the breakthrough had been a scorching summer of dramatic, faltering victories, this was the perfect storm. Each of the game's three aristocrats – Cork, Tipperary and Kilkenny – was picked off; Tipp (sorry about that) twice for good measure.

On a personal level, the final hadn't gone strictly according to plan. O'Connor, after an unsatisfactory (by his own exacting standards) final in 1995, came into the dressing-room at half-time in 1997 frustrated. Here he was, back in the All-Ireland final, his side were four points down, and the game was passing him by. 'At the end of the day, the All-Ireland is the big day. That's the day you judge yourself on,' reflects Seán McMahon, his teammate with Clare and St Joseph's Doora Barefield. 'He probably felt he didn't perform in 1995, so he probably didn't want it said that he didn't play well in an All-Ireland final. But at half-time, he hadn't played well in the first half against Tipperary, so I just thought he must be putting wicked pressure on himself – "Jeez, I didn't play well in 1995; I'm not playing well now" – but he turned it around completely in the second half. That was, for me, one of his greatest days.'

'Early on in the second half [manager Ger] Loughnane came over,' says O'Connor, 'and said, "Do you want to switch wings?" … I remember thinking afterwards that even though there's mayhem around you in a championship match – it appears – in the middle of it, we were very cool. We were focused on what we were doing. There was no madness. Okay, you're wired going onto the pitch, but once that ball is thrown in, what happens between the four lines – that's all that matters … we were thinking clearly. I can vividly remember that. That Loughnane was obviously thinking clearly; I was thinking clearly. We had that chat: "Do you want to switch wings?"

'"No. I'm starting to get into it." And I did get into it.'

He sure did. 'The last thirty minutes, Jamesie was just awesome in that All-Ireland final,' enthuses full-back Brian Lohan – before adding with evident respect: 'He was helped a lot by [Ollie] Baker; Baker did some awful beltin' that afternoon.'

Writing for the *Irish Times*, Tom Humphries felt O'Connor 'had almost single-handedly turned the tide of the game in the second half', popping over three majestic points from play. Each one picked off from the left-hand side, even though he was playing right half-forward.

Out of position like that. A surprise? Of course not. When O'Connor played hurling, he roamed the park untrammelled, foraging for ball like a forest animal. It was his coach on the Fitzgibbon team at UCG – current Tipperary selector, Eamon O'Shea – who turned him on to this roving, opportunist style. 'He was a great mentor to me,' says O'Connor, who called on O'Shea throughout his career for advice. 'He was the first guy that I could talk to as a forward. I didn't have anybody like that in Clare. He would have spoken to me about different aspects of my game and movement, and running off the ball. I tuned into that.

'He was obviously a highly intelligent fellow and a real thinker about things. I just found this guy was on a wavelength that nobody I have ever spoken to was on because Loughnane was a back, and a lot of people you spoke to weren't thinking at the level this guy was thinking at. In the modern game, you couldn't stand up in a particular zone with [a] Brian Whelahan or with [an] Anthony Daly and expect that you are going to score three or four points from him in that zone. You have to move. We played the training matches in Cusack Park, and I just ran everywhere. I just took off.'

O'Connor was blessed with incredible stamina, and in his bachelor days admits to having had an ambivalent approach to Mike Mac's infamous winter boot camp, recalling one stretch in November 1996 when he clocked up twenty-two training sessions in twenty-one days. 'It was tough. Jeez, it was tough. There's no question about it,' he says, laughing half-heartedly. 'There was a sense of dread going to Crusheen and more of a sense of dread going to Shannon. But we were young, right. And I would have minded myself. I'd have been in good shape, reasonably athletic.

'I don't know what way to put it. I won't say there was a perverse enjoyment out of it, but there was nearly a feeling sometimes of having done a really, really tough physical session – you nearly felt good about it. Plus, as well, you knew the benefits of it. Take 1997, 1998 – I was certainly getting scores in the last ten minutes of matches because of the work that I'd done, and when the game started to open up, you were able to keep going.'

He acknowledges that as a secondary-school teacher, having the summers off enabled him to rest appropriately and prime himself for the championship; and it was rare that toxins entered his system. Teetotal, judicious in his diet, he was a paragon of good health. 'If he came in there now and he turned around, there could be wings on him like a chicken – the amount of chicken he ate,' reckons his old inter-county teammate, Fergie Tuohy. 'We'd all be shovelling in steak and hamburgers, and he'd have chicken with salad, like.'

He was the identikit modern-day hurler, a professional in amateur's clothing five years before Seán Óg Ó hAilpín began to spread his ascetic creed. The Corkman actually marked O'Connor in his own Munster championship debut in 1997 in Limerick's Gaelic Grounds, and again in the following year's championship. 'He was a livewire, like. Jamesie was a livewire,' he says in jaunty Leeside tones. 'For what he lacked in height he made up for in everything else – skill, speed, stamina, hard work. He worked his socks off. He ran everywhere – ran, ran, ran everywhere.

'When the high balls were raining down, he was at the bottom of the pack, getting ready for the crumbs. He was a great comber. In Aussie Rules, he'd be a great "rover" – the rovers in Aussie Rules, when the big guys contest, they're down at the bottom of the pack, feeding off breaking ball.'

O'Connor's touch, his ability to control and scoop up a *sliotar* on the fly in the middle of a mêlée – like a pickpocket in a crowded market – was rare. 'Jamesie was the consummate stickman,' says ex-Cork manager, John Allen. 'He was in the same vein as the O'Connors, Ben and Jerry – the hurley being an extension of their hand. A sweet hurler, he'd be called in Cork.'

One score in particular stands out from his walkabouts, remembers Christy O'Connor, who played with him for both club and county, and points out that his brother's favourite position was as a defensive midfielder: 'He got a score in the 1998 Munster final – the drawn game – against Waterford. He literally ran nearly the length of the pitch. I remember him saying to me afterwards, "I've gone this far, I better make sure to put it over now."'

In total, he knocked over 151 points in forty-three championship games, including nine points against Kilkenny in 1997 – five from play. It was arguably his finest hour. The story goes that having watched one point sail over the bar, Eddie O'Connor – the Kilkenny corner-back – turned to his keeper, Adrian Ronan, and said, 'Don't bother puckin' that ball out anymore.'

O'Connor only bagged two goals in championship play – both against Tipperary, in the drawn game in 1999 and in 2003. Micheál Ó Muircheartaigh sees no fault in this, invoking the game's greatest goal scorer to prove his point. 'Christy Ring used always say, and I heard him saying it myself – even though he used also say, "You won't win All-Irelands without scoring goals" – that "It takes a hurler to score a point. Anyone could get a goal because goals happen. You get a chance. A lot of goals are ones that shouldn't be missed anyway, but you have to hurl better to get points at times," he said, even though he was a goal scorer himself. He had great time for the classy point and Jamesie got many of those, didn't he?'

He seemed to have that blinding burst of pace to pull him away from defenders, too. 'No,' corrects Michael O'Halloran, cornerback for Clare on their two All-Ireland-winning teams in the 1990s. 'I think what he had was that he took up good positions. A classic example of that would be the [winning] point against Tipperary [in the All-Ireland final in 1997]. He's moving fast, but when you're picking the ball in space and hitting the ball on the run, it looks like you're after burning somebody, but the thing is you're after picking up a good position and you're after coming on to the ball and you take it on five or ten yards.

'I don't think he had blistering, burning pace. D. J. would have had explosive pace. Kevin Broderick might have been another one, but I don't think Jamesie was overly fast. He'd great stamina. His greatest thing was that he was intelligent. He knew how to play his position. He just timed his runs better. I think he'd say himself he played particularly well off Conor Clancy. He'd let Clancy win the ball, horse a tackle or two, and he would suddenly appear at the right time, coming on to the ball at pace to take the pass from Clancy.'

It's true – O'Connor has huge respect for Clancy, and laments the fact that Clare lost the likes of the Kilmaley man and P. J. O'Connell in the later years of his own career – a year or two prematurely, he feels. 'We had six ball-players when we maybe didn't have enough dogs,' he says wistfully of the Clare team that reached the 2002 All-Ireland final.

For all the regard that O'Connor has for Clancy & Co., hurling analyst Liam Griffin argues the Clare forwards of the 1990s weren't as powerful a unit as the one that the other great forward of the era had to draw from. 'Jamesie wasn't playing on the most potent forward line like the likes of [D. J.] Carey was playing on. While he had good players, there was no Henry Shefflin on one side and Charlie Carter on the other. To Jamesie's eternal credit, within that forward line he still was almost uncontainable at top level when he was at the height of his fame and when Clare were going really well in the mid-1990s.'

During Clare's pomp, O'Connor – or 'Jamesie', as he was universally known – was the team's poster boy, their talisman; like D. J. for Kilkenny, he was the only one of the county's players on first-name terms with his fans. 'He was a popular player as well, wasn't he – with the crowd?' asks Ó Muircheartaigh rhetorically. 'You see, he wasn't a big man, but he stood up to big men, and crowds like that – a fella that's fiery – fiery in the playing sense – and Jamesie was that.'

In full flow, he was a sight to behold. What a scrum-half he would have made in rugby with that step he had. Loughnane described him as being 'poetry in motion'. Having stepped down as Clare manager in 2000, he spent time in the stands in 2001 – the year his *Raising the Banner* was published – watching O'Connor and the crowd's response to him. 'It is a joy to watch the reaction when Jamesie is on the ball,' he wrote. 'They are just awestruck. Not just the Clare people – everyone's "looking out of their mouths", as we'd say at home, with the runs he makes and the way he moves. He sends a kind of current through everybody watching.'

Three years later – again with his anthropologist's hat on – Loughnane observed a different mood among Clare supporters, as O'Connor – after an indifferent 2003 campaign – struggled with injuries and patchy form in the early part of the 2004 championship. Writing in his column for the *Star* in typically trenchant language on the morning of Clare's qualifier game against Offaly, he reflected on O'Connor's performance in the previous clash with Laois. 'Even more distressing for all the supporters was the embarrassment suffered by Jamesie O'Connor in that game,' he wrote. 'I hoped he would be taken off at half-time, and when he reappeared for the second-half, you could see the Clare supporters visibly cringe. There is nothing worse than seeing a once-great player being humiliated on the playing field.'

'We met in the Radisson [hotel] before the Offaly game,' says O'Connor. 'We'd a bit of a chat and [selector] Fr Harry just made a point that "We had to stick together and stand up and be counted … what Loughnane has written about Jamesie." I was wondering what that was all about,' he says, laughing at the oddity of being the rallying cry for a conspiracy he knew nothing about. 'The following day, I was inside in the shop [his parents' newsagents] … just went in to get the papers or whatever, and I just said to my sister, "Are yesterday's papers inside in the back, there?" She said, "They are, yeah. Dad wasn't even going to go to the match, you know." When I heard that: "Right, okay. What did he say?"

'As I said at the time, I didn't need anybody to tell me that I was playing poorly. I knew I was playing poorly. Loughnane could have phrased it differently – "That his best days are behind him. Clare really need to be looking at an alternative now" or whatever, and everybody gets the message, but to say that the crowds visibly cringe when he reappeared for the second half … this kind of stuff – I knew myself at the time that that was out of order. He actually wrote to me afterwards. Now I have no problem with Loughnane. I've met Ger subsequently and spoken away grand. That's Loughnane – he doesn't give a damn,' laughs O'Connor.

'I got enough plaudits over the years. When you don't perform, you have to accept the criticism. It cuts both ways. The point of it was when I heard that about my parents. That's different.'

O'Connor's parents had brought him to Clare in 1982. Until then, he had lived in Ballinakill, County Galway. He arrived in St Flannan's College, where he teaches today, in September 1985.

'I remember going down to a match somewhere against North Mon,' says Bishop Willie Walsh, who was teaching in the school at the time and later was a Clare hurling selector when O'Connor made the senior panel. 'Hugh O'Dowd had this under-15 team, and I remember going over to him after ten minutes and saying, "Who's the lad you have wing-back?" Ah, I thought that he was a beaut. He was very small. A pure natural, though.'

O'Connor won two Dr Harty Cups and an All-Ireland colleges' title while a student – captaining the team in his final year at school. That autumn, his club minor side – having lost an under-16B final two years earlier – took on their town rivals, Éire Óg – who had five of his Harty Cup teammates in their line-up – in the county final. It was in the days before Ollie Baker stalked hurling grounds like a human wrecking ball. He lined out as sub goalie that day, and might have had to bring out the oranges at half-time as well. He looked on in awe at O'Connor. 'I remember him inside in the dressing-room after the game. He was vomiting because he had run himself into the ground so much. Physically, he had given everything. It stood out in my mind that you have to push yourself to the limit if you're going to be successful. What he did that day – he won the match on his own. There was fourteen other players there and James.'

O'Connor and Baker went on to enjoy unprecedented success with St Joseph's – capturing three county titles and reaching back-to-back All-Ireland club finals, and winning the 1999 crown. Their national odyssey started in the autumn of 1998, after what *Irish Times* journalist Keith Duggan has described as the Clare team's 'hurling summer of discontent'. First up was Waterford's Mount Sion, which afforded a chance to re-engage with old acquaintances, Tony Browne, Ken McGrath and Anthony Kirwan.

'The championship had gone on late because they had held it up for [Colin] Lynch to serve his suspension, so we were playing the following weekend, and we'd played very poorly in the county final. It was an anti-climax because we were expected to win, but we went down to Mount Sion, and we were organised and professional and ready, and I just remember walking into the dressing-room and they were maybe pucking the ball outside, and it was patently obvious to us that they didn't respect us. We went out and …' – he pauses – 'basically leathered them, to be honest with you,' he says, snaffling a laugh. 'I'll never forget the dressing-room after that game. It was, I suppose, the emotion that we should have shown after the county final coming out then instead. That dressing-room … top five moments of all time. Definitely.'

It almost seems to matter more with the parish. While playing against the Lohan brothers' Wolfe Tones in the quarter-final of the county championship in 2004, he received a nasty gash on the head before half-time. 'He was still groggy and slightly disorientated in the dressing-room, and he became emotional during a game for probably the first time in his career,' wrote Christy O'Connor in an article shortly afterwards. "I've never asked ye for anything," he said to his teammates in the huddle, with tears in his eyes. "But I'm asking ye to carry me now in the second-half."'

'By Jesus, we're going to carry him,' roared Seánie McMahon to the rest of the team. 'We'll die out there if we have to because that man has carried us all long enough.'

MAURA O'CONNELL

'Molly dear now did you hear/ The news that's going round/ Down in a corner of the Deep South/ A love is what you've found …'Nashville, Maura – who'd have thought it? Hot and humid summers, neon, country music and the Grand Ole Opry, bourbon and honky-tonk bars, all those cowboy boots and rhinestone suits – so, so far from your roots.

'She hated Nashville in those days. She thought it was really tacky. She had a very naive view,' says P. J. Curtis, the revered Irish producer/ broadcaster who spirited her there in December 1982 to produce her album, *Maura O'Connell*.

'Oh, Hicksville, no way!' she screeches. 'If you'd told me ten years previous that I'd end up in Nashville, I'd have laughed in your face. It just so happened that I'd a boyfriend who was there, to be totally honest, and there was a music thing happening there that was really, really exciting. The town itself was very uncool, as far as I was concerned. I'd have looked down my nose – "Oh, you're just not hip,"' she says, bursting into that big, throaty laugh of hers.

She moved there for good in 1988, after a few years of ferrying backwards and forwards from Ireland. The 'boyfriend' of the time was none other than Béla Fleck, who has more Grammy awards than you could shake a banjo at. Fleck was playing with the New Grass Revival when they met – a progressive bluegrass band that, along with dobro player, Jerry Douglas, opened up a new and intoxicating world to O'Connell at a time when she was despairing of the live music scene in Ireland in those basket-case days in the 1980s. 'It was an incredibly bleak place, particularly if you were a solo singer without any guitar or song-writing skills! Oh, it was poverty-stricken. There were a couple of venues, if you were doing really well – the Olympia [in Dublin], the Ulster Hall in Belfast, the Opera House in Cork. After that, you were going down a tier or two. For the most part – if you wanted to earn money – most of us opened up for basic discos in noisy places. I used to lose my mind. It was awful. It was awful,' she sighs. 'Oh, I'd be in a sanatorium! I'd have quit …'

Instead, she was swept away by Music City, USA. Easy to see how when you consider the recording milieu she found herself in. In addition to Fleck and Douglas, the working musicians who pitched in on her first solo album included Bobby Whitlock – who had just come off the road with Derek and the Dominos – and Bob Moore on bass, who has played on 17,000 recordings, it is calculated, including sessions with Bob Dylan, Frank Sinatra and all the Elvis records post-1958.

No trouble for O'Connell to hold her own. 'We were doing a take one day in the studio,' remembers Curtis. 'Dr Hook – the guy with the patch – he was wandering through the control rooms to pick up tapes that had been in a side-office, and as he came through the studio – we were sitting at the control desk and Maura was inside, doing her take, headphones on and eyes closed – he stops and goes, "Holy shit! Who is that dame?" Maura O'Connell, an Irish girl. "Wow, that chick sure can sing."'

Because she only does the occasional live gig in Ireland these days, it's difficult to appreciate how big a star she is, particularly in the United States. 'How many Irish artists have been nominated for Grammys?' asks Mike Hanrahan, her one-time collaborator; the question is, of course, rhetorical. O'Connell's album *Helpless Heart* was short-listed for one in 1989.

Nashvillians can't get enough of her. While on a fellowship in Vermont in 2002, the artist Mick O'Dea – a friend of hers since days in their youth spent knocking around Ennis – spent a few days with O'Connell and her family in Nashville. (O'Connell married her husband Mac – a property investor – in 1993; they have a son, Jesse, born in 1996.)

'She's quite a celebrity there,' says O'Dea. 'She showed me some of the local countryside. On one occasion, putting petrol in her car – or gasoline – some guy came up, "You know, we really like your music." She's used to it, and can bat it. She brought us to a great venue for a bluegrass gig. Even then, there was a buzz at the door. We were let in. We'd great seats. I felt like Lord Muck. I was the guy with …' – he pauses to intone, reverently, a pair of inverted commas – '"Maura O'Connell". Her presence there brought a frisson. She's very respected.'

Curtis concurs. 'She's so well respected in Nashville. You've got no idea. Dolly Parton would call her up and say, "Maura, will you sing on my album?" She's the friend of a friend. This is not just an Irish *cailín* living in Nashville in a quiet corner. They all know her – from Emmylou to Bonnie Raitt … Maura O'Connell is a named artist.'

She has certainly collaborated with some giants of the business: Van Morrison, James Taylor, Nanci Griffith, and, of course, the inimitable Ms Parton. 'Dolly, for sure, is a character,' says O'Connell. 'When I first met her it was ten o'clock in the morning. I'd just flown in from Ireland the night before. I had jetlag. My throat was killing me, but I really wanted to go down and do [the recording], and she looked like she had just walked out of a movie set – with five-inch heels, the make-up, the hair, the whole thing. She's a caricature, but she plays at it, and honestly she might be one of the nicest ladies in the world. She's just as nice and as sweet. She knew I was nervous when I first met her, and she made me tea and said …' – adopting that famous drawl – '"I'm gonna go out now for a while …"'

She reckons T-Bone Burnett – the producer of the soundtrack for *O Brother, Where Art Thou?* on which O'Connell did vocals – looks like one of Clare's most famous adopted sons. 'He's very tall and strangely looks like de Valera – like a really tall, wide de Valera. I told him that once, and he was like, "Whaaa?"'

O'Connell was born in Dev's constituency in November 1958. The fish shop that her grandmother, a widow, had started in the marketplace in Ennis was the hub of her early life, ensuring that she got to soak up whatever flotsam floated around in a sleepy Irish market town in the late 1960s and 1970s. The fish shop used to open for the week's business on a Wednesday, and was, remarkably, the only shop open on a Thursday afternoon. On a sunny Thursday, she vividly remembers all kinds of shadows falling across the market, as the town would have been deserted. 'There's no quiet left, now,' she laments, at the risk, she says, of sounding like 'the returned Yank'.

One of the first recordings of her singing was unearthed recently. Originally, it had been conceived as something for a Yankee audience. 'The neighbourhood was sending good wishes to one of the Keanes who lived next door to us [and] who was getting married in America,' she explains. 'We all gathered 'round this newfangled machine, a reel-to-reel – big old thing – and 'twas very much "Dear Mary" like they were reciting a letter. In between, they played songs like "When Irish Eyes Are Smiling", and then my mother sang a song, and there was a bunch of blessings, and then myself and [two of] my sisters, Aileen and Alisheen, sang. It was the most precious thing you could imagine.'

O'Connell came third amongst four girls. It was a case of 'first up, best dressed', she says, with relations between them the normal mix of emotions: 'We got on well but fought like dogs, as siblings do.' Music was part of the atmosphere in the house. As Amby Costello's daughter, it was expected that she would always have a song to perform. Her mother – a star of local musicals who passed away in 1988 – used to serenade them with light opera.

Having spent the first three years of her secondary schooling as a border in Spanish Point, the action at the youth club at the Friary Hall ('which was really kind of rockin' for people') passed her by. Discos gave her ire: 'I hated them. The music was horrible. I can't stand being around horrible music!'

Although The Bothy Band blew her mind, the trad music scene that swept the country in the 1970s – when everyone was a musician – left her bemused. 'In Ennis, every weekend, it seemed to be a constant array of *bodhrán* players and one tin whistle. I was sick to death of it, actually,' she says wearily.

Brogan's pub on the appropriately named O'Connell Street was where it kicked off for her. 'It was where I first started to edge my way into sessions, trundling along, hoping somebody would ask me to sing,' she says, laughing. It wasn't long before she was leading her troops. Having joined a band called Drake's Tail, the name left her cold so she got them to change it to Corcomroe (after the Burren church). 'I wasn't in a wet week and I was bossin' them around!'

Shortly after, T. V. Honan got her together with Mike Hanrahan – around 1976, Hanrahan reckons – and while with Hanrahan their act went through a few colourful name changes, too – from Tumbleweed to Busy Silence to the fantastically named, The Natural Disaster Band. 'She's an exceptional professional. Even at that time, if we were going collecting money, and it wasn't a whole lot at the time, if we were having any trouble, we'd just call Maura. She'd come from that background of business – the shop. Maura suffered fools very badly. She was tough,' says Hanrahan.

Tumbleweed would do anything but Irish music. They would do some of Hanrahan's original compositions, new country music – Gram Parsons, Emmylou Harris, Willie Nelson, Richard and Linda Thompson, for example – and listened to obscure folk blues like Mississippi John Hurt, Dock Boggs, and all the greats once they came under, she says, 'the College of P. J. Curtis', where they feasted on the music collection he kept out in his house in Kilnaboy, County Clare.

They were 'divil may care' days, rehearsing practically every night, recording demos in the back of Honan's house, or availing of his green Volkswagen beetle to ramble up to Dublin for gigs, playing in places like the Oscar Theatre in Ballsbridge or the Meeting Place, and across to Bobby Clancy's folk club in Carrick-on-Suir. Notably, they played in the first Lisdoonvarna Music Festival in 1978. 'We got the big band out for that one,' says Hanrahan jokingly. 'She was a great singer,' he adds. 'She has a very infectious personality on stage. With Maura, there was never any bullshit. She's maintained that all her life.'

O'Dea remembers going out to see them performing in the Highway Inn in Crusheen, a folk club run by Joe Galligan, and, apart from the voice, there was a 'freshness' about her personality that set her apart. 'There was no sense that she was appeasing herself for something else,' he explains. 'She was very much herself. When Maura was in a place, you knew she was there. There was good *craic*. Even when the door would open – and I remember many times in [local bar] O'Dea's when Maura would come in – there'd be fun. There'd be a laugh, people turning around.

'She'd often come maybe with a few of her friends. There was loads of chat. There was always a sense that having Maura as a customer in the bar and coming into a place … always there was a sense of occasion. She was like a breath of fresh air, and one never tired of her. She is a very intelligent woman, very well versed, and then has this incredible voice on top of everything else.'

'She was like a huge big presence in the room. Maura bursts in the door and everyone knows she's there,' adds Sharon Shannon, who has known her since 1992 and their days touring with 'A Woman's Heart'.

By the end of the 1970s, Tumbleweed had run its course. 'I always remember when Stockton's Wing invited myself and Maura to join the band,' says Hanrahan. 'We sat down. Maura said to me, "I don't want to join Stockton's Wing because I don't see my future in traditional music, but you should go. I don't know what I want to do." My big worry was leaving Maura behind because we'd worked so hard, but we both knew that the next level had to be a different gear, but she had said that she didn't want to join a traditional band. Then six months later, we met each other on a tour. I was with Stockton's Wing and she was with De Dannan! We had an awful laugh about that.'

O'Connell was with De Dannan for two years, lured into the band initially by the promise of a six-week tour to the US in 1980, which was exciting – arriving in New York, especially – but also wearying to be living out of a suitcase and loafing from digs to digs. 'It wasn't all that comfortable. I remember that first tour, thinking, "If I have to meet another new person, I'm gonna die, I'm gonna die." Back then, we stayed in people's houses. That was when I learned that no matter what happens, you have to have a hotel room or a motel room or a bucket or something.'

Disentangling herself from the informal, rolling contract she had with De Dannan wasn't a problem, particularly as they 'landed on their feet' with Mary Black as a replacement, she points out. 'I never joined the band as far as I was concerned, and because I didn't have a broad repertoire anyway; my contribution was mostly pop songs of the early 1920s, 1910s. I didn't add anything to the canon of traditional singing. And I thought since I was already in the business at that stage, I might as well carry on.'

Being solo has always fitted her well. The notion of a band puzzles her. 'A band is a democracy? It's not,' she chuckles. 'There's no such thing. I would have felt very penned in. My interests were very different. Having had the hit with 'Molly' was a bit of a shock – a huge shock to the system – and I thought, rightly or wrongly, that I have to make sure that people don't think this is the only thing that I do. My first instinct was that I've got to do the least like this thing ever.'

It was a curious phenomenon. De Dannan's hit song 'My Irish Molly-O' became an anthem, a rejigging of a 1920s come-all-ye emigrant classic of American ballrooms. In Ireland in the early 1980s, as a result of overplaying, it morphed from a catchy tune to a schmaltzy irritant that you couldn't escape from. One can only imagine what it must have been like to perform it incessantly and to become synonymous with it. It has certainly left O'Connell with ambivalent feelings. 'It was wonderful in so many ways. It was a No. 1 hit. It was like "A Woman's Heart". It was everywhere and kids following you [screaming] "Molly!" I was young and I wasn't prepared. Fame back then in Ireland was a much more modest affair than it is now or even was during the "Woman's Heart" thing. Even at that stage, I wasn't very good at it. I used to get all kinda freaked out. It was a very strange time, having people recognise you all the time. You can get above yourself, too. It was just the shock of the initial thing,' she says, laughing. 'I liked it on one level – like anybody else. I felt on show a lot, but also I had a great time!'

Whatever about the recognition, as she eked out a solo career, the glory wasn't translating into pounds, shillings and pence. 'One thing about Ireland – you might be as famous as anything but you mightn't have tuppence to rattle!'

Having released the successful album *Maura O'Connell* in 1983, the scene – playing in clubs and hotel ballrooms – left her despondent. 'Ireland at the time? There was more happening in Timbuktu,' booms Curtis. She honestly thought she would see out her days in the fish shop, which was hers for the taking. But then Nashville came a-hollerin'.

Typical of her forceful personality, the first thing she ensured as she bedded herself into the Country & Western capital of the world was that she wasn't pigeon-holed as an Irish chanteuse. 'One of the things I had a hard time with when I moved over to the States … unlike now, people expected someone who was billed as an Irish singer to be someone in a green dress, and we didn't sit well together. In fact, in the beginning, I had it in my contract that I couldn't be advertised as an Irish singer – both myself and the audience would be disappointed. It sounds like I was embarrassed, but it was just that I didn't want to keep disappointing people.'

Twenty years on, she has remained an outsider – hovering around the edges of country, folk, blues, but never being consumed by any one genre in particular, and managing to avoid the neat boxes that music critics love to imprison artists in.

With O'Connell, it has always been about the voice, especially when it's unadorned. Sure, wasn't it the voice that sent Martin Scorsese scampering for her to appear in a cameo role in his 2002 flick, *Gangs of New York*? 'It's pretty lusty,' says Liam Clancy. 'She's a courageous kind of singer, you know – whereas some people would play it safe, she seems to do it with great abandon.'

Her accent still fluctuates wildly depending on her company. 'The minute I come home, the minute my ear hits the wind at home, I'm "Jaysus Chhrist, howzit ghoin?", but then I lapse because I'm over-compensating. Then what happens is that if I'm around American people, I'm all twang.'

Her last album, her tenth – *Don't I Know* – was released in 2004. She still revels in doing live gigs. At her peak, she used to get through 150 a year; now it's down to a more manageable fifty to seventy-five. She adores the adrenaline it produces. 'There have been times in my life when I've felt more comfortable and more in control of myself and my life while I'm on the stage than I have when I've been off of it. I feel very comfortable on the stage. I always tell my son Jesse, "I sing for free, I travel for money." And I like to be paid well, but that's beside the point. I love it, and I just can't help it. I'm a hound. I'm a big, old folk diva, so I am.'

As to why she isn't a songwriter – she once had T-shirts made to that effect – she is forthright. 'I don't want to sing bad shit. Truly. I used to go on at length about the fact that it's only in the last thirty years – now forty years, probably – since a singer has been expected to write his or her own song. Or be considered an imbecile. I suppose that's the most hurtful thing for me in a way, although I'd like the money, too!

'It doesn't come naturally. I don't wake up in the middle of the night going, "Oh, Jesus, I must write this down." And I know that everyone tells me it's ninety-nine per cent hard work and one per cent inspiration. I'd like to see the one per cent before I go sitting down working on it. I'm not motivated in that way. I probably could write a decent something that I could sneak on a record, but I wouldn't. I wouldn't do it.'

It is quite a testament that her voice has carried her so far. 'To the people who knew, she was obviously a real, real, universal talent,' says Curtis about the 'shtick' she had starting out. The fact that it's the Knitting Factory in New York or the Birchmere in Washington, DC rather than the old Highway Inn in Crusheen doesn't seem to have altered her approach.

'I think it was [Irish poet] Patrick Kavanagh,' says O'Dea, 'who talked about the difference between the parochial and the provincial – that the provincial are people who have, all the time, their eyes on what people are doing in the centre or what is perceived as the centre, and they're always pale imitations of it. So you get the provincial in France or in Ireland – they often don't see what's local, but they are all the time making yellow-pack versions of what is happening in what's perceived to be the centre.

'Whereas the parochial or the local – or, according to Kavanagh, your own ditch – is where the universal is tapped. I always think that Maura is very informed by her origins – where she's from, her own area, her own ditch, and it's that very familiarity she has that makes her universal, that transcends provincialism, nationalism, and makes her the artist that she is. That's the kind of insight she has.'

DESMOND LYNAM

Des Lynam used to cover Wimbledon tennis on TV for the BBC every summer. One afternoon, rain had stopped play. While waiting to resume coverage, he was reading out some sports results when, out of nowhere, this jaunty piano music piped up. He was startled for an instant, but then quick as you like, 'You must excuse me, but it's hard to read these and play the piano at the same time.'

King of Cool. Mr Unflappable. It was a vintage Lynam moment – calm, suave and with that killer line to leaven proceedings. As a producer on air, there is nobody you'd rather have in a tight spot. For a bloke, there's no one you'd rather have down in the pub to mull over a weekend's sport.

For the ladies, as playwright Arthur Smith – who penned a television play, *My Summer with Des*, following Lynam's triumphant coverage of Euro '96 – remarked, he's 'a kind of housewives' Samuel Beckett'.

That he appeals so much to the fairer sex is kind of a wonder, given his two great sporting passions are probably soccer and boxing – those male bastions – but Lynam doesn't trade in laddish gags. He's got a keen sense of the absurd, something which marks him out amongst sports broadcasters – a realm renowned for bombast.

He's that slight bit detached. He would never overplay the levity of a sporting occasion. It was, after all, only sport, which may explain, in part, how he always managed to remain so unflustered on air. All he had to do was raise one of those bushy eyebrows, not out of alarm, nor from ennui, just from bemusement.

As football manager Martin O'Neill once said: 'When people tune in to him they think everything's all right with the world because there's the voice, the look, that knowing little wink he gives, which makes people think: "Hang on a minute, it's a nice place to be, the world, you know." There's almost a reassurance about him, sort of: "Hey, listen, we'll be all right, everything will be okay." If he does have to work at it, he does it magnificently to make it look as natural as possible.'

He's a master of the cutting jibe, the kind that would crack up a locker room. During the 1998 World Cup, the Romanian team had all dyed their hair blond. Back in the BBC studio, comically, Jimmy Hill – Lynam's great friend – considered it a useful ploy: 'anything that helps you pick out a teammate quickly is good,' he mused.

'Doesn't do a lot for the Swedes,' quipped Lynam.

Or during the following World Cup, after a game in which France had failed to score against Senegal, Paul Gascoigne – one of his analysts on ITV – said he didn't know where Senegal was. 'I think you'll find it's been part of Africa for some time,' shot Lynam.

Whenever a bit of gravity did encroach on sporting affairs, he was invariably sure-footed. During the 1972 Olympics, when the Palestinian terrorist group Black September killed two Israeli athletes and kidnapped nine others (who were later killed in a shoot-out), the Games were suspended temporarily amidst all the chaos. Lynam was working for BBC radio at the time, and drew plaudits for the even-handedness of his reporting; so much so that when he returned home, there were moves to lure him from sport to the news department, but he resisted.

Like Michael Parkinson, his career has made him a prince amongst broadcasters in the UK – something that has been acknowledged by the awarding of an OBE in the 2008 New Year Honours List. When he moved from the BBC to ITV in 1999, there was a national outcry that he was leaving Auntie Beeb, the public broadcaster. It was the lead item on the BBC, ITV and Sky news programmes. In an article entitled, 'Des is gone and England with him', the cultural critic Bryan Appleyard was moved to comment, 'Des Lynam is taking from the BBC to ITV a character he has perfected, the laconic but indomitable spirit of Middle England.' A nation wept, but not the one he was born in.

Lynam was born in Clare on 17 September 1942. 'My father was in the British army in the Second World War and my mother gave birth to me in Ennis. I was born in [what was] called the New Hospital [Ennis County Hospital] at the time – it's a very ancient hospital now, and we lived with my grandparents for probably the first five years,' he explains. After that, he moved to Brighton with his parents, but, as was the fashion with Irish immigrants in the UK in the 1950s, he used to spend summer holidays, two or three weeks a year, back in Ireland, right through his teenage years. In fact, the family once travelled over by motorbike and sidecar. His dad had a 500cc BSA with a Watsonian sidecar capable of seating his mother, with Lynam behind her, singing away, as they moseyed their way through Wales to the boat train at Fishguard.

'I only remember him as a small, little lad,' says Seán Spring, the barber, aged seventy-one, who grew up on Abbey Street, around the corner from Lynam's grandparents on Francis Street. 'He was kind of pampered. We'd be a bit more rougher than he was. The grand-mother minded him. She wouldn't let the wind blow on him. She'd have him all decked up,' he laughs. 'Ah, he was only about five, you must remember.'

Lynam has vivid memories of the time. 'When I was a kid, in the west of Ireland, it was really the horse-and-cart age,' he says. 'Towards the end of the war years and the early-1950s, it was horse transport everywhere. It was no surprise to see donkeys and carts all over the marketplace.

'Of course, my grandfather [Packo Malone] was a blacksmith. He was as busy as hell. All round the yard, there'd be about twelve horses or donkeys waiting to be shoed. That was his business. He did it, physically, till he was about seventy-six. He was a tall man. I'm about the only other person in the family that's the same height as him – six-foot-one-and-a-half. All the other cousins are shorter people; not short people, but shorter people.'

'He's a bit like his grandfather,' adds Spring. 'Packo was a tall, straight man. Frank [Lynam's uncle] – the son that was a blacksmith with him – was more stocky and heavy. Lynam's great-grandfather, Stephen Malone [also a blacksmith] was a big heavy man. Frank's boast was that they used to have to bring him to the square to turn him.'

Packo Malone had his forge on Coach House Lane, a side street, which was part of a host of lanes and tenements that were blasted away to make way for what is now the car park at the back of Abbey Street. 'There was an abattoir next door to it,' says Lynam. 'As a young boy, I used to go in and watch the sheep and cows being killed. It was a bit of a gory thing to do, I suppose. I always felt sorry for them as they were going in. I used to look at the sheep and think, "You're for it. You're about to get done." The sheep always had this terror in their eyes as though they knew as well.

'I used to spend many hours pulling the bellows in the forge, keeping the fire going. You'd spend half an hour doing it. Other kids … who would come in from school would do the same for him. There was kind of a boy's club there.'

A large, imposing figure – a kind of paternal presence – Packo Malone used to counsel the kids, and, for amusement, send them scampering around the town on hoax errands to the local hardware stores, such as Kenny's or Rowan's, for 'glass anvils' and 'rubber nails'. He was a sportsman of repute. From 1904 to 1915, he won seven county medals for the Ennis Dalcassians, and played at the Ennis Showgrounds on the Clare team that came up against Kerry in the

1912 Munster football final, losing by 0–3 to 0–1. Lynam has a picture of the team in his office in London. 'All looking,' he says, 'like soldiers from the front at the First World War. They've got those sort of haircuts and moustaches and things. They're very young men, I would think, but they all look in their fifties.'

Packo Malone was also a good hurler, an angler and was fond of shooting. Indeed, an incident long before Dick Cheney ever went a-duck-shootin' his mate, gives an indication of how hardy a man Lynam's grandfather must have been. 'He went out shooting with the old Dr Harry Bugler; he was very impetuous. He discharged his gun – accidentally, we'll say – but it was dangerous to be around him. He pepped Packo with a fair amount of pellets in the back of the neck so he spent half of the day taking them out, but he never got them all out. That I can tell you is true. Till the day he died, there were a certain amount of pellets sticking in the back of his neck,' says a contemporary of Lynam's from growing up.

On Sundays, Lynam would traipse after his grandfather to hurling and football matches in Cusack Park – located on the same stretch of road as Francis Street – and bask in 'some reflected glory' afforded from being caught in the slipstream of a local sporting hero.

Lynam's father was from Borris-on-Ossery in County Laois, so the young Desmond also spent time holidaying with his paternal grandparents. Lynam's paternal grandfather was a signalman on the railway, and Lynam's grandmother, Bridget Lynam seems to have been quite a character, with a stream of old nonsensical sayings. About someone always complaining about their aches and pains, she would say, 'He's never without an arse or an elbow.' If she saw an odd-looking couple, she would remark that 'Every old shoe meets an old sock.' Or on seeing someone strange, she might say, 'It's amazing what you see when you haven't got a gun.'

Some of her wit must have rubbed off on her grandson, for it wasn't long before he began to have success in the dating arena, although the etiquette in which he was being schooled over in Brighton got him into a spot of bother on one summer trip to Ireland. 'I had taken a beautiful local girl from Ennis to the pictures,' he writes in his autobiography, *I Should Have Been at Work!* 'Her name was Maura Gorman, and I had given her a kiss in the back row. I had been spotted and was marched off to see my Uncle Frank, who took me to one side: "We don't do that sort of thing in public," he said. I was mortified, feeling that I'd let the family down. Mind you, Maura had enjoyed it as much as I had.'

Lynam met his wife Susan while she was still at the girls' grammar school. They married several years later – she was twenty-one, Lynam was twenty-three – and have one son, Patrick. However, the marriage broke down after only seven years, just as Lynam's career in broadcasting was taking off.

It wasn't a bad time to be single, as his work took him around the world, covering World Cups, Olympic Games, prize fights, and, as he 'was living his twenties in his thirties', his beguiling charm landed him a string of girlfriends before he met his current partner Rose, with whom he has lived for over twenty years.

There was, however, one unusual encounter during his time as a single bloke. Having been on a couple of dates with a 'sultry looking', six-foot female, he got an anonymous phone call warning him to be careful with her because she was born a boy and that the press were on to her. 'I had tried to get Caroline into bed after our second date, but she would have none of it. Now I wanted to find out the truth,' he writes in his autobiography. 'At our next meeting I was examining her like an antiques expert with a Louis XIV chair.' The relationship went no further. His informant had been correct, and the tabloids continued to hound her. It turned out that she was an ex-Bond girl and model, but no one had any suspicions of her past until the press revelations.

Of all the sporting stars he has encountered, Muhammad Ali looms largest. During almost twenty years as a boxing commentator for BBC radio, Lynam covered a lot of fights in the second half of Ali's career, as well as being lucky enough to interview him on a number of occasions, including a visit by the boxing champ to the BBC in 1983 in which he personally requested an interview with Lynam. His arrival in the studio – at a stage when he was already showing signs of slowing up – prompted the whole crew, usually blasé about celebrity, to rise to their feet and give a round of applause. It was something Lynam had never seen, before or since. 'He was a one-off, wasn't he?' says Lynam rhetorically. 'He was a different kind of guy altogether. He was brilliant at what he did and he was prepared to tell everybody about it, and with a twinkle in his eye and a sense of humour.'

While Lynam was covering the 'Rumble in the Jungle' in Zaire in 1974 for BBC radio, he sat beside Ali for an interview one day, along with a gathering of British boxing writers. Ali was doing a demonstration for the media entourage – jabbing air punches at Lynam for illustration – as he explained how he was going to undo Foreman. Initially, Lynam flinched, but reckoning that if Ali connected and drew blood, it would make a fine scoop, he began to edge forward bit by bit. When he finished, Ali threw him that wry look of his: 'You're not as dumb as you look.'

Lynam also got to know one of the other great sporting personalities of the 1970s and 1980s: Brian Clough. 'He said to me once – a great quote that I treasure – "You and I have got something in common, son,"' intones Lynam, a dead ringer for Cloughie's nasal drone.

'I said, "What's that, Brian?"

'"I'm good at what I do and you're good at what you do."

'I said, "Well, thank you very much."

'He said, "There's no thanks. It's not thanks. I'm not saying it to be thanked." He damned you with faint praise.'

Lynam is certainly a pro, the ultimate TV link-man. For the viewer sprawled on the armchair, it is difficult to appreciate how tricky a job it is: working long slots live on air (five hours for *Grandstand*, eleven for Wimbledon, etc.); making sure to be thoroughly briefed; taking in a producer's directions while also listening to the interviewee; reading autocues seamlessly; adjusting to sudden changes; ad libbing humour.

Inevitably – although nothing to compare to Murray Walker's repertoire – Lynam has had his gaffe or two on the job. On *Grandstand* one afternoon, while commenting on live soccer results that were coming in, he blabbered: 'Southampton won 2–0, the same result as last year when they won 4–1.' On another occasion, he started reading a cue, only to realise that he didn't quite recognise the lines and that they should have been read by Steve Rider. The director had popped Lynam up in vision by mistake. Lynam got a fit of the giggles as he was reading, only to discover to his horror that the cue ended with somebody's death. And in what he thought was 'the end of my career', he momentarily went blank on screen before the start of the England–Cameroon quarter-final match in the 1990 World Cup at Napoli's ground. At the last second, he had decided to change his opening words, but got stuck between his rehearsed script and his new opener. As it was in front of fourteen million viewers, it was a bit more alarming than your normal after-dinner freeze at a wedding, but he regained his composure after a few seconds, blurting the immortal phrase, 'See Naples and dry.'

'He was mortified,' said Bob Wilson, working for Lynam's competitor, ITV at the time, 'but it helped all of us, I can tell you that. It showed he was human. It helped me because I thought, "If that can happen to Des Lynam …"'

It had shown he was fallible. Nothing more. 'I went home to the realisation that I wasn't as good as I thought I was,' he writes in his memoirs. 'I hope, as a result, that I became a better and more humble person. Perhaps it was something I needed and had been lying in wait for me. Never again in the next 14 years of my career as a sports broadcaster would I take for granted that it was all a piece of cake.'

Perhaps his finest hour came at Aintree, which, given he isn't a horsey type, is the sporting broadcast he admits to having had to work the hardest at to prepare. In 1997 IRA bomb warnings meant the race had to be postponed until the following Monday. Peter O'Sullevan – the doyen of racing commentators, who was there for his last broadcast – was fulsome in his praise afterwards: 'Des handled his aspect of that drama just as immaculately as one would expect … His great characteristic is so well known – he is so exceptionally composed.'

Lynam is not so composed that he is unable to completely betray emotion, though. That afternoon, the trainer Jenny Pitman, who was about to marry her long-time partner, suggested it was about time Lynam made Rose 'a respectable woman'. Known for being very guarded about his personal life, his eyes went cold. 'Thank you for sharing that with the nation,' he replied. Back in the BBC's production recording truck, the Princess Royal got a great laugh out of the exchange. 'She was roaring with laughter,' his producer, Martin Hopkins, told Lynam afterwards.

A few years earlier, during 'the race that never was' – as O'Sullevan described the void Grand National of 1993 – Lynam scurried around the course, elevating the TV coverage to unexpectedly high levels of drama. 'Wasn't [it] the most brilliant piece of live television coverage you have ever been gripped by?' wrote Esther Rantzen in the *Daily Express*. 'The place to be was watching BBC1. That team did not miss a shot, or an interview. Desmond Lynam held it together with interviews that vividly expressed the rage and disbelief of riders and trainers.'

Lynam also did his bit for Irish patriotism that afternoon. 'This wouldn't even happen in Ireland,' moaned trainer John Upson live on air. 'As I say, I go to point-to-points in Ireland – you know, a backward little country like Ireland.'

To which Lynam jumped in: 'Be careful now, I come from there,' prompting an embarrassed Upson to cough up a quick U-turn: 'I don't believe it is a backward country at all.'

Lynam is a member of Lahinch Golf Club in County Clare. He goes over to Ireland every now and again to 'show how bad a golfer' he is, and remembers watching the 1995 All-Ireland hurling final on television – which Clare won – some eighty years after his grandfather had represented the county – days when Packo Malone would have been blissfully unaware that his grandson would one day become one of the great wits of broadcasting on these islands.

Again at Wimbledon, rain had scuppered play for three, long days in 1999. At one point, as a camera ranged over the saturated courts, Lynam, exasperated and giddy, dead-panned: 'This is live rain you are watching, not recorded rain.'

KEVIN SHEEDY

Kevin Sheedy is the greatest Clareman to ever lace a pair of soccer boots. Greater even than Mannix from Avenue United. Except, unlike Mannix, Sheedy wasn't born in Clare. He qualifies under the granny rule.

His dad Michael grew up in Daragh. Having left school, he worked for three years in Connellan's Hardware near the Old Ground Hotel in Ennis. The money was derisory – £3 10 shillings a week – so Michael up and left for London in 1951. His brother Stephen stayed at home on the family farm; Stephen's sons – his namesake Stephen, who won an All-Ireland hurling medal in 1995, and Martin – were the barnstorming backbone of Clarecastle's successful hurling club side of the 1990s.

After a few years in the UK, working in heavy steel, Michael Sheedy washed up in Builth Wells, a quaint market town in north Wales, with his Welsh wife, Jean. They ran a pub there, The Plough Inn. Their second son, Kevin, arrived in October 1959, born on the premises; little did they know what he would go on to achieve.

When Everton's supporters came to vote on their all-time greatest Everton XI to mark the club's one hundred and twenty-fifth anniversary in 2003, Sheedy was nominated left of midfield.

His goal-scoring record is phenomenal. He averaged, approximately, one every four league games. For Ireland, he bagged nine goals in forty-five appearances. To put that in perspective, Johnny Giles got five in fifty-nine games; Liam Brady, nine in seventy-two. Another Irish midfielder, Eamon Dunphy, drew a blank in twenty-three outings. Dunphy is a big fan. 'He was an outstanding player, technically very good. He did extremely well for Ireland, and because he had such a good left foot, that was quite rare and very valuable. It's hard to find left-sided players, and he fulfilled an important role for Jack [Charlton] to give the side balance.'

That left leg of his was like a wand, whether it was whipping in those arcing crosses or unpicking defences with a clever, threaded ball for his strikers to run on to in an era when defenders, obsessed with the offside trap, used to push up close to the midfield line. Or, most memorably, from a dead-ball situation. He scored his first free-kick for Everton against Peter Shilton. One time, he scored a free-kick against Ipswich in a league game. The ref disallowed it. Sheedy shrugged, replaced the ball, and struck it into the other corner past a flailing Paul Cooper. Years after he finished playing for Everton, if they won a free near the opposition's box, their fans would growl, 'Sheedy, Sheedy, Sheedy'.

One free in particular endeared him to the Goodison Park faithful. Playing away to their rivals across the Mersey – against the club that had discarded him a few years before – Sheedy flashed a corker into the top left-hand corner. Liverpool's keeper, Mike Hooper, stood rooted to the ground as Sheedy took off on a celebratory run, changing his trademark finger-in-the-air salute into two fingers as he wheeled away from the goal-line. Merseyside derby. The Kop End. Up yours. In terms of inflammatory gestures, it was atomic. 'I got hauled before the FA, then,' says Sheedy in a discernible Scouse accent. 'I had to go down and explain my actions. As it was in those days, the FA had people in their sixties and seventies who didn't really have a clue about football. It was quite hilarious. They put the video on and they said, "Explain your actions."

'I said, "Well, I've just scored a goal at the Kop End."

'Someone stopped the tape and said, "How do you know it's the Kop End?"

'It was farcical, really. So I managed to talk my way out of it and get away with it. Myself and Adrian Heath, who got called as well – we just looked at each other and shook our heads in disbelief. That's the sort of people who were there at the time.'

Still sporting that boy-next-door haircut, flecked with grey around the temples, Sheedy's hardly changed in twenty-five years. The fact that he's decked out in shorts, a navy Everton training jersey – with K.S. initialled on the front – adds to the illusion. He's taking a break from training. He's back at Everton, coaching the sixteen to eighteen-year-olds, and loving it.

As a player and coach, Sheedy's football odyssey took in the three clubs in Liverpool. He spent a decade with Everton, from 1982 to 1992, during the club's most successful period; he worked for five years as assistant manager to John Aldridge at Tranmere Rovers in the late 1990s when the club reached a League Cup final and twice reached the last eight of the FA Cup; and he passed a frustrating spell at the start of his career at Anfield.

His professional career began with his local team, Hereford United. When he was four, his parents moved to Hereford to take over a pub, the Tram Inn, located outside the town. In Sheedy's last year at school, as a fifteen-year-old, his schoolmaster allowed him to train with the club in the mornings and take classes at school in the afternoon. The deal was that if he ever got to a cup final, he'd get him a pair of tickets. Years later, Sheedy gladly coughed up, sending him two tickets to the 1984 League Cup final, in which he played for Everton against Liverpool.

Sheedy made his debut for Hereford United aged just sixteen. It was their last game of the season in the old Third Division. They had just been promoted. He made a further fifty appearances. At the end of the 1978 season, his mate got him a ticket for the European Cup final at Wembley when a Kenny Dalglish goal helped Liverpool retain the crown. Four weeks afterwards, Bob Paisley – Liverpool's manager – came looking for Sheedy. It was boyhood-dreams stuff, but Sheedy was hesitant. He knew the club had a reputation for leaving young players wallowing in the reserves. Once he saw the stadium though, all reservations quickly dissipated. 'A couple of weeks later and I'm getting changed beside Dalglish,' he says, almost still flushed with schoolboy disbelief.

At the time, Liverpool was in its pomp. The famed Boot Room Team – Paisley, Joe Fagan, Ronnie Moran and Roy Evans – was on autopilot. Renowned for their tea-drinking, they had little else to do, it seems. 'Because they had such a great side at the time, Liverpool, they didn't need coaching – the players. I was there for four years and I never saw anyone do any coaching. Their method [of training] was just playing games, five-a-sides, just passing and moving. The players were that good that they didn't need organisation. Whereas now,' says Sheedy, with reference to his work at Everton's youth academy, 'you've got to coach the back four, the midfield, the strikers. They just had internationals throughout the team.'

It is true. England played an international against Switzerland in 1977 in which seven of the starting team were from Liverpool. Throw the Scots – Dalglish, Alan Hansen and Graeme Souness – into the mix and you've got the bones of, arguably, the greatest British club side ever. Souness played across the middle with Jimmy Case, Terry McDermott and Ray Kennedy. 'They never really got injured, so you were fighting a losing battle,' says Sheedy of a formidable unit.

On a four-year contract, things progressed okay the first season, but he was struck down with a back injury in the second season. They tried everything to cure it, including a spell in hospital in traction. Nothing seemed to work. The Boot Room Team didn't like what they read in their tea leaves. 'In the end, they started to doubt me, mentally. Thinking, "Is he strong enough? Is he tough enough? Has he got a back injury?" Basically, you're pushed to the side, a little bit,' says Sheedy, at long enough of a remove to speak dispassionately about a dispiriting time for a teenager with his career in the balance.

Acupuncture – 'a last resort' – sorted him. He bounced back and made a couple of first-team appearances in his third season when injury struck again. He was playing for the Ireland under-21s against England at Anfield when he went over on his ankle, putting him out of action for four weeks. Ray Kennedy was injured at the same time, and Sheedy's fellow Irish under-21 teammate, Ronnie Whelan – who was sharing digs with Sheedy – was called up to cover. He took his chance and went on to become a mainstay in the side.

Sheedy was back in the wilderness – unable to break into the first team, but good enough that clubs were sniffing around. Paisley, nervous of releasing players that might come back and bite him in the ass, offered him a move to lowly Blackpool. Sheedy declined. Derby, a first-flight club, came in for him. Sheedy was keen to go, but Paisley scotched the move. 'They were just trying to palm me off. That's how it works,' says Sheedy.

The last season was 'really frustrating', but he resolved to see out his contract and, buoyed by his parents – who would go to see him in every reserve game – his form held. He used to go along to Goodison Park midweek to watch Everton's home games, and could see the 'nucleus of a young team' forming – Graeme Sharpe and Kevin Ratcliffe had just made their debuts; Heath had just been bought for the princely sum, at the time, of £850,000. 'It was the last game of the season; we were playing Preston in the reserves,' he says. 'I got a phone call from a press man and he said, "Would you be interested in going to Everton?"

'And I said, "Yes."

'So he said, "Put the phone down and Howard Kendall will ring you." That was the old-fashioned way of what you'd call 'tapping up'. He was on his way. And he couldn't have timed it better. The team practically picked itself. Neville Southhall minded goal. Although he looked like a pub soccer player, no other keeper has won the Football

Writers' Association Player of the Year award since he picked it up in 1985. Pat 'Psycho' van den Hauwe and England international, Gary Stevens were at full-back; 'Dangerous Derek' Mountfield and Ratcliffe at centre half; Sheedy in midfield, with Trevor Steven, Paul Bracewell and the old English bulldog, Peter Reid; Sharpe and Heath were up front.

Gary Lineker also played for a season – 1985–86 – the year, bitterly, that Liverpool pipped them for both the league and the FA Cup. Sky pundit, Andy Gray, also arrived for two seasons.

From 1984 to 1989, Everton won a European Cup Winners' Cup, reached four FA Cup finals – winning one – played a League Cup final, and won two league titles. 'We never lost a semi-final,' he says proudly. 'We could play the big occasion.'

There was none bigger than the second leg of the European Cup Winners' Cup semi-final in 1985 – treasured by Everton fans as the club's greatest night. Playing Bayern Munich, who won the German league title that season, the first leg had been a scoreless draw. 'We went a goal behind,' says Sheedy, describing the second leg. 'It was quite eerie because you could hear a pin drop when the ball hit the back of the net. It was, like, a full house of Evertonians. We used to try and kick away from the Gladys Street End in the first half, and then the second half, always, was like the cavalry charge.

'It was just a case of get the ball in their box and go for it. We had Andy Gray and Graeme Sharpe up front, and they just battered their centre-backs in the old-fashioned way. We got the equaliser and the whole place came alive. There was no way we were gonna lose on the night.'

And they didn't, winning 3–1. They repeated the score line in the final against Rapid Vienna. Sheedy scored a cracker to kill the game. It is his all-time favourite goal. Bar one. That one came on a greasy June night in Cagliari during Italia '90. Trailing England 1–0, with twenty minutes left in the opening game of the pool stages, Sheedy dispossessed Steve McMahon – ironically, an Everton-turned-Liverpool player – and let fly. 'As soon as it left my boot, from years of doing it, I knew it was in. I caught it as sweet as I could,' he says. It was the country's first-ever goal in the World Cup finals. For some, it was as good as a match winner.

Cocooned in hotels during the tournament, videos used to be sent to the squad from RTÉ, along with others people had filmed. 'After dinner, we'd have different stuff to stick on and some of it was quite funny,' remarked Niall Quinn years later. 'I can remember one girl – she said after we'd drawn with England, "It's brilliant. We wouldn't have won without Kevin Sheedy."'

The country went la-la. 'I was back in Ennis not long afterwards,' says Sheedy, 'and I went for a drink with my cousins and my dad. Someone was telling me a story that when the England game was on, and they'd all be in the bar watching it, one of their mates would go to the toilet and they'd give it, like, ten seconds and then they'd all jump up as if we'd scored, and he'd come running out. And then the lad who was telling the story said he was in the toilet and they've all jumped up and shouted and whatnot. He let them off. As it happened, I'd scored the goal.'

As regards the maths in the group, Ireland wouldn't have progressed without 'the goal' – ultimately, it was the difference between qualifying for the next round.

Sheedy was instrumental again when it came to the famous penalty shoot-out against Romania. Having missed two in his football career 'from I don't know how many', he was an obvious choice when Big Jack scouted for five volunteers amongst the players. He said he'd take the first, as there was no point in saving himself for last, as 'there mightn't be a last one'. He had about ten minutes from the time of the final whistle to the time of his penalty kick to compose himself. The kicks were taken into the goal where all the Irish fans were lodged, including his parents. Then there was the long walk up. He's never experienced pressure like it. He decided to hit it high, down the middle. With all that adrenaline, surely, you'd think, he was at risk of ballooning it over the bar. 'Why there?'

'From experience', he explains. 'Usually, I'm thinking: the first penalty, the goalkeeper will have to dive. He's not going to stand there. He's gotta dive. He's not gonna just stand there and let me roll it into a corner. The reason for it being high was that if he did dive, then he leaves his legs there. Then he can save it with his legs.'

Sure enough, Sheedy smashed it home, as did his four other team-mates, and Ireland progressed. Losing to Italy in the quarter-finals was crushing, though. Giuseppe Bergami, a World Cup winner in 1982, was detailed to mark him. He took his brief seriously. 'I was never marked tighter or closer. I couldn't move,' bemoans Sheedy. 'There was no getting away from him. He was by far the hardest opponent I played against.'

There was nothing between the sides on the night. 'I just remember the referee was very biased towards them,' he argues. 'Every fifty-fifty decision went their way, and when it's such a close game sometimes that tips the scales.'

They fancied themselves against an ageing Argentinian side that knocked Italy out in the semis. 'We probably did as well as we could have done, but when you get that close you still feel maybe …'

It was the pinnacle of the Charlton era. For such a stylish, cerebral player, he denies – when responding to a question he has fielded before – ever finding the long-ball, 'put 'em under pressure' Charlton tactics suffocating. With full-backs like Denis Irwin and Steve Staunton, it was never a case of kick and rush like a Watford or Wimbledon, he points out. Unusually for international football at the time, they used to close down the opposition in their half instead of dropping off and letting them come into the Irish half. It meant strikers rarely lasted more than an hour. If a defender passed to a midfielder and he was dispossessed, it was the defender who got the berating. There was a method to the system. New players could easily fit into it. Charlton was a clever bugger, Sheedy stresses.

'We played Wales one time,' he says, 'and Jack had their team written on the back of a cigarette pack. It was when he was getting the names wrong. He'd say, "Alan Malcolm", and somebody would say, "It's Malcolm Allen, Jack." I don't know [if] in a roundabout way he was trying to psyche us up – these aren't very good – or whether he was that bad.'

Whether Charlton was a master psychologist despite himself is unknown. We do know, though, that he had a Machiavellian streak. He used it tellingly in the way he exposed and ditched Liam Brady – another player whose name he used to get muddled; he would sometimes call him *Ian* Brady – the Moors Murderer. Ouch! Brady had been the ringmaster of Irish soccer teams for over ten years by the time Charlton came along. He didn't fit into Charlton's plans, and suffered an ignominious end to his international career as a result. 'We were playing [West] Germany, who were the best team in the world at the time, at Lansdowne Road, and he played Liam at midfield and they were just sort of machines, the midfield,' says Sheedy. 'After about twenty minutes, we were getting overrun in there, and Jack took Liam off and that was his sort of way of saying to the crowd, to the press: "He can't play to this system." That was Liam's last game. He was quite shrewd in some of the things that he did.'

In a neat piece of symmetry, Sheedy played his own last game for Ireland against Wales – the land he forsook in a move he never regretted given the success he had with Ireland – in February 1993, scoring in a 2–1 victory. He had made his senior debut ten years beforehand at Dalymount Park in a game against a Dutch team that included van Basten, Gullit and Rijkaard – the Irish forfeiting a 2–0 lead, eventually losing 3–2.

Two years later, the Irish played host to Italy, the reigning World Cup champions, again at a packed Dalymount Park, narrowly losing 2–1. 'Me mum and dad went, and they said there were people walking to the game and putting ladders up against the wall and just getting over, sort of thing. That was what they call a full house,' he laughs.

Paul McGrath made his international debut that day. When pressed about the great players that Sheedy played with and against in the old English First Division during the days of Kevin Keegan, Glenn Hoddle and Bryan Robson, he singles out two: Dalglish and McGrath. 'Because he never trained much,' Sheedy says of McGrath, 'and during games when it was a hundred miles an hour, he was just sort of cruising. It was easy for him. When you're playing with people like that, it stands out – how they're making it look easy.'

Sheedy walks gingerly himself these days. His knees are in a bad way. 'The price you pay,' he says stoically. And, of course, he's got a few stitches in his head courtesy of a famous headed goal. 'When we played them [Manchester United] at Goodison, we won 5–0. I scored – I didn't score many headers – but I scored a header from the edge of the box and there was a challenge from Kevin Moran. Kevin had sort of headed the back of my head, helping to generate the power for it to go into the top corner. He was stretchered off and went to hospital. I got taken off and had stitches in my head and came back on. I'd seen him loads of times afterwards, but a few years ago he rang me up. He was playing golf and I'm a member of the local club where he wanted to play, so I signed all his brothers in and we played. Then we were having a drink afterwards. We were just talking football with all his brothers, and one of them said, "What's the best goal you ever scored?"

'I said, "It was the header against Kevin when I rose above him and scored."

'He said all he was trying to do was put me off. In those days, every game he played he was cuts and bruises. His way of putting me off was head-butting me in the back of the head. That's the way he was. He wasn't a dirty player. He was wholehearted.'

There were some tough dogs around that time. He once nutmegged Souness in training while they were both at Liverpool. The Scot just laughed. Sheedy did it to him again during a League Cup final. This time, Souness smashed him in the face with an elbow. Different when it's the real thing.

'Jimmy Case, he was the silent assassin,' he says, adding to the list. 'He wouldn't say much, but if someone needed sorting out … and then in our team, Kevin Ratcliffe.' The Welshman and Sheedy were best mates and used to room with each other. 'He used to ask me to roll him fifty-fifty balls if there was somebody who needed a kicking,' he says, grinning. 'He'd say, "Next time you get it, don't pass it to me; give me a fifty-fifty with him. That'll sort him out."'

JIMMY SMYTH

Jimmy Smyth was playing a club game for Ruan on one occasion. With time running out, they were trailing by a couple of points. Gathering the *sliotar* out in midfield, he took off on a solo run, bearing down on goal. 'Throw it over the bar,' someone screamed, eager for him to play the percentages; another demanded that he ferry it into the full-forward line, before a lone voice of reason called out from the bank behind the goal: 'Take no notice of them, Jimmy. Make your own arrangements.' Seconds later, he flashed it to the back of the net.

'He'd a great run at a goal,' explains RTÉ's Micheál Ó Muircheartaigh, who broadcast dozens of his matches. 'He carried the ball. He went in a straight line. He had the physique. I never saw Mick Mackey, but they say he used go the same way.'

Smyth was a scoring sensation, particularly of goals. In 1953 he got 6–4 in a match against Limerick – a tally clocked up in the days of sixty-minute games, and which still stands as a record for the Munster championship. A year later, playing against the billboard Wexford team of Nick O'Donnell and the Rackard brothers – a team that played in every All-Ireland final from 1954–56 – Clare were trailing by four points with a few minutes to go in the Oireachtas final at Croke Park. 'Jimmy got a fantastic goal,' remembers Ó Muircheartaigh. 'He ploughed through several and had nothing on his mind but a goal. There'd be no film of it but it would rank as one of the greatest I ever saw.'

It seems to have been the product of a mazy run like a soccer player would make. He gathered the puck-out from the Clare goalkeeper, Mick Hayes, slipped past two Wexford defenders, and headed for goal. 'I normally hit the ball with the left,' said Smyth in an interview in Raymond Smith's 1972 book, *The Clash of the Ash*. 'I tried to do so on this occasion, but the Wexfordmen were aware of this gambit – hence the way was barred. Turning to hit with the right, I was also anticipated. Being reasonably hefty, I went through the middle, meeting Bobby Rackard – I think – on the way. I was spun around, but, luckily, I found myself facing the goal. Going on again, I hit the ball from the twenty-one-yard line. Art Foley stopped the shot – the backs failed to clear and I was lucky enough to be up to score.'

Within a couple of minutes, Smyth added the equalising point from a free, and helped Clare win the replay on a bleak November afternoon shortly afterwards.

Ó Muircheartaigh first took proper notice of him in 1949 when Smyth turned out for a Munster colleges' football team against Leinster. One of his teammates that day was Team of the Millennium member, Seán Murphy. Apart from his scores as a hurler, what impressed Ó Muircheartaigh was Smyth's physique. 'He was a big young fella. I mean to look at him – he'd a huge back,' he says. When he was hurling fit, Smyth weighed fifteen and a half stone, a prodigious size for a hurler of that era, given that Colin 'Pinetree' Meads, New Zealand's fearsome lock forward of the late 1950s and 1960s, was sixteen stone when playing.

'He was a big strong man,' agrees Liam Griffin, the son of a Clare man, who remembers seeing him score three – if not four – goals from play against 'the great Ollie Walsh' in Nolan Park. 'He was a fierce strong man when he got the ball. He could carry a ball. He just strode around the game like a colossus. Any time I saw him play, whether Railway Cup or with Clare, he always seemed to be a dominant force. He wasn't the kind of fella that disappeared in a game.'

Neither has his stature in the game dissipated over the years. He was commemorated on a stamp as part of An Post's GAA Hall of Fame collection in 2002. Eamon Cregan once remarked that he was among five of the best hurlers of all time. John Doyle, who won eight All-Ireland medals, said that, next to Christy Ring, he was the finest hurler he ever played on. But perhaps the most enduring plaudit came from Ring himself.

Cloyne's finest came up to Ruan in 1971 to help publicise the re-opening of their pitch. After the game, he repaired to Smyth's mother's house. After half an hour of tea and chat, he got up to go. Perhaps a touch sentimental, though understandably so, he left her to dwell on these words: 'Do you know, missus, your son is the best hurler in Ireland.'

As for Ring, Smyth is effusive in praise of his mastery. Along with Nicky Rackard, he remains a hero. 'No matter what position he was in, he was always a figure of art,' he says. 'What he did with the ball, it was always artistic. Balance more than anything else. I've seen him score, his body flat along the ground, his arm stretched out, and he'd be able to strike the ball and bury it in the corner. Oh, he was deadly. I've never seen anything like him.'

'What about D. J. Carey?' I wonder.

'He was better than D. J. D. J. would probably have more skills than him in some areas, but Christ, he couldn't touch him for determination and power to enthuse people. He had this power. Thousands came to see him. He was the last word.

'He had something special. People were attracted to him. He didn't have to say anything. I always say it about Ring, "When he came out onto the pitch, every daisy got a sudden death."'

Smyth – who was an accomplished track athlete – would burn Ring by ten yards over one hundred, but 'from here to the wall,' he says, pointing to the other end of his sitting room in Clontarf, County Dublin, 'nobody could beat him. He didn't sprint, he bounded. He seemed to be here; then he was gone.'

Ring had that mental resilience, too. 'He silenced many opponents with the steel of his stare, and the cold stillness of his eyes could see into the tops of your toes. The mind to Ring was everything,' wrote Smyth in the chapter, 'Memoir of a Hurling Life', which opened his book, *In Praise of Heroes: Ballads and Poems of the GAA*.

As for the heat in Hell's Kitchen – where Messrs Doyle, Maher and Carey webbed all before them, as part of Tipperary's notorious full-back line of his era – Smyth says it has been exaggerated. 'They were just hard, tough men, but they were fair men. I played on John Doyle for a number of years, and he was tough, and he used his legs and his arms and his hips, everything, and his hair would be askew, and he'd be running out, and his socks would be down, and he'd be taking everything in front of him, and he looked tough, but I never got a dirty stroke from him. Never. It was only fairy tales,' he says, tossing his head dismissively.

He has great regard for the skills of today's backs, although the smothering tactics that modern defences employ have changed the nature of the game – doing away with the art of doubling in the air, for one. 'I think back play is out of this world today, certainly better than it was in my time,' he says. 'The forwards may not be as good, but the backs are twice as good as when I was playing because there are always four or five backs on you now. In our time, except against the great Tipperary team, you were always only playing one man. It was easy because you weren't crowded out. It's very difficult to score now.'

The 'great Tipperary team' he refers to – the best he has seen until Brian Cody's three-in-a-row outfit emerged – is the one that went two and a half years unbeaten from 1964–65, league and championship – a team that included Jimmy Doyle, Len Gaynor and Babs Keating. Smyth refereed the Munster finals both those years in which they easily beat Cork.

Year in year out, Smyth played Railway Cup with Ring *et al.* at a time when the annual Gaelic football and hurling Railway Cup finals at Croke Park on St Patrick's Day were one of the great days in the country's sporting calendar. He played in twelve Railway Cups from 1952–64 – a record for a Clareman – winning eight finals. Amusingly, he reckons he only ever received two passes in all those appearances, as players vied to prevent players from other counties from stealing any limelight. 'There was a Corkman injured badly in one match, and I remember Jim "Tough" Barry saying to him under no circumstances was he to go off – a Tipperary man would be coming on in his place. That's Cork for you!'

As it happens, Jim 'Tough' Barry's role was largely superfluous. 'Management in those times really meant nothing,' says Smyth. 'Jim Barry had a fierce reputation as a manager of a team, but, sure, he never spoke to me and I was there about eleven years. Jim "Tough" Barry had great fellas with him,' he points out sagely.

'Really, he was ploughing a lonely furrow. Clare had a lot of good players around at that time, but you hadn't anybody as strong as he was. He was a bit like Tony O'Reilly making his name with the [British and Irish] Lions in that he played some of his best games for Munster in the Railway Cup,' argues Dermot Kelly, drawing an analogy with another Irish sporting star of the 1950s.

Perhaps this is an overly harsh assessment of Smyth's county teammates from the man who tormented Clare in the 1955 Munster final, amassing an incredible 1–12 as hopes of Clare's first Munster final victory since 1932 foundered on a stifling hot July day.

'For me to remember a team that played fifty-three years ago is a great compliment. I can still remember the names of the players on the Clare team that day,' says Babs Keating about the 1955 Munster semi-final game against Tipperary. 'They were outstanding players. You'd Mick Hayes in goal; Dan McInerney, full-back. You'd [Donal] O'Grady and [Dermot] Sheedy, and Des Dillon was exceptional, and [Haulie] Donnellan and Matt Nugent. It's a bit like the Down football team – they created an impression.'

Smyth refrains from isolating any one of the Clare team in particular for their prowess, deeming it 'a bit hurtful' to do so. As to the rumours that some of the players were drinking on the night of the 1955 Munster final, he is dismissive. 'I don't know anything about that,' he says sharply, before laughing, 'I know I didn't go wild, anyway. I don't know anything about what the other fellas did. You'd hear all kinds of stories, and I'm sure every story you hear is a lie.'

Clare were run-away favourites going in to the 1955 Munster final, having recently defeated Wexford, the previous year's All-Ireland finalists, in November's Oireachtas final; Cork, the three-in-a-row All-Ireland champions in the first round; and Tipp in the semi-final. But complacency and an electric performance by 'Mackey's Greyhounds' caught them out. It was the end of that Clare team. That they had underachieved is indisputable, riddled as they were with an age-old inferiority complex. As Smyth has remarked, 'Even the language of the supporters carried the wail and woe of what was said and unsaid. I hated the question, "Will ye win?" People knew the answer when they asked you. What they were really saying was, "We want you to win, we know you can; but you won't."'

That the epoch-ending defeat came against Limerick was tough to take, as Limerick were Clare's most intense rivals of the period, with each county interchanging periods of ascendency over the other. 'I remember going to a match between Clare and Limerick, and this is something that always remains with me,' he says of an abiding memory of his days as a kid going to matches. 'Larry Blake was playing. He'd a great match, but Limerick beat Clare. I think it was the first round of the championship.

'Coming out, Larry was with his son Michael – Michael was killed afterwards; he played with Clare – and I remember somebody put a Limerick badge on Michael's coat, and Larry caught it and threw it to the ground, put his foot down on it, as if to say, "That's it!"'

Smyth was born in Ruan on New Year's Day 1931, a fortuitous date for those playing Gaelic games. Born a day earlier and he would have missed out on a year of playing minor hurling. Not that it would have mattered much. Smyth played Clare minor hurling for an astonishing five years in a row. He also played on St Flannan's Harty Cup team for five years, reaching the final in each year – winning the first three and losing the last two, one as captain. Bishop Willie Walsh – a selector for the Clare hurling team in the early 1990s – remembers arriving in St Flannan's College in September 1947 and being 'agog' as Smyth was the senior boy attached to his row of seats in chapel. 'He was outstanding,' he says. 'Just for a natural hurler, he had it every way. He had a tremendous physical presence, but also, for a big man, he could turn in a very small space – he could hit a ball in a very small space.'

Smyth learned his hurling in the expanse of Porte Hill, a thirty-acre hill and field at the back of his house. As a child, he played six and seven hours a day with old broken bits of hurleys pieced together, or 'straight sticks'; these were hazel sticks with a loop at the end that they'd manufacture themselves. They used to call them 'spocks'. He didn't get a proper hurley until he was about ten or eleven years of age.

He went to school at Kells National School, where his mother was principal. She was a devout hurling fan, as her brothers played for Clooney. Although she wouldn't let her charges sit in a draught in case of catching cold, she happily let them play hurling in a downpour. 'When it came to hurling, she had her values right,' says Smyth mischievously. His father was a sergeant with the gardaí, and was stationed in barracks during the week – often in other counties, such as Mayo, Galway and Kerry – so Smyth and his three brothers and sister would only see him at weekends, as was customary for children of a garda at the time.

He would get to see him and his mother less once he began boarding in St Flannan's – entering during the war years, so he got to experience an especially Spartan regime. 'We had the black bread and the auld patter, yellow butter,' he says, his face contorting at the memory. 'Then we had Mass at half past six in the morning, and we were in bed at nine. It was a fairly tough old tenure, I can tell you.'

After school, he got a job with Clare County Council. He won the first of five county championships with Ruan in 1948. The final is remembered for eighteen minutes' extra time that the ref allowed, but it was against Clarecastle so nobody in the rest of the county was too perturbed. The 'Magpies' were the team to beat in those days, and the town/country divide was even more pronounced back then. 'Ah, there was always a divide between the town and the country,' he says. 'Larry Blake used always say to the townies when they'd go out to Tulla, "Lads, when ye go out past Corrovorrin, you're on your own." It's different now because country fellas are more up-to-date then they were in my time. There was this little bit of jealousy by the countrymen of the townies. They were always sleeker. They dressed nattier, and they got the women. So they always had something on us, and we were jealous of them, and then when they came over with a stylish flow on the hurling field, you'd cut 'em asunder. You vented your jealousy on them,' he says with a laugh.

For dances, himself and his mates would cycle into Ennis. None of his teammates on the Clare team would have had a car, with the possible exception of Dan McInerney. Smyth married a Clare woman, Vera, and they have four children and twelve grandchildren, all living in Ireland.

Having worked for fifteen years with the council, he moved to Dublin to take up a post as an executive officer at Croke Park, where he worked until his retirement in August 1988. He went back to university in 1989, studying philosophy for four years at Trinity College, which accounts for the inquiring, intellectual approach he has to hurling. Interestingly, he suggests that if a team took to ground hurling again, it would revolutionise the game and break up this cloying, smothering defence that teams adopt in the present era.

As to the other big questions about life outside hurling, his answers are less decisive. 'I eventually formed the decision – because I got a good honours degree in it, you know – that we'd talk about anything and get no place,' he says, tumbling in laughter.

After his jousts with philosophy, he earned a master's degree at University of Limerick, completing his thesis on 'The Poems, Songs and Recitations of the GAA in Munster'. It was a labour of love, as he's a renowned ballad singer himself, and it later helped inform his books, *Ballads of the Banner* and his magnificent tome, *In Praise of Heroes*.

He still lives in Dublin. The house he bought in Clontarf is the one in which Maureen Toal (or Teasie in *Glenroe*) was born in. His heart is still back across the Shannon, though. 'I'm in Dublin forty years but I'm still a Clareman,' he says in his broad Clare accent. 'I never settled down here. You never do. When I go down to Nenagh, when I'm shoving in to Clare, I get a breath of fresh air.'

The county has given him much; and him the county much. After that championship game against Limerick in 1953 in which, according to the *Clare Champion*, he 'bedevilled the Limerick backs to the tune of 6–4 with wizardly accuracy', an elderly lady approached him by the side gate outside Cusack Park after the game. 'She smiled into my face, and caught me by the back of the jersey,' he says. 'Without a word and with her hand still on my jersey, she walked by my side to the Queen's Hotel doorway, where she smiled into my face again, and then walked silently and smilingly away.'

MICK O'DEA

Portraits don't always bring pleasure to the sitters. Winston Churchill felt that Graham Sutherland's likeness made him look as if he was passing a troublesome stool. When the old bulldog passed away, his wife had the canvas burnt. Manet took no such chances – he had Degas' portrait of himself and his wife torn up immediately. No doubt painting portraits is a daunting business for the subject and, indeed, for the artist on occasion.

'I've had people storm out of rooms,' says the portrait painter Mick O'Dea. 'I've had people cry, shriek with terror, look for mirrors, look at the mirror, look at themselves and then at me, and in a kind of broken way say, "I suppose that's the way you see me." It made me feel like an assassin when all I'm trying to do is honestly paint the person in front of me.

'I have been forced to question myself after the few extreme reactions to my work by the sitter because I'm not in the business of trying to character-assassinate people. It's very hard to hold your nerve then.'

'When I was that bit younger, I was tougher. I think I might be a little bit more sensitive to people now, which could be a mistake. At one stage, even, I was doing portraits of people without clothes on or just in their underwear or T-shirt on the basis that everyone's the same,' he says, adopting a mock serious voice: 'Strip them of all their props. Let's have no books there or anything to show that they're this, that or the other thing.

'And how I would have had opinions of people would have affected how I would have painted them. Then I was looking at particular representational artists – usually German or Austrian, tough kind of painters, in the early twentieth century, who were uncompromising – and that's what I'm interested in.'

It's this unbending vision of O'Dea's that can cause the upset, particularly, he points out, for the unsuspecting sitter unfamiliar with his work. Of course, anyone who says that they're not vain is a liar, so to run the gauntlet and have one's physical image thrown into harsh light, exposing facets of one's personality and laying bare the ageing process, must be an unnerving experience. As George Orwell once remarked, 'At age fifty, every man has the face he deserves'.

'In the beginning, it was traumatic because people have ideas about portraits,' explains O'Dea. 'Maybe people would have an idea that a portrait painter has the ability to see in them everything positive that they've done in their life, and that what I'm in the business of doing is seeing all that and bringing it to the fore, whereas they don't realise: I can only paint what I see.

'I'm not good at not being able to paint what's in front of me. I was told by my wife, at the time – Elizabeth – she said, "Mick, if you want to become a successful portrait painter, you need to wear dark sunglasses smeared with Vaseline." As it is, I'm all too sharp.'

'All Mick's portraits of people are the key to him,' argues the poet Theo Dorgan – a friend and fellow member of Aosdána. 'He'll try and see: who are you? Straight away: who's in there? He has a genuine interest in other people, but he also has a very serious sense of himself as an artist without being in the least bit po-faced. The way to talk to Mick is to talk to him with a brush or a pencil in his hand because that's who he is.'

Elected to Aosdána in 1996, O'Dea is one of the country's pre-eminent artists. By his own admission, he is a 'fair-weather landscape painter', and every Wednesday he paints nudes, but it is for his portraits of many of Ireland's more prominent people (in their clothes) that he is best known.

People from the arts and media world alone who have sat for him include the writers Roddy Doyle, Gerry Stembridge and Colm Tóibín, the actor Michael Harding, artistic director of the Dublin Theatre Festival, Loughlin Deegan, and journalists Lara Marlowe, Catherine Foley and Aidan Dunne.

It is, however, for a work to do with another journalist – Ireland's foremost investigative reporter, Veronica Guerin – that brought him to nationwide attention at the end of May 2003. O'Dea endured a week of frenzied media debate – most notably on Joe Duffy's *Liveline* show on RTÉ radio – for putting forward a portrait of Brian Meehan, the convicted murderer of Guerin, as part of the annual RHA exhibition.

O'Dea submitted the painting as one of his six to hang with more than four hundred others in the academy for its six-week-long exhibition. Earlier that season, O'Dea had carried out a two-week workshop at Portlaoise Prison entitled, 'How to paint somebody standing up at an easel'. The prison organised the models, one of which happened to be Meehan.

'When it came towards the end of the year, I had to select work,' explains O'Dea about his duty as a member of the RHA to submit a selection for its annual exhibition. 'I had all the stuff laid out. My girlfriend was with me. She said, "That is the best portrait."

'I said, "I know it's the best portrait but there could be fallout."

'At the same time, one of the things that I've always attacked artists for is self-censorship. Never mind censorship from everywhere else – that's there – but the biggest offender when it comes to censorship are the artists and the writers themselves in that they don't want to show the full story. I was in a situation then where I had to make a decision, and I said, "All right, I was going to put it in."

'I put it in and nothing happened for a week, and then somebody noticed it and the shit hit the fan. I could see where it was coming from, and at the same time the only way that I could answer was that I had to make the decision that I had made. I think people reacted in the sense that here is another case of the perpetrator being lionised at the expense of the victim.

'The biggest problem that a lot of people had was the fact that it was being shown at the annual RHA exhibition, so it was the context. It was a major society exhibition, and the portraits of the RHA every year are of the great and the good, so Cardinal [Desmond] Connell, for example, was up there. People tend to view portraits there as the Hall of Fame, and if your portrait is hanging in the RHA, it's because of achievement or your contribution to society. Here was somebody – hanging up with all of those – whose contribution to society one could question. I don't have the stereotypical view of portraiture that it's like that – as far as I'm concerned, it's something else.'

This was what drew the ire of Willie O'Dea, junior minister for justice at the time. The moustachioed minister, leading the political community's charge, felt that the portrait was giving Meehan 'a status that he did not deserve'. Another problem was that Meehan didn't look like he was suffering, which shocked the public in the way that the sheer ordinariness of the Nazi Adolf Eichmann's appearance unsettled people around the world during his 1961 trial in Israel for his role in the Holocaust, which culminated in his execution.

'He didn't look like he was repentant,' says Mick O'Dea about the portrait of Meehan. 'He didn't look like incarceration was making him suffer, and that outraged a lot of people – the fact that he looked ordinary and that he looked relaxed. That in turn was clear evidence that the artist had no insight into the true nature of the man because, if he did, he would have portrayed a completely different kind of man. It's a bit like the notion that the artist is meant to see into the soul, so in some way I would have a kind of Dorian Gray unveiled, I would have a Dorian Gray in the attic rather than the veneer.'

Supported by the RHA's committee, O'Dea held his nerve and the painting remained on exhibit although it was withdrawn for sale, having being listed for €3,000. The controversy was a fascinating case-study – albeit one that O'Dea acknowledges caused a lot of 'hurt and upset' to folk at the time – into the expectations that people sometimes have about art; that, in the instance of Meehan's portrait, it should cohere with the emotions and preconceptions of the beholder of the work of art rather than represent truth. As Professor Brian Maguire – who ran the art course in the prison at the time – rightly remarked, 'When we paint someone in prison, we paint the human being and not the crime.'

O'Dea had been working with prisoners in art programmes for fifteen years when the Meehan ruckus blew up. Before becoming the establishment figure he is today, he juggled a variety of part-time jobs with his painting, teaching art in prisons, hospitals and primarily in art schools such as Dún Laoghaire School of Art and the National College of Art and Design, where he taught from 1981 until 1999.

He admits that his compulsion to be a portrait painter comes from his fascination with history and his desire 'to contribute to the faces of time'. He has always wanted to paint people, and surmises that his comfort in the company of his fellow man may come from the fact that he grew up in an old-style pub-grocery business, working as a messenger boy – a routine that exposed him to people and their stories, and afforded him the time, while on call, to doodle on a sketch pad.

O'Dea was born in Ennis, County Clare in 1958, growing up in a pub at the end of the town's main street, O'Connell Street, and a few doors from the Pro-Cathedral. His brother John still runs the pub, which in their youth played second fiddle to the grocery side of the house. On returning from over a decade working in Boston, their father, also Mick, started the business, O'Dea Bros, with his brother Tom, a veteran of the republican side during the War of Independence and civil war.

O'Dea's first memory of art came while he was in the town's old convent school, which is now a museum opposite the Temple Gate hotel. He was about five. 'At the time,' he explains, 'junior and senior infants still didn't use paper – we used chalk and slate. Everyone had their own slate. I liked the chalk on the slate. I remember the nuns would give us *marla*, or plasticine, and the first thing that I ever made, the nun came along and asked me – Sr Malachy was her name – she said, "What are you making?"

'I said, "A graveyard." Because the slate was the land and then I had all these tombstones.'

Fortunately, as he points out, there were no child psychologists in the early 1960s school system to try and unravel the impulses behind his creative tendencies. Later attending the local CBS, O'Dea applauds the encouragement given to him by Cyril Brennan, one of his teachers. Interestingly, O'Dea painted a portrait of Brennan's son, a diplomat, also named Cyril, in 2006, while O'Dea was in Paris by invitation of the Irish College to complete a series of portraits.

After the Christian Brothers, O'Dea went to St Flannan's College where he came into contact with the school's art teacher, Jim Hennessy, who, due to his bald pate, went by the nickname 'Hairy', and like all teachers was prone to bouts of sarcastic ribbing. 'When he'd lose the cool,' remembers O'Dea, 'for his most extreme reaction, he'd say, "If I was your father, I'd stop feedin' you." We'd be on the corridor waiting for the class to open and you'd hear these steps going down the stairs overhead, and lads would say, "Hairy comes," and then he'd pass by – "Hairy goes."

'But he was a big influence. He created a very good climate in the art room. He challenged us. He'd have pictures up on the wall – Picasso and other artists. I think a lot of young fellas are reactionary, and I think we were no different to anyone else. For instance, when we went into the art room at thirteen or fourteen, fellas would be saying, "That's not art, sir. He's got two eyes on the one side of his head. Sure, anyone could do that, sir."

'Jim would say, "You're ignorant, boy." And he was right. It was through exposure and his non-judgemental approach – other than telling you that you were ignorant – that we were lucky to be there.'

Hennessy must have fired their imaginations if the statistics are anything to go by. O'Dea's Leaving Certificate class was the first to send a crop of students to art college. Five, including O'Dea, went on to carve careers in the art world: Mike Fitzpatrick is current director of Limerick City Gallery of Art; Harry Guinane is a wildlife artist; Dermot Kelleher is a noted local sign writer; and, completing the circle, Brendan Howard is the present art teacher in St Flannan's.

Where study in art college might lead for their son was never a concern for O'Dea's parents, despite the uncertain employment climate in mid 1970s Ireland. His father, from Daragh, and his mother, from Crusheen, thoroughly supported his decision, oblivious to the precariousness of a life in the art world or the perceived lack of practicality in studying art. O'Dea suggests that the potential for teaching at the end of the degree offered something tangible to appease, if necessary, but in reality his parents seem to have been remarkably philosophical in their hopes for him. O'Dea says that his dad used to even try and get him to work in the shop during the Leaving Certificate exams, and says he would have liked for O'Dea – who showed interest – to have become a farmer on the land that the family had outside town.

'In a way, they had rebelled themselves,' says O'Dea. 'He had travelled a bit. He'd gone to America in 1927–28 and came back in 1939. My mother was in England during the war as a midwife. She went there in 1938, came back in 1946, so they had a bit of experience. They weren't anxious for us. If you needed to do something, you fled the nest. You did it.

'I think country people are like that. Maybe it's because they didn't have a middle-class value system, that they were country people who had to go abroad and came into the town. They were respectable, and they had to work hard for anything they got, but they weren't all that conscious about middle-class values.

'My father's education didn't go beyond primary school; my mother's did, but the fact that I even had the desire to do something – to go to art college, for instance – if I showed that initiative – fine. If I didn't have any initiative maybe it would have been a different case.

'I think [my father] was quoting George Bernard Shaw when he said, "Never let your schooling interfere with your education." He was always acutely aware of that. He was always aware that it is in the world that you'll get your education. So they never valued education if the person was unpleasant or not a nice person because they were dealing with people in the bar and the shop all the time. They didn't discriminate. Education and the kind of person you were, were two different things.'

O'Dea – not surprisingly, given his artistic bent and feel for history – paints a vivid portrait of life in Ennis during his school days: a town that at the time had a population of 8,000 people, a third the size of the bustling satellite town it has become for neighbouring employment centres, Galway, Limerick and Shannon today. During the 1960s and early 1970s, the town was 'quite intimate' – people lived in the town. His neighbours, the McCulloughs, for example, had about thirteen in the family.

O'Dea despairs of the reconstruction visited on the nearby cathedral, ushered in following the Second Vatican Council, changes that caused the church to lose its 'nice railings' and much of its ornate interior. 'A lot of lounge-bar building skills were employed,' he says wistfully, pointing out that so many things were associated with poverty – wood in particular – which meant everything exposed had to be 'painted or pebble-dashed' in a rush to embrace modernity, or, worse, they were burned. With the onset of electric light, he kids, you could see dirt for the first time, which meant beautiful old, solid pine surfaces were replaced with Formica, while walls were adorned, for the first time, with the wonder of washable wallpaper.

'Every generation sees a transition of one sort,' he says. 'I saw the pre-television transition. When we were younger, we didn't have telly. The first television shop opened opposite the church – a place called

RTV Rentals. The televisions were left on in the night-time. I'd be down there trying to get in to look, and there'd be about fifty or sixty people all gathered around looking,' he says, shifting in his seat to ape the jostling. Television, like, was coming. There was one series on called *The Gallant Men*. I've never seen it since, but I think it was a kind of Second World War series. Everyone was trying to see *The Gallant Men*.'

The town had a splendid cinema – the Gaiety Theatre on O'Connell Street – which closed around 1972 or 1973, he reckons, being replaced with the Burren Cinema. 'I remember Fr Ryan,' he says, 'on the pulpit condemning a film called *The Sweet Sins of Sexy Susie*. Not that anything much happened in the film – it was kind of old-style stuff. And I remember the black marker used to be still employed in posters. When you got low-cut dresses, you'd get the black marker filling up the cleavage. There was a lot of creativity on display all over town at that time.'

O'Dea remembers the first people to flaunt flairs and mini-skirts around the streets, and also the first local women to wear trousers. Before that, tourists might be seen in them occasionally – to the dismay of some locals. 'You'd hear people commenting,' he says, "They were wearing trousers."'

Meanwhile, if you were a fashion cad, the greatest compliment to receive would be if someone remarked that your clothes were very 'swanky', a variation, he reckons, on the progressive style being paraded by Yankee tourists. Yet despite the dowdiness of the fashion and the strictures of the Catholic Church, there was tremendous acceptance of difference. 'There were great characters around the town,' says O'Dea, 'like Michael Tierney who was kind of extrovert gay, a great man for wearing women's gear. He'd a great collection of hats. My father would be there and he'd say, "How's your knickers today, Michael?" and he'd have a smart comment for my father, and all the other heterosexual men in town were not in the slightest bit threatened by Michael. He was camp and great fun.

'At the same time, Michael would have tours, magical mystery tours, where all the women went on the tour with him. A fifty-two-seater bus would arrive, maybe outside the church. Michael would take them off for the day up to the Burren or somewhere. They'd end up coming back a bit tipsy one way or the other. Michael would entertain them along the way; they'd stop for dinner and Michael would have a chance then to wear his different hats.

'There was a lot of tolerance for eccentricity. There was a lot of tragedy – not in Michael's case – but a lot of the characters had major drink problems, but, nonetheless, they were accepted as part and parcel of the scene. A lot of people had come from the same background. The class thing wasn't there. It was about people. It was more character-based because it was people that were important, not what the people had. It was about what you could contribute, like what song you had. There was singing in every bar. Every man had a song, and regardless if it was heard every Sunday, the Sunday wouldn't be the same unless that song was sung at the same time.'

What is striking about O'Dea is that he is about the least eccentric person you could meet. Sure, he's independent-minded, but there is an earthy, unpretentious air about him. You get the sense that he's very comfortable in his own skin, and although he's learned, he is – as his friend, the writer Eoin McNamee says – as happy discussing Clare hurling as he is about Flaubert.

'There's a good no-nonsense quality to him,' adds the writer Eamon Delaney – another friend. 'He's straight up. It's great at a time when there's so much bullshit in the arts, so much of it is impenetrable and about theory. It's great just to have somebody who's got traditional, artistic values. Back to what art used to be.'

TOM MORRISSEY

Did you know that Tom Morrissey crossed the Canadian border to get back into the United States in the back of a bread van? Or that he travelled up to Leitrim with the Clare football team on crutches, having reefed his foot on a rusty nail at work in Ennistymon a couple of days earlier. Clare were getting thumped, so Morrissey gritted his teeth, threw the crutches to the side, and went on for the second half, scoring a goal as Clare, heartbreakingly, lost by a point. If only he had started the game.

Of course the stories are apocryphal, embellished with the telling over the years. There are so many stories about the man, enough to fill a book; not your Hans Christian Anderson variety, though – more of the kind to be savoured over a few drinks in the local. 'Lads at home, now,' says a former Cooraclare clubmate, 'would sit around a bar for a night and tell Tom stories: "We'll have a Tom story session."'

Unlike the English singer of the same name, Morrissey is a big rogue, full of bluster. He was blessed with an inordinate gift for Gaelic football but cursed by a short career, having played his last championship game for Clare aged twenty-five. A talent squandered? Unquestionably so, but the man made sure to enjoy – if not capitalise on – his brief brush with celebrity, and managed to pick up a Munster football championship medal along the way. And there aren't many of those men alive outside Cork or Kerry.

Morrissey grew up on a farm in Cooraclare along with his eight brothers and four sisters. He came fourth in the brood, all of them 'football crazy', he affirms, including his sister Eithne, who has won six All-Ireland medals and two All-Stars. 'They had to fend for themselves at a very early age,' says Gerard Kelly, the principal of Cooraclare National School. 'They're a very loving family and very caring. Like at school, if a child fell in the yard, they'd be the first over to lift him up and see if he was all right. Even though they were reared hard, there was no blackguardism involved.'

Morrissey's mother, Mary, is something of a folk legend, the original soccer mom. A few years ago, when there was a Morrissey boy in every line of the Cooraclare side, the story goes that if the ball went in towards the full-back line, the cry would go up from the crowd: 'Pat's ball'; if it made it to midfield: 'Tom's ball'; arriving at full-forward: 'Martin's ball'; and when it slipped out over the sideline: 'Mary's ball.'

One of the many mysteries about Tom Morrissey is that he was such a small, light fellow growing up. 'He was insignificant in those days, a small wizened little lad,' says Kelly. At seventeen, he was five-foot-five and seven and a half stone – small enough to be thrown out a school window. A year and a half later, he had shot up to six-foot-three and weighed in at thirteen stone.

After an undistinguished under-age career, the change in stature was enough to help get him on to county teams. He played under-21 for Clare for two years – playing midfield against a Maurice Fitzgerald–Noel O'Mahony pairing in a trouncing administered by Kerry in 1990 – and captained Cooraclare to an under-21 county title in 1991. His relationship with the county senior set-up was tumultuous from the start, though. 'I remember meeting him as a young fella,' says John Maughan, Clare senior football manager at the time. 'He certainly wasn't shy. The story was this young, raw lad,' he says, stifling a laugh, 'from Cooraclare would never play county football again – along the lines: "I'm never going to play for them feckers, dada, dada, da" –

because apparently he had some sort of a bad encounter where he had to walk home after being injured or going for treatment or something. Meanwhile, to the best of my knowledge, he was lighting up his Major at the same time. That's the type of character he was. He hasn't a care in the world, full of charisma, full of devilment.'

'If you want the real story,' says Morrissey – obviously used to amending details about the public's understanding of his biography – 'in 1990, Clare were in the All-Ireland "B" playing Sligo, and I was called into the panel. Brendan Brown and myself took off over to Ennis, and there was only sixteen players there, and we were playing above in Markievicz Park. No manager – Noel Walsh was missing. The only selector there was Donal Clancy.

'So off up to Sligo we went – the sixteen of us. Donal Clancy and Martin Flynn picked the team. Martin Flynn was captain because Miltown [Malbay] won the [county] championship in 1990. No one knew me so they left me on the sideline. So that was grand until about fifteen minutes into the game [when], next thing, Noel Walsh arrived in. "The Colonel" we used to call him. There was I standing above by the dugout and I smoking a fag. I'll never forget it. "Have you interest in playing football for Clare?" he says.

'"To be honest with you, Noel, not too interested now," I said to him.

'"Put out that fag!" he says.

'So I put out the cigarette, and in the second half Frankie Griffin was hurt and I went on, and I was on ten minutes when I got sand-wiched. Oh, busted two ribs up under my shoulder blade. I had to come off. Frankie Griffin went back on again.

'I arrived home and didn't go into the hospital or the doctor till the following day. My mother and father were going to Ballinasloe, and they brought me over to hospital. I got an X-ray – two ribs busted – and got a prescription for painkillers, and they sent me off on my way. I was out of work for about four weeks, and I put in an insurance claim and they gave me £21.90. That was £10 for the hospital fee and

£11.90 for the chemist, so I told them to go away. I wouldn't play senior. I'd only play 21s.'

His return to the senior panel could not have been timed better, as he played his first National League game against Tipperary in the spring of 1992. With the change to the open draw in Munster, Clare overcame Tipp a few months later in the championship semi-final to make their first senior interprovincial football final since 1949. Nobody, save Maughan and his courageous, bouncing-fit band of footballers, predicted the improbable 2–10 to 0–12 victory over Kerry in Limerick's Gaelic Grounds on 19 July 1992, Jack O'Shea's last game for the Kingdom.

'With about three or four minutes to go, the pressure was serious from Kerry,' remembers Martin Daly, goal hero for Clare that day. 'They were four points down, looking for a goal, and constantly pushing forward. [Clare goalkeeper] James Hanrahan took a kick-out and it was coming towards the stand side. We were hitting towards the Ennis-side goal, and Tom just went for a ball, and he was head and shoulders above anybody else. Just when you wanted it: "Let's win the ball and go up the field and make an attack for ourselves."

'That's typical of Tom. The lads would be slagging him because he's a super character, but when it comes down to it, you could count on him because he was that type of guy that could get the one hand in or the one catch or the one point that you'd need.'

'I remember some pictures of Tom catching the ball in the middle of the field, and he would have his feet up that height,' says Joe Considine, pointing at a bar table. Joe was a Cooraclare teammate and played midfield for Clare in the 2000 Munster football final. 'But it was the arc he could get on his body. He could catch a ball jumping, and his hands could be back here, catching the ball,' he says, with his arms raised like a soccer player taking a throw-in.

'A lot of midfielders catch the ball over their heads or in front of them. Tom had this ability to lean, arch. His only difficulty was keeping his feet. He was light-legged. If he got the ball, he might often be knocked over. But on his day, when Tom put his mind to it, when he was on form, minding himself and applying himself, you couldn't match him. When he had that year in 1992, it was off the back of anonymity. That was perfect for Tom.'

After the Munster-final win, the team went on a tour of the constituency to celebrate the county's first title win since 1917, finishing up in Miltown Malbay early on the Wednesday morning. 'We went over to training that Wednesday evening,' says Morrissey with that raspy voice of his, as dry and leathery as old cowboy boots, 'and Maughan, he says, "Lads, if we want to win the All-Ireland semi-final, there's one thing we have to do. What have we to do, Tom Morrissey?" I knew what he was hitting at.

'"I suppose we've to go off the drink, John."

'"Well done Tom Morrissey."

'Cooraclare played Kilkee in a club championship first round the following Sunday. We lost. By God, my tongue was hanging down to there,' he says, pointing at the ground. 'I didn't have one drink. No drink. We did – we stayed off the drink until the All-Ireland semi-final.'

Few of a certain age will forget the giddy excitement that took over the county in the run-up to the game against Dublin. For most Clare fans, it was a first-ever visit to Croke Park. More alarming, with the exception of Noel Roche, a compromise-rules star, it was the first time for all of the Clare footballers to play there. Not that it fazed Morrissey. 'I think that little garden will suit me,' he was heard to say to someone in the dressing-room before running out onto the pitch where he and his teammates were met with a back-draft of noise they'll never forget. 'Oh, Jesus Christ, the crowd,' he says. 'One thing I will never, ever forget is the run-out in Croke Park. I will never, ever forget the atmosphere in that field. Oh man, it just went straight through our heads. The roar. There was about 60,000 people there. It was fantastic.'

'Did it get to you?'

'No, no, I revelled in it,' he says, struggling for words to describe his enthusiasm. 'The bigger the crowd – the bigger I am. That's the way I was. I loved the crowd, being modest as I am,' he says, cackling in laughter.

Clare, possibly overawed by the occasion, surrendered an early lead to Dublin that they never managed to claw back, and, unlucky with two goal decisions, they lost in a high-scoring affair, 3–14 to 2–12. Morrissey excelled, but was cited after the game for decking Charlie Redmond with a box. The irony was that he mentioned in a broadsheet profile before the match that the use of video evidence was one of the ways in which the game could be improved. Observers say that the suspension cost him an All-Star. He did, however, pick up a Munster Player of the Year award at the end of the season. 'It was the most fantastic year of my life,' he says. He was twenty-two years of age.

The Maughan train continued on through a few more stations, reaching a quarter-final of the league in 1993 against Donegal in Croke Park, in which Morrissey scored a wonder goal.

But a moment of personal disaster lay in store for him the following year. 'Oh, Jesus Christ, 1994,' he says despairingly. 'A game I will never forget. We played Tipperary below in the Gaelic Grounds in the first round. We kicked seventeen wides the same day. Two minutes to go, Tipperary's Peter Lambert kicked in a ball from the sideline. I went in to catch it, dropped it into the net anyway. Down a point. Jeez, I'll never forget that game. I was after playing a fine game. I just wanted to bury myself into the ground that day. "Will you get out to midfield?" Horse [Aidan Moloney] said to me. That was 1994 taken care of. John Maughan left after that.'

John O'Keeffe took over the reins, leading Clare to a Munster final in 1997, but Morrissey was long gone from the scene by that stage. Himself and O'Keeffe endured a frosty relationship that resulted in Morrissey playing his last championship game against Cork in 1995. 'That day, he'd a bad run,' says a Clare teammate who played that afternoon. 'He was moved from midfield into centre-forward and full-forward, and nothing was working for him on the day. Nothing was working for any of us. We lost by six or seven points. But he was taken off with about ten minutes to go, and he walked over to [Cork manager] Billy Morgan and shook hands with him: "Ye have it now." Tom is gone off the field. There's no way we're going to win it now, like.'

Morrissey emigrated to Boston a couple of weeks later, working at 'everything and anything,' including construction (or 'destruction,' as he calls it, given the work entailed gutting premises); painting; and being a doorman for pubs. But mostly his time was spent having the *craic* and playing Gaelic football for the Kerry team in the city, alongside other inter-county stars such as Galway's Pádraig Joyce and Kerry's Anthony Gleeson.

Out of the blue, the parish came calling for him one early morning in September 1997. Cooraclare had won most of their county titles in 'the black-and-white-television era' according to Kelly, but they sensed an opportunity that year. 'Paddy Keane, who was over the [Cooraclare] team, rang me of a Monday morning at six o'clock. I remember it,' he says, still a bit dazed by a shot from the dark like that at the tail-end of a weekend. '"Morrissey," he said, "there's a ticket waiting for you in Logan Airport on Thursday morning."

'"What? Feck off, Keane. I'll ring you back later." What's wrong with that man, at all?

'So I started thinking then. I had a Munster championship medal and I had no championship medal. So I arrived back here of a Friday morning and had to go to [county secretary] Pat Fitzgerald to get the papers sorted out that Saturday evening, and togged out above Sunday afternoon against Ennistymon.'

With Morrissey on board, Cooraclare marched to a county final where they came up against their neighbours, Doonbeg, who were closing in on a three-in-a-row. Instead of being played in Cusack Park – the county's GAA headquarters – the game was to be played in Michael Cusack's pitch in Carron, the Burren. 'I was talking to Tom beyond one day,' says one of Cooraclare's selectors that year, 'and he said to me, "What are they bringing this county final up to Carron for?"

'So I said, "There's some anniversary to do with Michael Cusack and they're doing it in his honour."

'"Jaysus," he jokes. "That place can only take about 3,000. There'll be 3,000 come to see me alone." And he hadn't played inter-county for a few years.'

The day of the county final, the bus for the panel and mentors left Cooraclare at ten o'clock, took in mass in Cree – where some of the other panel members lived – and continued on to Ballyvaughan for lunch, with Morrissey belting out ballads from the back of the bus along the way. What better way to stave off the pre-match jitters?

The match was a dour battle. 'A war of attrition,' says Considine, who picked up the Man of the Match award. Morrissey's brother Martin scored the decisive goal for Cooraclare as they won their first title since 1986. Morrissey spent most of the game at midfield, cancelling out Doonbeg's Francis McInerney, who he credits as being 'the best footballer I've seen'.

'To win a championship is great, but to beat Doonbeg in a championship is fantastic,' says Morrissey. 'We were the underdogs, but we rattled into them like we always do. Ah, jeez, the scenes above after that. I won a Munster final, but I'll tell you one thing – the scenes with the club are much better. Ah, you're with your own, your closest, your own kin.'

Putting the kibosh on Doonbeg was the easy bit. The emigration officials at Shannon Airport a couple of weeks later proved to be a lot stickier. 'I went in below to the airport,' says Morrissey. 'I had my ticket bought and everything. I went into the bar. Everything was going great guns. Out to the check-in desk and next thing, "Mr Morrissey, can we speak to you a minute?" Off in to the office. Denis Riordan was head of US Immigration in Shannon, and he was a great football man, actually. He sat me down. He had the *Clare Champion* out there in front of him on a table and he had the *Examiner* beside it. "Now, look at that, Tom," he said. "Tom Morrissey returns after two and a half years illegal in Boston." Lovely. "And this: 'Morrissey, non-starter, going back to Boston tomorrow.' Sorry Tom, I can't let you back to America. If I do, I'll get fired." So, out the door; that finished that,' he says, laughing.

At the end of January, he went over to England, jumped on a flight to Toronto, got a bus to Montreal, and was picked up by a guy who drove up from Boston and smuggled him back over the border. Six trips a year he does, says Morrissey, for $1,200 a pop.

Morrissey spun out another couple of years in the United States, but came home to work the land. 'I came back,' he says, 'to farming, sure, but I'd say I'm the only farmer in history that got a P45 from it. I came home from holidays one time and my mother said, "I'm leasing the land to your brother." Okay, so. Good luck. That finished that.'

He's managed to evade marriage so far. 'I came close once or twice,' he says. 'I just didn't want to, I suppose. I was over in America when I asked this lady, a Kerry lady, to marry me. She said, "Yeah."

'The following morning, she woke up, a big smile on her face. "Did something happen last night?" I said. "I don't remember a thing."

'"Ah, yeah. Ah, yeah," she says. "Well damn you." That was that.

'There was one or two girls I let slip away from me – the mother would be telling me that – but 'tisn't the mother that's marrying them. But no, I'm happy. I'll tell you one thing: I have twenty-seven nieces and nephews.'

He works as block-layer these days, but the body is in poor shape. He needs a hip replacement and both his knees are a bit gamey. If he's to play golf, he has to use a buggy. 'I'm dragging away, but I'm used to it now,' he says without a trace of self-pity. He still pines for football, mentioning that Aidan Moloney is still at it. He hasn't kicked a football himself since 2001.

'He came home that year in 1997,' says Martin Daly, another old soldier from the 1992 team still playing at club level, 'and I hadn't played championship with him in 1996 or 1997. He wasn't around. For the 97–98 league campaign, he was there for the beginning. He came down, we played against Cork in Páirc Uí Chaoimh, and I remember making a run in behind the defence, and Tom was in midfield, and he gathered the ball, and he was looking at the left-hand side of the field, and he just turned and gave this perfect pass into my chest, and we got a score out of it.

'And I was just saying to myself, "That's one of the things we're missing." That's the vision and the ability he had, and I was there, "It's great to have this fella back. He's going to be such an addition for the coming year." But then he was gone again, you know?'

ACKNOWLEDGMENTS

Have you noticed the expression on Keith Wood's face on the cover of this book? He looks forlorn, at best bewildered; kind of resigned to this cockeyed task he has been assigned. That is how I thought Greg, the illustrator of this book, must have felt in the middle of this project.

Greg is a mate and the most selfless individual you could meet, but Greg is from Dublin so he's not as preoccupied and as familiar as some of the rest of us are with Clare's heroes. Greg would sit patiently while excitedly I'd feed him crumbs of detail about the people he was to portray, about the nuances he was to somehow capture, petering out with an unstated but vague hope that he would, as a theatre director once famously screamed, 'give me more genius'. And he would. For that, I am eternally grateful.

I am indebted to Christy O'Connor also, a friend since primary school and days shortly afterwards when we used to sit together in Mike McInerney's English class in St Flannan's College, days when we were more interested in the Harty team than Hemingway; Mike Mac, too, if truth be told. Christy's fingerprints are all over this book. His integrity and forensic analysis as a journalist has long been a benchmark to aspire towards. Time and again, he was there with sound advice, calmly fielding calls at 11 p.m. despite having to worry about the sleep patterns of a six-month-old baby. Hurling is an important pursuit, you know?

At Mercier Press, I was fortunate to work with the coolest commissioning editor in the business – Eoin Purcell. The guy is composure personified as well as being utterly professional and good humoured. Dominic Carroll both frightened and delighted me with his attention to detail and judicious suggestions in the copy-editing process while

Patrick Crowley beat the drums tirelessly and effectively on the publicity front.

For help with research and in sourcing on-the-ground contacts, Pat and Brian Connellan were able assistants; two men, in another life, who would be coveted by the private eye trade. Others who kindly assisted on the research trail and with advice included Brian O'Connell, John O'Dea, Noel Crowley, Dermot McMahon, Tony and Shane Mulvey, Pat Cotter, Nicola Fahey, Louis McRedmond, Colum Flynn, John Madden, Kieran Ryan, my two wise not 'wizened' aunts, Ann and Mary, and Ray McMahon (if I could write like he tells stories, I'd be a bestseller). And to Richard Murphy, hat's off for giving me the best tip in the book – Fr Bernard's story.

The big pleasure of this book was in conducting the interviews. Of all of them, there was probably none to match the couple of hours I spent with Ollie Baker, one of Clare's giants, for insight and wit.

My brother, Finbarr, and his wife, Edel, the best thing that has happened to our family, were an invaluable help in sounding out sections of the manuscript, of doctoring my thoughts, as it were. Thanks be for their intuition. I want to thank the battalion of proofreaders who were cajoled/strong-armed into helping with the draft – Donn McClean, Jane Morgan, Barry Ryan, Cormac Little, Paul Horan, Joe Considine, P. J. Curtis, one of life's truly original men, and Joe Ó Muircheartaigh, who was extremely helpful as well with research and fact-checking, not to mention moments of private humour thanks to his wonderful book, *The Time of Our Lives*.

So many people generously helped with photographs, including Séamus O'Reilly, a top man to while away a few hours chatting, Ollie Byrnes, whose book *Saffron and Blue* was well-thumbed throughout the writing of this book, John Power, Nuala Pollard, Garry Shannon, Ella Street, Eamon Ward, Anne Kearney, Michael Guerin, Peadar Derrane, Jean Sheedy, Peter O'Connell, Daithí Turner, Irene McMahon, Gerard Kelly, and particularly John Kelly, whose pictures bring so much life and animation to the characters profiled.

I must also mention Jed and Mary for their wise counsel in the final selection of photographs; although I found some of their assessments to be unnecessarily cutting.

I'd like to take the opportunity to thank my editor at the *Irish Examiner*, Fionnuala Quinlan. She's such a relaxed person, a paragon of good sense, accommodating and a mighty laugh to boot.

My heartfelt thanks to Micheál Ó Muircheartaigh for taking the time to write the foreword for this book. It is a huge honour, as my friends know what high regard I hold him in. He is the quintessential Irishman.

To my parents, for whom this book is dedicated, I owe everything. Any success I've had in life is a result of the confidence my mother's unconditional love has fostered in me. My dad is my great hero; his curiosity and puckish sense of humour has always been an inspiration.

Lastly, word up to some of the influences I've been lucky enough to have in life, to Anna Murphy, Noel Pyne, Liam Ashe, John Sheehan, Eddie Ryan, God be good to him, Pago, and, of course, the crew – Barry, Milky, A, Eamon, Greg, Lava, Coff, Big John, Johnny, Glenn, an adopted son and a man who lives life in The Comfort Zone, and the great George Mulvey – folk who embody elements of what makes Clare people special: pride of place, a dollop of madness and a wicked sense of *craic*.